DIRT, SHAME, STATUS

*Perspectives on Same-Sex Sexuality in the Bible
and the Ancient World*

THOMAS KAZEN

WILLIAM B. EERDMANS PUBLISHING COMPANY
GRAND RAPIDS, MICHIGAN

Wm. B. Eerdmans Publishing Co.
4035 Park East Court SE, Grand Rapids, Michigan 49546
www.eerdmans.com

First published in Swedish as *Smuts, skam, status* by Makadam.

Book design by Lydia Hall

Printed in the United States of America

30 29 28 27 26 25 24   1 2 3 4 5 6 7

ISBN 978-0-8028-8434-3

Library of Congress Cataloging-in-Publication Data

A catalog record for this book is available from the Library of Congress.

CONTENTS

FOREWORD

In many communities the issue of same-sex relations has become a matter of contention. In many instances, assumptions and values inspired by religious traditions have been a source of sometimes passionate objection to anything other than the view that all people are heterosexual; and attitudes, passions, and behaviors deviating from that view are a manifestation of a morally corrupt age. Such outrage has even contributed to the motivation to impose such orthodox values on countries deemed in danger of corruption by the West, as in Russia's invasion of Ukraine.

In any such conflict of values it becomes essential to take time and give attention to listening to all points of view and engaging in careful consideration of all available data. Where values are strongly rooted in religious tradition and religious tradition strongly rooted in attitudes and values of cultures and times long past, listening entails scholarly research to engage in cross-cultural encounter in a way that enables the past to be heard and understood.

The discipline of such cross-cultural encounter needs to be aware of vested interests that can sometimes seek to authenticate cherished views by reading preferred views into ancient texts. On the issue of same-sex relations, that can happen along both wings of the debate. Some on the left, wanting to justify their affirmation of same-sex relations, mount the argument that ancient authors, if only understood correctly, can be seen as confirming their conclusions. Such quasi-fundamentalism from the left finds its echo in the fundamentalisms of the right, and both operate under the banner of claiming the

Bible as their authority and so invest their stance with a passion born of their faith commitment.

Such heated issues are best served when scholars commit themselves to listening to ancient texts, whether the Bible or elsewhere, and seeking to articulate what these texts say in their own right, whether it matches their own values or not. That entails also the discipline of listening to other scholars with similar commitments to avoid failing to see aspects because of personal blind spots. Let's try to hear what ancient texts were saying in their terms, whether we like it or not. That is genuine listening.

It is this spirit that informs the current work by Thomas Kazen, a scholar well versed in ancient value discourses. In this work he invites the reader to listen to that world on its terms without prejudgment or the distortions that filter out the strange and uncomfortable. Context matters, and so reading what biblical writers expressed in the light of what was being said in the world of their time is simply good listening. Kazen helps the reader listen, and not just the scholar but readers with general interest who may often find themselves engaged in ethical discussions about sex and homosexuality.

The book goes beyond helping us hear texts as they echo in their world. It also invites readers to reflect on major changes in attitudes toward human life and human relationships that have taken place since those ancient times, including assumptions about shame and honor, hierarchies, and the function of sex. Some of these will be less obvious than the fact that we have long since found ourselves comfortable with not sharing ancient views about the earth as flat or creation as barely a few thousand years old. At the same time, it invites readers to reflect on abiding values, some reaching back to the radical tendencies generated by Jesus, obvious but easily lost—not least, love and respect. Joining this engagement with the ancient world, including cherished religious traditions, will be informative and formative for many, a rewarding journey.

WILLIAM LOADER
Professor Emeritus
Murdoch University
Perth, Australia

PREFACE

A negative view of same-sex relationships is still present in large parts of the world, including many societies in the West. Through history, it has often been linked to the Bible and its interpretations. In this book, I take biblical texts condemning same-sex sexual acts as my starting point and I examine them from the perspective of three ancient paradigms: notions of ritual purity and impurity, social power structures with clear patterns of superiority and subordination, and the ancient (and for that matter still prevalent) game of honor and shame. These are issues that have interested me for two decades.

In December 2010 and January 2012, I was granted funding from the Royal Swedish Academy of Sciences, Torsten Amundson Foundation, for a project with the working title "Impurity, Shame, and Subordination: On Early Jewish and Christian Understandings of Same-Sex Sexuality." The project consisted of two parts: research on ancient history and texts, and public education work, the latter in the form of lectures on homosexuality and biblical interpretation in the light of ancient culture and history. Over the years I have given a number of such lectures and seminars, and in 2018 I published my book *Smuts, skam, status* (in Swedish) with the publisher Makadam. I subsequently received grants from Åke Wibergs stiftelse, Stiftelsen Längmanska kulturfonden, Stiftelsen Lars Hiertas minne, and Magnus Bergvalls stiftelse for making an English edition of the book and for research periods in Cambridge, during which I have done most of the revision and translation. Chapter 3 was translated by Cian Power. Ida Simonsson has annotated part of the bibliography.

This book is intended for a broader readership than biblical scholars or scholars of antiquity. I analyze and discuss not only biblical texts but also a large amount of material from ancient West Asia as well as from Greece and Rome. The translations of the texts are, unless otherwise indicated, my own. Some of these texts display values, attitudes, and expressions that in our time are offensive and, in some cases, could even be subject to public prosecution. It may need to be pointed out to some readers that a book such as this largely adopts a descriptive perspective and thus attempts to understand ancient texts, beliefs, and behaviors in terms of their given conditions and contexts. The fact that expressions and phenomena are often described rather than criticized does not imply an acceptance of the values and practices associated with them. However, I think that the first and last chapters indicate my own position quite clearly.

A recurring problem in the interpretation of texts, especially prescriptive ones, is that they do not convey an objective picture of reality but represent someone's perspective. Moreover, since the art of writing was not widespread in antiquity, its texts often represent the perspectives of the powerful or the elite. To the extent that we learn about how the general population lived and what they thought, the information is therefore biased. When a text describes or prescribes a certain behavior, it does not necessarily mean that this was the way all people behaved. However, even between the lines, texts can reveal cultural patterns of thought and action.

Perhaps something should also be said about the role and function of biblical texts in confessional contexts. It is a common misconception that sacred texts are always regarded as normative by religious practitioners. In fact, all religious traditions engage in interpretation, discussion, and negotiation of their texts. In practice, sacred texts often have a formative, rather than a normative, function—and this has been the case throughout history. No texts have ever been unconditionally applicable because all texts are contextual. This is why exegesis and hermeneutics—textual interpretation—are essential ingredients of all text-based religions.

Interpreters can thus take a mainly historical-descriptive approach to their material, but they can also undertake a theological-hermeneutical task within the framework of a particular tradition. In this book, I am mainly concerned with describing and analyzing historical texts, but I do not avoid theological-hermeneutical discussion. On the other hand, I make no attempt to "rescue" biblical texts by reading and interpreting them *against* what I perceive to be their historical context and original function or meaning. Texts can certainly be used in a variety of ways, and the history of reception presents many examples of how old texts can be used and given renewed relevance beyond more original contexts by reading them in new ways. Such maneuvers can range from biblicist attempts to find positive and egalitarian features in obvious subordination texts to experiments in queering texts by searching for cracks and gaps that can be filled with intimations and new potential interpretations. I try to avoid such readings for the simple reason that I do not want to engage in any kind of wishful thinking. For me, a good understanding of the historical context of the texts is the best prerequisite for dealing with them responsibly today, whether in relation to religion, culture in general, or social life.

A webpage with numbered images is available at https://www.ehs.se/dss. Throughout the text footnotes direct readers to the correct figures.

The book is dedicated to all who have ever felt discriminated against because of the interpretation and use of biblical texts.

ABBREVIATIONS

'Abod. Zar.   'Abodah Zarah
Aelian
   Var. hist.   *Varia historia* (*Various Histories*)
Anth. pal.   Anthologia palatine (Greek Anthology)
Aristophanes
   Ach.   *Acharnenses* (*Acharnians*)
   Eccl.   *Ecclesiazusae* (*Women of the Assembly*)
   Nub.   *Nubes* (*Clouds*)
   Pax   *Pax* (*Peace*)
   Plut.   *Plutus* (*The Rich Man*)
   Ran.   *Ranae* (*Frogs*)
   Vesp.   *Vespae* (*Wasps*)
Aristotle
   Eth. nic.   *Ethica nicomachea* (*Nicomachean Ethics*)
   Probl.   *Problemata* (*Problems*)
b.   Babylonian Talmud
CH   Code of Hammurabi
Clement of Alexandria
   Paed.   *Paedagogus* (*Christ the Educator*)
Epictetus
   Diatr.   *Diatribai* (*Discourses*)
Euripides
   Iph. aul.   *Iphigenia aulidensis* (*Iphigeneia at Aulis*)

Giṭ.   Giṭṭin

Herodotus

   Hist.   *Historiae* (*Histories*)

Hippocrates

   Artic.   *De articulis reponendis* (*Joints*)

HL   Hittite Laws

Lucian

   Dial. meretr. *Dialogi meretricii* (*Dialogues of the Courtesans*)

4 Macc   4 Maccabees

MAL   Middle Assyrian Laws

Martial

   Epigr.   *Epigrammata* (*Epigrams*)

Musonius Rufus

   Diatr.   *Diatribai* (*Discourses*)

PG   Patrologia Graeca [= *Patrologiae Cursus Completus*: Series Graeca].
           Edited by Jacques-Paul Migne. 162 vols. Paris, 1857–1886

Philo of Alexandria

   Abr.   *De Abrahamo* (*On the Life of Abraham*)

   Agr.   *De agricultura* (*On Agriculture*)

   Leg.   *Legum allegoriae* (*Allegorical Interpretation*)

   Spec.   *De specialibus legibus* (*On the Special Laws*)

   Virt.   *De virtutibus* (*On the Virtues*)

Plato

   Leg.   *Leges* (*Laws*)

   Phaed.   *Phaedo*

   Symp.   *Symposium*

Plutarch

   Amat.   *Amatorius*

   Lyc.   *Lycurgus*

   Pel.   *Pelopidas*

   Quaest. rom. *Quaestiones romanae et graecae* (*Roman and Greek Questions*)

Seneca the Elder

   Controv.   *Controversiae* (*Declamations*)

Seneca the Younger

   Ep.   *Epistulae morales* (*Letters*)

   Nat.   *Naturales quaestiones* (*Natural Questions*)

Sirach   Sirach (Ecclesiasticus)

Soranos of Ephesus
    Chron. pass. *Chronicae Passiones* (*On Chronic Diseases*)
Strabo
    Geogr.   *Geographica*
Tatian
    Or. Graec. *Oratio ad Graecos* (*Discourse against the Greeks*)
Tertullian
    Pall.   *De pallio* (*The Pallium*)
T. Levi   Testament of Levi
Vd.   *Vendidād*
Wis   Wisdom of Solomon
Xenophon
    Anab.   *Anabasis*
    Lac.   *Respublica Lacedaemoniorum* (*Constitution of the Laedaemonians*)
    Symp.   Symposium
y.   Jerusalem Talmud
Yebam.   Yebamot

HOMOEROTICISM AND HUMAN SEXUALITY

A Negative Attitude

"With a male you must not lie as with a woman, that is an abomination," rules the Holiness Code in Leviticus. "Their females exchanged the natural intercourse for that which is against nature, similarly males also abandoned the natural intercourse with females and were inflamed by their desire for each other," says Paul in Romans. And in 1 Corinthians he exclaims, "Don't you know that no unrighteous person will inherit the kingdom of God? Don't be misled: neither *pornoi* [sexually indecent people] nor idolaters, nor *moichoi* [adulterers], nor *malakoi* [lit. "softies"], nor *arsenokoitai* [lit. "male-bedders"] . . ." This last term also appears in 1 Timothy.

On the one hand, this is pretty much all that is explicitly said about sexual acts between people of the same sex in the biblical corpus. On the other hand, these few texts clearly express the same negative attitude toward homoeroticism that has characterized both religion and society for much of Western history. And between the lines and beneath the surface there is much more. Not everything we find is equally condemning. As we will see, texts about sexuality do not always say what we think at first glance. We will find explanations for the negative attitudes to same-sex relationships but also stories of same-sex attraction in the texts we discuss.

This book is about biblical texts in their context, which means it is just as much about other texts: texts from ancient West Asia, Greece, and Rome.

In our time, at least in the Western world, a new understanding of what we now call homosexuality has emerged. It is a development that has taken place very rapidly and mainly in recent decades. In some regions of the world, and in certain ideological and religious contexts, there is still much resistance. It may be worth recalling that the Judeo-Christian tradition is probably no more homophobic than most other religious traditions. And perhaps it is even more important to remind ourselves that religious people are not necessarily more homophobic than others, even if it may sometimes seem so. The feelings and beliefs that underlie fear and lack of understanding today are in many ways similar to those that can be traced in ancient texts. Human beings have not changed that much.

It is sometimes said that ancient cultures, particularly the Greeks, had a very different and much more positive view of same-sex relationships than the culture that came to dominate the Christian West. This is true in a way but at the same time misleading. It is, in fact, the ancients' view of sex in general that is the underlying problem, as it lives on into modern times. A negative attitude to same-sex sexual acts is not based on specifically religious beliefs but on deeply held notions of power relations. We will examine three such areas, three opposing pairs of concepts, all of which play a major role in the biblical texts that express negative views of same-sex relationships. They are important for understanding the biblical texts, precisely because they were so important in the ancient cultures that made up the world in which the biblical texts were written. The three pairs of concepts are purity and impurity, superiority and subordination, and honor and shame. These concepts can help us understand not only ancient views of sexuality but also our own.

Nature and Culture

Humans are fundamentally biological beings. Like all mammals, we give birth to live offspring that are initially entirely dependent on us. Our babies are among the most helpless mammalian offspring and remain heavily dependent on their parents for a long, long time. We are also a socially advanced species, the most advanced on the planet, as far as we can tell.

Evolution has provided us with drives and emotions that have enabled our species to survive and become highly successful. The sex drive ensures human reproduction. Desire and pleasure facilitate the whole process. But in addition, we carry in ourselves an incredibly complex set of emotions that underlie what we call affection, friendship, love, loyalty, and responsibility. Such qualities have helped people to stick together. They have stabilized relationships and enabled humans to survive successfully as a species, even though our offspring is so vulnerable.

It may seem provocative to some to begin a discussion of sexuality by talking about biological functionality. Biological arguments have sometimes been misused to argue, for example, that men and women are inherently suited to different roles, or that homosexuality is unnatural or dysfunctional. But an evolutionary explanation of *why* and *how* basic human emotions and behaviors have evolved does not tell us how we "should" or "must" act. Moral values cannot be derived from the underlying biology of humans.

Everything we are and feel as human beings has its necessary basis in our biological body, which is the result of a long evolution. But all that we are and feel has, at the same time, been formed in interaction with other human beings in the context of social communities and of a culture that is at least as complex as our biological systems and has prehistoric roots. Moreover, our brains are so intricately designed that the formatting of the signaling system itself is not a given from birth but is influenced throughout our youth and—according to some researchers—does not fully stabilize until around the age of twenty-five. So, the eternal question of inheritance and environment has no simple answer. Nature and culture are intimately intertwined and, in many ways, represent an indissoluble entity.

It would therefore be completely wrong to draw deterministic conclusions based on human biological conditions. Many of our emotions have evolved because they have benefited us as a species. They are part of our constitution, whether we like it or not. They influence us and underlie our behaviors, our drives and our desires, our capacity for pleasure. Our emotions and behaviors have evolved for a "purpose," that is, they are—or have been—functional. They continue to be part of our lives regardless of whether their "purpose" is fulfilled or not. Their adaptive function may shift or disappear. The adaptive function is the cause of their emergence. But emotions and behaviors can receive other, actual functions that are wholly or partly different. A person who experiences closeness, friendship, love, security, or pleasure feels good about this! This is true quite independently of whether it leads to reproduction or success for humans as a species.

Same-sex relationships cannot lead to biological reproduction. But feelings of closeness, love, and desire can be experienced by people in same-sex relationships, just as feelings of closeness, love, and desire are experienced by people in heterosexual relationships. This is not very strange.

When we examine concepts of impurity, subordination, and shame in antiquity, we discover that they are often linked to what is perceived as natural. People in antiquity had reasonably the same biology as we do. But what they perceived as natural rarely had to do with human biological conditions, but instead concerned cultural notions of what they considered appropriate. In contemporary research on what sexuality really is, there are widely differing views on the relationship between heritage and environment, nature and culture, biology and social systems. To discuss and interpret biblical texts about homoeroticism and sexual acts between people of the same sex, we must navigate a minefield: that between biology and cultural construction.

Sexual Categories

Some argue that the concept of sexuality is in some ways a modern invention. We are not talking about sexual acts, sexual attraction, or sexual desire. The sexual drive is, of course, older than the human species and has accompanied us throughout our biological evolutionary history. But the way in which we understand sexual identity and sexual orientation today has no obvious counterpart in the ancient world.

This is particularly true of the categorization of people as heterosexual or homosexual. The terms are modern, and the first use of "homosexual" can be traced back to the German writer Karl Maria Kerbeny, who used this neologism in a letter in 1868 and in a couple of writings the following year. The concept of homosexuality then spread in Germany and was translated into English toward the end of the century. The first known occurrence in an English text is from 1892.

The concepts of homosexuality and heterosexuality are mutually dependent. They assume that people can be divided into somewhat clear categories describing their sexual identity, orientation, or preferences. Today, this division has been further developed to include more categories: heterosexual men, heterosexual women, homosexual men, lesbian women, bisexuals, asexuals, and transgender people. In some contexts, it almost seems as if we consider these different categories as separate genders.

At the same time, the division of human beings into sexual categories has been problematized. If people perceive their sexual identity as fixed or fluctuating in so many different ways and to varying degrees, into how many categories do we actually need to sort ourselves? Historical and anthropological research indicates that people in different cultures, both past and present, have perceived and categorized gender identity in different ways.

To simplify, one could say that, in the past, people of the same sex who performed sexual acts were usually not considered a special category with different orientation than others. They were not seen as belonging to a particular gender, but as people (men and, sometimes, women) whose actions transgressed certain boundaries. In some contexts, certain same-sex sexual acts could be performed as part of a ritual or counted as part of an accepted social interaction. In other situations, such acts were considered morally reprehensible and punishable. This is, of course, a simplification, and we will soon see that even the ancients could put labels on categories of people with deviant sexual behaviors. But we will also see that these categories usually do not correspond to ours but were constructed according to completely different guidelines or starting points.

Of course, there were people in premodern times who felt greater attraction to people of the same sex than they did to people of the opposite sex. We also have ancient texts that discuss such cases or express such feelings. But the starting points are still not quite comparable to how we usually think in our time because the basic understanding of how sexuality shapes human identity looked different, and our modern categories were not available. We will soon look at examples that illustrate this.

Biological Basis—Social Construction

Thus, one can say on good grounds that the ways in which we think and reflect on our sexuality and our sexual identities in a given culture are social constructs. At the same time, human sexual behaviors and sexual attraction—in many different forms and variations—existed long before anyone formulated a terminology for it, just as we can speak of religion even among peoples who lack words or concepts for this phenomenon because they do not distinguish what we call religion from life in general.

There has long been a tug-of-war between those who see homosexuality and heterosexuality as results of biological factors (genes, hormones, brain neurotransmitters, etc.) and those who argue that these categories are social constructions. Sometimes the battle has been fierce. One could perhaps say that ideological factors have played a role in this tug-of-war, but that it is not entirely clear what is at stake in defending one view over the other.

Considering homosexuality to be an innate orientation has made it easier for a lot of people in the West to accept and "understand" homosexuality. If attraction to people of the same sex and homosexual behavior is seen as an expression of a person's "nature," then it is easier to relate to one's own feelings and behavior. It becomes more difficult to perceive homosexuality as something "unnatural" or perverse. Such an approach—sometimes called "essentialism"—has also been the starting point for many homosexuals in their formation of a positive identity. In particular, the understanding of homosexuality as biologically determined has served as a defense against those who claim that homosexuality is merely a result of various factors in upbringing or environment and can therefore be treated or cured.

At the same time, a focus on the biological conditions of homosexuality has been perceived as problematic by people who emphasize the individual's right to choose. Not everyone perceives themselves to have a definite orientation of one or the other kind. Is it the case that homosexual relationships can only be legitimized if they are an expression of a clear and irreversible preference for people of the same sex? Or how much "disposed" in one way or another would one have to be for it to be considered morally acceptable to choose what one wants? Why not rather regard sexuality as a social construction? Different societies construct sexual relations and gender roles in different ways. Anyone who does not fit into the dominant patterns is considered "queer," and being queer (or choosing to be queer) can be regarded as a protest against social hierarchies or establishments and a struggle for individual freedom.

Both approaches are associated with problems. As mentioned earlier, a biologistic view has been misused in arguments about men's and women's roles. In the discussion of homoeroticism and same-sex relationships, a biologically based approach has sometimes been perceived as feeding notions and prejudices about how people take on different roles in homosexual relationships. A biologically based essentialism may simply be suspected of legitimizing stereotypes. Some, however, have pushed the view of social construction so far that it may seem that it is only social structures, learned patterns, and underlying values that govern our sexuality. Without being governed, we could in principle direct our sex drive in any direction—and in doing so we might free ourselves from the control exerted by social structures and gender role patterns. While some people affirm such a view, it does not correspond to the way in which many others experience their own sexuality. Many people perceive themselves and their sexuality to be driven by internal rather than external forces. This applies in particular to those who find themselves attracted to people of the same sex, even when their surroundings do not provide room for or allow it, and they themselves would be more than happy to conform to the majority if only they could.

Surprisingly often, representatives of different positions seem to talk past each other, and the reason is often that we are sloppy with our definitions. Sexual attraction is definitely biologically founded, and it would be very difficult to deny that important variations in attraction, expressing themselves in different preferences for one's own or the other sex, must have basic biological causes. Our interpretation of this attraction, however, is governed by how we model our analytical categories, and the ways in which we express our attraction are shaped and constrained by the social contexts we construct. Human expressions of sexual attraction will therefore display great differences over time and in different cultures.

Social constructivism is a completely necessary starting point for being able to interpret and understand ancient texts about sexuality. Without such a starting point, we become the victims of our own anachronisms—we will read and interpret based on our quite different contemporary ways of thinking. However, social construction cannot explain the origin and cause of sexual attraction, whether it is directed toward people of the same or different sex. For this we need biology—and a combination of explanations based on evolutionary, biological, developmental, and neuroscientific models. Together, such perspectives can help us understand why we feel the ways that we do, why we think the ways that we do, and why we behave in the ways that we do in different situations and relationships.

Is Homoeroticism Normal?

For a long time, homosexual acts in the West have been regarded as a pathological deviation or perversion. One of the starting points for such views has been a functional understanding of sexuality associated with reproduction.

From such a perspective it becomes logical to resist contraception and sex in circumstances that do not lead to conception. This has been a common approach throughout history.

Today, such views are less common, although they are still held by some groups. Most people realize that sexuality fills more functions for human beings than mere reproduction. Most people also consider these different functions as meaningful and legitimate, although reproduction is the biological explanation for the rise of sexual attraction far back in evolutionary history. One could perhaps take the mouth as an analogy: we use the mouth for a number of purposes, even though the evolutionary explanation of the mouth's appearance is probably food intake. Not many people would think that because of this it would be inappropriate or immoral to speak with our mouths. It is, of course, true that a number of things have evolved in the mouth and throat—things that are not absolutely necessary for eating but are more suitable for talking. Similarly, our sexuality has evolved beyond what is necessary for reproduction to fill other functions too. Evolution often develops already existing functions for more purposes rather than "inventing" new ones. From such a perspective, a sexual relationship can obviously fulfill the same function in relationships between people of the same sex as in relationships between people of the opposite sex.

The question of how homoeroticism may have arisen can be discussed at different levels. There are no simple answers, and the uncertainties are many. For example, theories that homosexuality would be related to exposure to extraordinary high levels of sex hormones during fetal development cannot be corroborated by evidence from scientific studies. In any case, such theories do not suffice as explanations. However, it seems that genetic factors can play a role and that tendencies toward same-sex attraction can be part of a person's genetic inheritance. It still does not explain the origins of homoeroticism. A gene can accompany the genetic material as a by-product. The question why it is there is still not answered.

From an evolutionary biological point of view, sexual attraction is an adaptive trait, that is, a trait that evolved because it facilitated reproduction and survival. The question is whether attraction to people of the same sex can be explained in a similar way or is a kind of "noise," an evolutionary by-product without specific function. The latter would perhaps be a possible explanation for various forms of bisexuality but is not a good explanation for homosexuality, many researchers say, because so many homosexuals find themselves uniquely attracted to people of the same sex. From an evolutionary point of view, this would counteract reproduction and survival, that is, same-sex attraction would have a negative function.

It is more reasonable to assume some form of indirect adaptive function for homoerotic attraction. Some people think of it as an exaptation, that is, a trait that evolved for a certain function but then acquired another. Others speak of it as a biological spandrel, that is, something that initially had no specific function but emerged as a by-product of another functional feature. Spandrels are often shown to provide evolutionary benefits at a later stage, thus becoming exaptations. Without using terminology from evolutionary biology, we could simply say that attraction between people of the same sex may have evolved into something functional that has contributed to human survival, regardless of origin.

A possible explanation can be sought in human prehistory. Many researchers argue that prehistoric hominids—from whom we descend—lived in small groups held together by kinship ties and with a fairly high degree of gender segregation. The latter, of course, was linked to a certain division of roles between men and women far back in prehistoric times, much of which had to do with the helpless and vulnerable offspring, which needed maternal nursing and care for an extended period. Sexual attraction provided survival benefits and could bridge barriers between family groups, thus facilitating social interaction outside of their own groups.

At the same time, there were numerous problems associated with the type of social structure in which our distant ancestors lived. Some conclusions can be drawn from studies of other primates where, for example, dominant or aggressive males prevent others from accessing the females, and major conflicts arise due to intragroup competition. We can also study the problems that arise among primates when new members from other family groups become integrated, leading to the renegotiation of social relations and hierarchies. Quite often sex, including acts between individuals of the same sex, has a positive function in resolving conflicts and facilitating social cohesion in such situations, with the best-known examples being the bonobos ("dwarf chimpanzees"), who frequently engage in mutual sexual stimulation for bonding and tension-relieving purposes. Questions about competition, integration, and the complicated social game required for group stability are familiar to us from modern human history, including our own time. Today, much of the social interaction in our societies also occurs in more or less gender-segregated groups. The ability to connect to each other in such groups and bring about functioning social interaction depends on our capacity for positive feelings toward people of the same sex.

It is a pretty good hypothesis that homoerotic attraction evolved, based on given biological conditions, because it facilitated collaboration and relationships in the sex-segregated groups in which human ancestors spent much of their time. Attraction to individuals of the same sex proved to be an advantage in the difficult and threatening situations faced by our predecessors. Homoerotic attraction reduced tensions and sometimes lethal competition, facilitated the integration of strangers, and had positive effects for group cooperation. This could also have led to more people having access to sexual partners of the opposite sex. Ultimately, both reproduction and survival would have benefitted.

Thus, evolutionary biology provides good explanations for human same-sex attraction and for some kind of predisposition for such attraction varying in a population. The social environment—in a broad sense and during the multimillion-year-old history of hominids—has been one important factor in this development. Historical as well as anthropological studies indicate that homoeroticism can actually have a cohesive function, from ancient Greece— which we will look more closely at later—to initiation rituals among hunter-gatherer communities in New Guinea. Most of us probably have some kind of potential to be attracted to both sexes, although we do not express this in sexual behaviors. Social and cultural frameworks play a crucial role in how this inherent potential develops. In that regard we can certainly affirm homosexuality as a social construction.

The question is nevertheless whether this train of argument can explain what we have recently mentioned, namely that many homosexuals find themselves uniquely attracted to people of the same sex. What would be the adaptive benefits of such an exclusive orientation? One possible interpretation could be that a uniquely homoerotic attraction is simply a by-product of a multifunctional "bisexual" attraction. Paradoxically, this then also ought to apply to an exclusively *heterosexual* orientation. Neither would be entirely optimal, because survival is not just about reproduction but also requires social interaction and functioning group dynamics. And since it is beneficial for human beings as a group to be predisposed for attraction to both one's own sex and the opposite sex, both capacities come to expression in a population to a larger or lesser degree, and sometimes—or often—an exclusive attraction takes over on the individual plane.

The reasoning engaged here represents some of many possible interpretations and in extremely simplified forms. It is also not the task of this book to give an exhaustive description of different theories. The main task in this chapter is to point out how sexual attraction to people of the same sex can be explained intelligibly through a combination of evolutionary biological factors and our sociocultural history, from prehistory to modern times. What we call sexual orientation is reasonably the results of biological and cultural factors in collaboration. From such a point of view, homosexuality cannot be regarded as something "abnormal," not even (or especially not) from an evolutionary perspective.

"Normality" is otherwise a concept that has stirred up many emotions. A slogan used to question a common use of the term reads: "heterosexuality is not normal; it is just common." But in fact, "normal" often means nothing more than "ordinary" or "common." From that perspective, heterosexuality is "normal"—although it could be argued that this applies less to exclusive heterosexuality than to the ability to feel at least some attraction to both sexes! The problem with the concept of "normality" is that it is associated with "norm" and "normative" and is often used as a value statement. This also applies to the term "deviation." From one point of view, homosexuality is a biological deviation. From another angle (or is it ultimately the same evolutionary perspective?), homosexuality is a *natural* deviation, meaning variant. Neither nature nor culture provides simple guidelines.

$$\boxed{2}$$

THE BIBLICAL TEXTS IN CONTEXT

The Pentateuch

The five books of Moses, known as the Pentateuch, represent the first section of the Hebrew Bible, or what in the Christian tradition is called the Old Testament. In Jewish tradition the Pentateuch is commonly called "Torah." The Hebrew word *tôrâ* is often translated as "law." A more accurate translation would be "guidance" or "instruction." These books consist of a blend of narratives and instructions. The Pentateuch's instructions gradually took on the role of legally binding legislation, especially from the Hellenistic period (about 300 BCE) and beyond, first under the influence of Greek and then Roman law. But to begin with, these laws had a more flexible status.

The Pentateuch was not written by Moses, as all scholars agree. The material has evolved over time. The first book, Genesis, contains mainly narratives divided into primeval history and patriarchal history. Some of these traditions have older roots, but they were related to each other and shaped into a coherent narrative only after the Babylonian exile during the sixth and especially the fifth centuries BCE. The book of Exodus describes the exodus of the Israelites from Egypt and can be dated similarly. In its second half, which contains civil laws and instructions for the cult, we find the so-called Covenant Code (Exod 21–23). This collection is one of the oldest parts of the Pentateuch and was possibly composed around 700 BCE. The first part of Leviticus contains sacrificial and purity rules, which were compiled after the exile during the Persian period, mainly in the fifth century BCE. The second part (Lev 17–26) is commonly referred to as the Holiness Law or Holiness Code, because it focuses on the holiness or separateness of the people of Israel in relation to other peoples and with regard to certain behaviors and customs. It complements the first part of Leviticus and today is often dated toward the end of the fifth century BCE. The book of Numbers complements Leviticus with various supplementary rules within the framework of a travel narrative that depicts the people's wanderings in the desert. It probably belongs to the most recent material in the Pentateuch and was redacted during the early fourth century BCE, close to the Pentateuch's final editing. Deuteronomy purports to contain laws that Moses proclaimed to the people after forty years of wandering in the desert. In actual fact, this book, whose name means "the second law," is an update and extension of the Covenant Code. This reworking appears to have begun toward the end of the seventh century BCE and continued during the Babylonian exile, and the book of Deuteronomy was then completed during the Persian period after the exile.

The Holiness Code

The texts that lie at the roots of the Judeo-Christian tradition's predominantly negative attitude to same-sex sexual relations are found in the Holiness Code, that is, in the second part of Leviticus. This section holds together various Israelite cultic instructions and reflects the perspectives of a priestly elite that attempted to consolidate the temple state of Jerusalem and its territories in the Persian province of Yehud in the fifth century BCE. One of their goals was to strengthen Israelite group identity, which, among other things, expressed itself in an emphasis on specifically Israelite customs and practices. The Holiness Code emphasizes the people's separate status—their holiness—and warns of behaviors associated with other peoples (Egyptians and Canaanites). Here we find lists of incest rules, which include discussions of sex with animals and sex between men. We find Sabbath rules and prohibitions against participation in other cults, some of which probably had earlier roots. We also find special holiness laws for priests and sacrificial animals, and we find new updates of civil laws known previously from the Covenant Code and Deuteronomy. Finally, we encounter violent threats about punishment for disobedience: the land will vomit the people out and they will be expelled again if they do not follow the instructions.

Some of the instructions in the Holiness Code talk about concern and compassion for fellow human beings and about social justice. It appears evident that many people lived in a vulnerable situation and unity was considered important. The Holiness Code also reflects a situation in which the Israelites did not always have the upper hand—their society was not homogeneous. The texts not only call for humane treatment of compatriots but also for tolerance toward strangers. Immigrants should be treated as native and are expected to follow the same rules and holiness laws as the Israelites. There is a fear that the new and fragile identity emerging in Persian period Yehud will be destroyed. The underlying idea is that past catastrophes struck the Israelites because of their disobedience to the law and improper worship of other gods.

The Holiness Code puts a lot of effort into trying to regulate sexual behavior. Lists of prohibitions in two similar versions can be found in Leviticus 18 and 20. In addition to various incest rules, the prohibitions against lying with a woman during menstruation, having sex with animals, and sex between men are all repeated.

LEV 18:22

With a male you must not lie woman-lays (*miškəbê 'iššâ*), that is an abomination (*tôʿēbâ*).

LEV 20:13

And a man who lies woman-lays (*miškəbê 'iššâ*) with a male, the two of them have done an abomination (*tôʿēbâ*). They shall die indeed. Their blood [guilt] is with them.

We begin by noting some important details. First, the perspective is all male. This is almost always the starting point in ancient texts. Second, the language used here is very specific. The texts literally talk about "the lyings of a woman," "the beddings of a woman," or "woman-lays." In the context and culture of these texts, the Hebrew phrase *miškəbê 'iššâ* cannot really mean anything other than intercourse with penetration. The texts clearly specify the meaning of the prohibition; it cannot be misunderstood. Lying with a woman is understood as penetrating her and this, says the text, is prohibited to do to a male. It is something a male does to a female. When the possibility that a man could do so to another man is nevertheless envisaged, we must assume that the expression refers to anal intercourse.

Third, a very strong value judgment is expressed: the act is described as something "abominable." The word *tô'ēbâ* means "loathsome" or "abominable" and is an expression of disgust. This term never appears in the purity and sacrificial laws of Leviticus 1–16, but it is widely used in the Holiness Code along with threats that the land will spew or vomit out the people if they engage in abominable acts. In the Holiness Code, *tô'ēbâ* is closely associated with "impurity" (*ṭum'â*). This becomes clear in the summary of prohibitions against a number of sexual behaviors in chapter 18.

LEV 18:24–30

Do not defile yourselves (*tiṭṭammĕ'û*) with any of these, for with all these did the peoples defile themselves (*niṭmĕ'û*), whom I am driving out before you. And the land became impure (*wattiṭmā'*), and I brought its sin upon it and the land vomited out its inhabitants. But you shall keep my practices and commandments and you must not do any of these abominations (*hattô'ēbōt*), the native as well as the immigrant who lives among you. For all of these abominations (*hattô'ēbōt*) did the men of the land who were before you, and the land was defiled (*wattiṭmā'*). So do not let the land vomit you out by your defiling it (*bĕṭamma'ăkem*), like it vomited out the people who were before you. For anyone who does any of these abominations (*hattô'ēbôt*), the one doing it will be cut off from the midst of their people. You shall keep my instructions so as not to do any of the abominable (*hattô'ēbōt*) practices that were done before you; you must not defile yourselves (*tiṭṭammə'û*) with them. I am Yahweh, your god.

In the summary of chapter 20 we find another expression of disgust, which we recognize from the food rules of Leviticus 11. In that text, certain small animals are classified as disgusting (*šeqeṣ*). The corresponding verbs (*qûṣ; šāqaṣ*) are used to describe God's reaction to forbidden sexual acts and to eating forbidden food.

LEV 20:22–26

You shall keep all my practices and commandments and do according to them, so that the land I will bring you to live in will not vomit you out. You shall not walk according to the practices of the people that I drive out before you, because they did all these things and I got disgusted (*wā'āquṣ*) by them. And I said to you: You shall possess their soil and I shall give it to

you as a possession, a land flowing with milk and honey. I am the Yahweh,
your god, who has separated you from the peoples. And you will separate
the clean and the unclean (laṭṭəmēʾâ) animals and the unclean (haṭṭāmēʾ)
and the clean birds. So do not make your lives disgusting (tĕšaqqəṣû) by any
animal or bird or anything that creeps on the soil, which I have separated as
unclean (lĕṭammēʾ) for you. You shall be holy to me, for I, Yahweh, am holy,
and I have separated you from the peoples, to be mine.

Both summaries are motivated in similar ways: it is important that the
people follow the Holiness Code so as not to get into trouble again. The underlying premise is that the people are separated to be holy and therefore must
not behave like the surrounding peoples. The question, of course, is how other
peoples behaved. We will return to this in a moment.

First, an additional detail requires a comment. The two prohibitions regarding male same-sex penetration are similar but not identical. The first
text (Lev 18:22) simply forbids a man to penetrate another man and calls
the act abominable. The other (Lev 20:13) begins similarly, but then says
that *both* parties have acted abominably and are to be punished with death.
A somewhat similar turn is found in the prohibition of lying with another
man's wife a couple of verses earlier (20:10), which begins by saying that a
man committing adultery shall certainly be put to death, then adding that
this concerns the adulterer as well as the adulteress. These nuances in the
text are not apparent in every translation but suggest to some scholars that
the prohibition originally applied to the perpetrator only—which in fact
seems to be the case in the first text (18:22). The editing and reworking of
the material resulted in certain changes: both parties are now regarded as
guilty, anal intercourse between men is juxtaposed to other prohibited sexual
behaviors, and all of these are seen as disgusting abominations associated
with non-Israelite behavior. Thus, we must turn to the question of same-sex
sexual acts among Israel's neighbors.

Ancient West Asia

Unfortunately, the material we have about sexual acts between people of the
same sex in ancient West Asian (Near Eastern) texts is rather meager. Both
sexual violence against, and erotically tinged friendship between, persons of

the same sex occur among gods and demigods in Egyptian and Mesopotamian myths. Some of these we will return to later, as they illustrate conceptions about power, subordination, and honor. However, these stories tell us little about how the people of ancient West Asia viewed same-sex sexual acts in practice.

The Egyptian Book of the Dead contains burial texts with very old roots. The famous chapter 125, known from around 1500 BCE, contains a long list of crimes that the speaker says he has not committed. Among these we find: "I have not had sex with any boy / man." It is unclear whether the text refers to a minor or just to another adult man. In any case, it is clear that this behavior was regarded as unlawful.

In the Code of Hammurabi, from about 1750 BCE, we find bans against incest similar to those of the Holiness Code, although they are not quite as frequent. The prohibitions concern relationships between father and daughter, father and daughter-in-law, son and mother, and son and stepmother (CH 154–158). In the Hittite laws from about 1650–1500 BCE (but which, unlike many other legal collections, were updated over several centuries), we find similar prohibitions: a man must not have sex with his mother, stepmother (as long as the father lives), daughter, or son (HL 189). The laws thus envision the possibility of a man having sex with his family members, including his son, and prohibit this, but we find nothing generally about sexual acts between people of the same sex. The son is simply mentioned as one of several others in the immediate family against whom it is not allowed to commit sexual acts. In the larger context (HL 187–200a), the Hittite incest rules are juxtaposed with prohibitions against sex with animals: cows, sheep, pigs, and dogs are forbidden but not horses and mules. In many legal collections from ancient West Asia, we also find regulations regarding rape. Sexual acts against slaves are never considered as serious as infringements on free people. Many of these issues are similar to the prohibitions against certain sexual behaviors that we find in the Holiness Code and in other legal collections of the Pentateuch. But there are also differences. In none of the other collections is a general ban on sexual acts between men expressed as clearly as in Leviticus.

This also applies to the Middle Assyrian laws from the eleventh century BCE.*

---

* The images referred to in this book can be viewed at https://www.ehs.se/dss. See figure 1, Akkadian cuneiform tablet with Middle Assyrian laws from the eleventh century BCE.

MAL A19–20

If a man secretly spreads rumors about his neighbor and says, "everyone fucks him," or in open quarrel tells him: "everyone fucks you," and further: "I can prove" but cannot prove and does not prove, then they shall give him fifty lashes; he shall serve the king for a whole month; they shall cut his hair; he shall also pay 3,600 shekels of lead.

If a man fucks his neighbor and they prove it and find him guilty, they shall fuck him and castrate him.

These laws are part of a longer section dealing with adultery, sexual abuse, and rumors (MAL A12–24). For example, just before this passage, there are laws about a man who spreads rumors about his neighbor's wife. I have chosen to represent the Akkadian verb with the term "fuck," despite its coarseness, since "sleep with" is far more neutral than the original language infers and in a modern setting suggests a reciprocity that would become anachronistic in relation to ancient texts. A possible alternative would be "screw." The verb *nâku* (*niaku*) suggests unauthorized intercourse not necessarily from coercion (i.e., rape), although this seems to be presumed in the second of the two cited laws above. I have also chosen to render the Akkadian *tappā'u* with "neighbor." The word can mean companion or colleague and is used for a clan member, someone with the same social status, an equal, or a peer.

From this we can draw certain conclusions. It was considered degrading for a man to be subjected to sexual intercourse by another man of the same social rank. To accuse a man of equal status of submitting himself to such an offense was punishable. Subjecting another man of equal status to penetration (arguably under compulsion) was considered extremely serious. The punishable behavior seems less to have been the sexual act as such than the disgrace and honor infringement incurred upon an equal. This is indicated by the fact that the perpetrator is supposed to be punished not only by castration but by being subjected to the same shameful treatment: penetration. Like the prohibition in Leviticus 18:22, but unlike the prohibition in Leviticus 20:13 (in its present form), the Middle Assyrian laws say nothing about punishing the man subjected to the intercourse. Nor do they tell us anything about how sexual penetration of a man of lower status would be perceived. The wording "his neighbor" suggests that the "moral" problem was about honor and shame in relation to a man's social status. This is presumably the problem behind the

Holiness Code's prohibition as well, but here we encounter an additional factor: the prohibition is subsumed, together with a number of other bans against prohibited sexual acts, under the conceptual umbrella of purity and impurity. Could this fact partly explain why both men involved in "woman-lays" are condemned? To this question we will return in the next chapter.

A possible background to the Holiness Code's vehement condemnation of sexual acts between men, together with its instructions to punish both parties involved in "woman-lays," might be traced to a development that Israelite religion underwent at the time when this text was formed. During the fifth century BCE, the Israelite province of Yehud was under Persian rule. The postexilic attempts to reconstruct social structures and recreate a religious cult took place in a context that has many affinities with a colonial situation. In the Persian Empire, Zoroastrianism was a power factor. It is possible to trace a certain amount of Zoroastrian influence on postexilic beliefs as well as on cultic issues, not least on purity rules, during Persian times when the contours of what is commonly called "Second Temple Judaism" first began to take shape. Zoroastrianism's attitude to sex between men was very negative. In *Vendidād*, which in its present form is of a later date but contains material that is considered by many to have roots in this period, both parties are condemned in a male-to-male sexual intercourse: both shall be punished. But *Vendidād* makes a distinction between coercion and voluntary acts (*Vd.* 8.26–27). The text says that for an involuntary act, the punishment is milder than for an intentional one. This part of the text can also be interpreted as referring to semen emission (masturbation?) but this is unlikely, considering that a little later the text is explicit about sexual acts between men:

VD. 8.32
The man who is penetrated and who penetrates, Spitama Zarathustra, he is
a demon (*daeva*) and he worships demons (*daevayaz*)

Thus, both parties, he who penetrates and he who is penetrated, are unambiguously associated with the demonic world. (The text continues to describe such a man as a lover or mistress of a demon.) On this point, therefore, the specific stance of the Holiness Code seems closer to contemporary Zoroastrianism than to earlier ancient West Asian conceptions.

There is a fairly widespread notion of cult prostitution being common in ancient West Asian cultures. Against such a background, the prohibitions of the Holiness Code could be interpreted as part of a struggle against the influence of foreign cults in ancient Israel. But the question is how widespread cult prostitution really was. The traditional image that emerged toward the end of the nineteenth century and dominated scholarship during the twentieth century envisioned Israel as surrounded by fertility cults with temples that in practice served as gigantic brothels. Behind this lies a statement by the Greek historian Herodotus that the Babylonians had a custom according to which every woman must prostitute herself in the temple of Aphrodite (Ishtar) once in her life (*Hist.* 1.199). This became the basis for an entire interpretive tradition: texts, images, and archaeological artifacts were interpreted from the belief in widespread cult prostitution. But it seems likely that Herodotus had misunderstood something, or perhaps he was just engaging in slander. Today, an increasing number of scholars are questioning these ideas, which otherwise were quite exciting for scholars as well as novelists to entertain. This whole paradigm is crumbling.

In Deuteronomy 23, male and female cult staff are referred to with expressions that have been interpreted within a context of temple prostitution:

DEUT 23:17–18(18–19)
There must be no cult servant (*qədēšâ*) among the daughters of Israel, and there must be no cult servant (*qādēš*) among the sons of Israel. You must not bring the wages of a prostitute (*zônâ*) or the payment of a dog (*keleb*) to the house of Yahweh your god for any vow, for both of these are abominations of Yahweh your god.

The words *qādēš* and *qədēšâ* are formed on the root *qdš*, "separated" or "sacred," and only occur in a few places in the Hebrew Bible. The roles they refer to can probably be associated with female cult servants in Mesopotamian texts (*qadištu*) and male cult servants in Canaanite (Ugaritic) texts (*qdšm*)—but neither of these categories seems to have had the task of providing sexual services. Speculations that poor Israelites engaged in temple prostitution in order to pay for thoughtless vows are quite groundless. However, sexual metaphors are often used rhetorically in the Hebrew Bible's polemic against foreign cults, and "idolatry" is often likened to prostitution. The text from Deuteronomy 23 can simply be read as a ban against Israelites serving in local cults while participating in the temple cult in Jerusalem. For such behavior, slurs such as "whore" and "dog" could be used. The word for "dog" (*keleb*) does indeed appear in ancient West Asia as a term for a faithful slave, which has led some to interpret *klb* in a temple inscription from Cyprus from the fourth century BCE as a category of cult servants—but the inscription might also refer to a literal dog. There is simply no certain evidence of male prostitution in the Hebrew Bible and nothing at all indicating that such supposed male prostitution would have involved other men.

We know, of course, that slaves were often used and abused sexually, which makes it quite reasonable to assume that cult servants, that is, temple slaves, could also have been exploited for sexual purposes. A text that may reflect some such practice is the story of Judah and Tamar (Genesis 38) where the term *qədēšâ* is used as a euphemism for "prostitute." But once again, this language might reflect Israelite value judgments regarding foreign cults and their practitioners. The notion of large-scale cult prostitution within the framework of a widespread fertility cult, with the aim of promoting fertility and improving the harvests, does not have as much evidence for it as some scholars previously thought. In any case, the Israelite prohibition against men lying "woman-lays" with other men requires other explanations.

One cult that seems to have been perceived as the greatest threat to the Israelite worship of Yahweh, at least in retrospect, was the cult of the Mesopotamian goddess Ishtar (Inanna in Sumer) or Astarte, who was sometimes conflated or blended with the mother goddess Asherah. In Akkadian texts we find three categories of cult servants who were faithful to the goddess Ishtar: *assinnu, kurgarrû,* and *kulu'u.* While their roles differed, according to the myths these cult servants were all created by the god Ea/Enki for Ishtar/Inanna's sake. One thing the three categories had in common was a kind of transgendered identity: they were basically men but dressed like women and wore women's adornments and makeup. They engaged in various forms of ecstatic exercises with dance, music, and performances, but also practiced ritual flagellation or self-mortification to trigger spiritual experiences. Some are described as Ishtar's lovers and were considered to have prophetic gifts; others acted as professional mourners. Some may have engaged in same-sex sexual acts, but the texts are difficult to interpret. In any case, Ishtar was considered to have changed their gender from men to women. We do not know if this meant that they were castrated. They were viewed with a mixture of devaluation and horrified respect by people in general, and they seem to have been poor but with some support from the temples. Maybe their roles had a safety-valve function for people with ambivalent gender identities in a society with otherwise fixed gender roles.

If some of Ishtar's cult servants actually engaged in ritual intercourse between men, this could at least in theory have provided part of the background to the Holiness Code's prohibition. But neither of the two statements in Leviticus suggests a cultic context, although other sections of the Holiness Code do focus on cult and ritual. Instead, the context is prohibited sexual acts in general and the interpretive framework is impurity. Would Israelite men have been able to buy sexual services from feminized Astarte- or Asherah-worshiping male cult slaves? Considering the lack of evidence, it is quite unlikely that this would have been the background to the Holiness Code's ban against men lying with other men as with a woman.

Noah and Ham

So far, we have mainly discussed legal material. In Genesis, which contains no legal collection but mainly narratives, there is a cryptic story about Noah and his sons. It is related to the fact that Noah is said to have been the first to plant a vineyard after the great flood.

GEN 9:20–27

And Noah, a man of the soil, began to plant a vineyard. And he drank of the wine and became drunk and he lay uncovered in his tent. And Ham, the father of Canaan, saw his father's nakedness and told his two brothers outside. Then Shem and Japheth took the garment and put it on their shoulders and walked backward and covered their father's nakedness and their faces were turned backward, and they did not see their father's nakedness. When Noah woke up from the wine and learned what his youngest son had done to him, he said: "Cursed be Canaan, a slave of slaves may he be to his brothers." And he said, "Blessed be Yahweh, the god of Shem and may Canaan be his slave! May God enlarge Japheth; he shall dwell with Shem and may Canaan be his slave!"

The text literally says that "Ham . . . saw his father's nakedness" (*wayyar' ḥām . . . 'ēt 'erwat 'ābîw*). The behavior of Shem and Japheth, on the other hand, is depicted as the opposite: they did not see their father's nakedness (*'erwat 'ābîhem lo' rā'û*). The whole thing may seem innocent, if it were not for the fact that the Hebrew term "see somebody's nakedness" is also an idiom for sexual intercourse. Examples of this are found above all in Leviticus in the Holiness Code, although the exact wording is not always visible in modern translations. For example, if a man takes his sister and "sees her nakedness and she sees his nakedness" (*wərā'â 'et 'erwātāh wəhî'-tir'eh 'et-'erwātô*) both shall be cut off from their people (Lev 20:17).

From rabbinic times onward, it has occasionally been suggested that the narrative could indicate that Ham raped Noah or possibly even castrated him. The problem is that the text is so terse and what Shem and Japheth do by walking backward and covering their father with a garment is described as the opposite of Ham's crime: they do *not* see Noah's nakedness. Their righteous action is described with the same idiom. For there to be any correspondence between what Ham does and his brothers do not do, the verb "see" must arguably be interpreted literally.

A further problem is posed by the fact that the expression "his father's nakedness" (*'erwat 'abîw*) is used in the Holiness Code's prohibition against having sex with one's father's *wife*. "A man who lies with his father's wife uncovers his father's nakedness" (*'erwat 'abîw gillâ*) (Lev 20:11). Does the story of Noah and Ham possibly suggest incest—that Ham should have raped his mother?

Any attempt to read something out of this story beyond what it actually says on the surface remains speculative. It is not impossible that the text retains a hint of some unaccepted sexual behavior in addition to the mere seeing of Noah's nakedness, as some interpreters smell a rat here. An older narrative may have been edited and rubbed down as various traditions were merged into a literary framework during Persian times. At the same time, the story may in fact reflect very old reminiscences without any sexual connotations: in an Ugaritic myth about the high god El and his three sons, Thukamuna, Shunama, and Haby, the first two help their drunken father while Haby treats him badly. What now remains of the story of Noah's sons is a kind of etiological myth, a justification of the Israelite view of the Canaanites and their status, blaming it on the crimes of their alleged ancestor Ham. Attributing negative traits, less status, and lower dignity to enemy peoples and competitors because of their origin was usually effective and can still be today. But if we look for some detailed information on ancient views of homoeroticism, this narrative provides nothing.

Sodom and Giva

A more well-known story from Genesis that has played a major role for the Christian cultural understanding of same-sex activities through centuries is the story of Sodom and Gomorrah (Gen 18–19). The two cities are usually located geographically to what is now the southeastern part of the Dead Sea. The passage has a complicated history, and it is clear that different traditions have been woven together. Some of the material about Abraham and Lot may possibly originate from the seventh century BCE.

The plot is as follows: Yahweh has determined to destroy the cities of the plain because of their wickedness. Three men visit Abraham and two of them then continue toward Sodom. Yahweh (who seems to be the third) decides not to withhold the information from Abraham but tells him: "The outcry from Sodom and Gomorrah is so strong and their sin so very heavy that I will descend to see if they have really acted according to the outcry that has reached me. If not, I must know it" (Gen 18:20–21). After this, a negotiation follows where Abraham manages to make Yahweh promise to spare Sodom if at least ten righteous people are to be found there.

The crux is that Abraham's nephew Lot lives in Sodom with his family. The two men heading toward Sodom, now called messengers or angels, reach the city gate in the evening, and Lot persuades them to stay overnight with him and invites them to a meal. Then the house is surrounded by the men in the city who want to "know" the strangers—a euphemism for sexual intercourse. Lot then goes out and appeals to the men not to hurt his guests. Instead, he offers his virgin daughters:

GEN 19:7–9
And he said: "My brothers, please do not do evil. Here are my two daughters who have known no man. Let me bring them out to you so that you can do to them what is good in your eyes. Just do not do anything against these men,

because they have come under the protection of my roof beam." But they said: "Stand back!" And they said: "This one came to reside here and now he acts like a judge. We will do more evil to you than to them!"

The guests then pull Lot back into the house and reveal to him what will happen. They also give him the opportunity to save his prospective sons-in-law, but they think it's all a joke. Lot is reluctant to leave, but at dawn the angels drag Lot and his family out of the city and ask them to flee. When they come to Soar, the sun rises and sulfur and fire rain over Sodom and Gomorrah. Lot and his daughters are rescued, but Lot's wife looks back despite the prohibition the angels had given and turns into a pillar of salt.

The story has given rise to the word "sodomy"—a pejorative term for homoerotic acts that was common in the past. Sodom's sin came to be perceived as sex between men. The problem is that this is not apparent from the story. It is clear that the men in the city want to rape the strangers, but does that have anything to do with homoeroticism? Note how Lot, in the narrative, instead offers the men his daughters!

It is interesting to compare the story of Sodom with the story of Giva in Judges 19–21. The book of Judges is part of what scholars call the Deuteronomistic History (Joshua, Judges, 1–2 Samuel, and 1–2 Kings), a collection of writings that, like the Pentateuch, received their final form during the Persian period. Like Genesis, Judges contains some older material. But Judges 17–21 differ from the core of the book, which is mostly about great ancient heroes. These chapters appear to be relatively late additions that mark a boundary to the books of Samuel and the subsequent Israelite kingdom. There are some conspicuous similarities between the stories of Giva and Sodom, which makes it likely that one story lends traits from the other, or that they were somehow aligned and coordinated during the editing process.

The story of Giva is about a Levite from the mountainous areas of Ephraim, whose concubine has run away to her father in Bethlehem. The Levite then travels there to fetch her. On their way home, they stay overnight in the Israelite town of Giva in Benjamin because they do not want to spend the night in Jerusalem, which at the time when the story is situated in the narrative world was inhabited by a foreign people. The Levite stops at the town square as was the custom, but no one offers them shelter. In the end, a kinsman turns up, an old Ephraimite who has settled in Benjamin, and offers lodging.

While the Levite is eating the evening meal with his host, the house is surrounded by the men in the city, and now the similarities with the story of Sodom appear.

Judg 19:20–26	Gen 19:3–11
²⁰ The old man said: "Peace to you! All your needs are only on me, just do not stay overnight in the square."	³ But he urged them so insistingly
²¹ So he brought him to his house and fed the donkeys and they washed their feet and they ate and drank.	that they turned aside with him and entered his house. And he made a feast [i.e., "drink"] for them and baked unleavened bread and they ate.
²² They were enjoying themselves when suddenly the men of the city, worthless men, surrounded the house (ʾanšê hā ʿîr ʾanšê bənê-bəlîyaʿal nāsabbû ʾet-habbayit) and while they were pounding the door they said to the old man who owned the house: "Bring out the man who has come to your house so that we shall know him" (hôṣē̂ ʾet-hā̓îš . . . wənēdāʿennû).	⁴ But before they went to bed, the men of the city, the men of Sodom, surrounded the house (wəʾanšê hā ʿîr ʾanšê sədōm nāsabbû ʿal-habbayit)—from the young to the old, people from all parts, ⁵ and they shouted to Lot and said to him: "Where are the men who came to you tonight? Bring them out to us so that we shall know them" (hôṣîʾēm ʾēlênû wənēdʿāh ʾōtām).
²³ The man who owned the house went out to them and said to them: "My brothers, please do not do evil (ʾal-ʾaḥay ʾal-tārēʿû nāʾ), since this man has come to my house. Do not do such a dishonorable thing.	⁶ Lot went out to them in the doorway and shut the door behind him. ⁷ And he said: "My brothers, please do not do evil (ʾal-nāʾ ʾaḥay tārēʿû).
²⁴ Here is my virgin daughter (hinnēh bittî habbətûlâ) and his (the guest's) concubine, I will bring them out now (ʾôṣîʾāh-nāʾ ʾôtām) so that you can abuse them and do to them what is good in your eyes (waʿăśû lāhem haṭṭôb bəʿênêkem), but to this man you must not do this dishonorable thing."	⁸ Here are my two daughters (hinneh-nāʾ . . . bānôt) who have known no man. Let me bring them out (ʾôṣîʾāh-nāʾ ʾethen) to you so that you can do to them what is good in your eyes (waʿăśû lāhen kaṭṭôb bəʿênêkem). Just do not do anything against these men, because they have come under the protection of my roofbeam."

Judg 19:20–26

²⁵ But the men did not want to listen to him.

So the man forced his concubine and brought her outside to them and they knew her and raped her all the night until morning and they released her to get up at dawn. ²⁶ The woman came back at daybreak and fell at the entrance of the man's house, where her master was staying, until daylight.

Gen 19:3–11

⁹ But they said, "Stand back!" And they said: "This one came to reside here and now he acts like a judge. We will do more evil to you than to them!" And they pushed the man Lot hard and approached to break the door. ¹⁰ Then the men stretched out their hands and brought Lot back to them into the house and closed the door ¹¹ and the men at the entrance of the house they struck with blindness, from the small to the great.

Unlike in the Sodom story, the Levite in Giva is not saved by any divine intervention. The rest of the story is even more uncanny: the Levite wakes up in the morning and finds his concubine dead at the entrance. He then travels home with the corpse, carves it up into twelve pieces, and sends these to all the tribes of Israel, whereupon a war of revenge breaks out in which the tribe of Benjamin sides with Giva and is all but exterminated. Except for six hundred Benjaminite soldiers entrenched on a rock, the genocide is complete. After this, however, Israel is struck by compassion for Benjamin, but since all people have sworn not to give their daughters to any Benjaminite, they come up with a brilliant idea to save the tribe from extinction. The people of Gilead, who refused to take part in the war, are simply slaughtered except for four hundred untouched virgins. These are then distributed among the surviving Benjaminite warriors after due negotiations. Those who go without a girl in the first round are given the opportunity to snatch one at the annual feast in Shiloh without reprisals.

The story in its entirety tells some quite interesting and appalling things about the view of women and the relationship between sex and violence in the ancient world—things that we shall find relevant later on. Right now, however, we are only focusing on similarities with the story of Sodom.

First, a comparison makes it even clearer exactly what sin the inhabitants are thought to have committed. One of the most sacred commandments of ancient West Asia was hospitality toward strangers, but the Sodomites behave in exactly the opposite manner. To rape another man of equal status was an outrageous affront that should be punished severely. It was, as we have seen, even a way to punish a perpetrator, and a known method of humiliating defeated enemy soldiers. The inhabitants of Giva are, if possible, even worse than the Sodomites, because they treat fellow Israelites (albeit from another tribe) as enemies. In both stories, the scandalous treatment of guests is at focus.

Second, we see that none of the stories concern homoeroticism in any reasonable sense, but they are all about sexual violence. The men of the city do not want to lie with the strangers because they lust for other males or are particularly homosexually inclined, but they want to lie "woman-lays," that is, they want to penetrate them and thus humiliate and degrade them. How then can Lot offer his daughters, the old Ephraimite his daughter, or the Levite his concubine? Is this just to save their own skin? Or was it not considered that evil to rape and penetrate a woman?

The world of these stories is thoroughly patriarchal, and the perspective is entirely male. The Levite's concubine is almost seen as his property; perhaps she is his slave, at least he owns the sexual rights to her. He has brought the woman back and he can make use of her sexually for himself, or let others use her. Daughters are a different thing; their virginhood and honor are usually defended. But in comparison with the alternative, that male guests would be humiliated by being raped and feminized, the daughters' honor weighs less—at least in the narrative. The audiences of this story would not have made light of such threats to their own daughters. The sacrifice that the protagonists had to offer to satisfy the extreme xenophobia of the townspeople in these two stories only proves the depth of their sinfulness and the justice in their being annihilated.

Interpretations of Sodom's Sin

Sodom's (and Giva's) sin is thus a lack of hospitality, which expresses itself in gross xenophobia. This is, in fact, how the Sodom narrative was usually interpreted in Jewish tradition. Few other stories from Genesis are quoted and referenced so often in the Hebrew and Christian Bible as well as in various Jewish and Christian apocrypha. Sodom exemplifies evil and destruction, and the city becomes a warning for judgment and punishment. What the sin consists of is rarely specified. But when the story is discussed in the Hebrew Bible, the context is usually about social injustice. Here are a few examples. Isaiah's book begins by making Jerusalem resemble Sodom and Gomorrah.

ISA 1:10, 15–17
Hear the word of Yahweh, you leaders of Sodom! Listen to the instruction of God, you people of Gomorrah! . . . Your hands are full of blood. Wash, make yourselves clean, remove your evil misdeeds from my eyes! Cease to be wicked! Learn to be good! Rebuke the oppressor! Be just to the orphan! Defend the widow!

Ezekiel likewise compares Jerusalem with both Samaria and Sodom.

EZEK 16:46–49
Your younger sister, who lived to the right [south] of you, was Sodom and her daughters. Have you not walked their roads and practiced their abominations? And you quickly became more corrupt than they in all your ways! By my life, says the Lord Yahweh, never did your sister Sodom and her daughters behave the way you and your daughters did! Look at this! This was the sin of your sister Sodom: she and her daughters had luxury, abundance of food, and a calm and easy life, while they did not support the poor and destitute. They became arrogant and practiced abominations before me, so I removed them when I saw it.

From the Old Testament Apocrypha, we can illustrate the same point with an example from the so-called Wisdom of Solomon, where the author compares Egyptian inhospitality with that of the Sodomites:

WIS 19:14–17
Some people [the Sodomites] did not receive unknown travellers, but these [the Egyptians] enslaved their foreign benefactors. And not only will there be a visitation of the former because they received the strangers with animosity, but the latter, after having received those who already shared the same rights as themselves, maltreated them terribly with labor. But they were also struck blind like the former at the door of the righteous one, when surrounded by yawning darkness each one tried to find their way through their doors.

And we find the same motif in the Gospels:

LUKE 10:10–12

Whenever you enter a town where people do not receive you, go out into its
streets and say: "Even the dust from your town which sticks on our feet we wipe
off against you. But you should know this: The kingdom of God has come near.
I tell you: it will be more endurable for Sodom on that day than for such a town."

From where, then, comes the interpretation of Sodom's sin as unlawful
sexual acts? The book of Jubilees and the Testament of the Twelve Patriarchs,
two so-called pseudepigraphs from the second century BCE (the latter with
considerable Christian interpolations, making some scholars date the whole
work to the second century CE), identify Sodom's sin as unlawful sex. Still,
they do not single out sexual acts between people of the *same* sex but rather associate Sodom with incest, adultery, and pagan women. In particular, Sodom's
sin is linked to the story of the guardians, the angels who, according to Genesis 6:1–4, had intercourse with human daughters and gave rise to the giants.
Both the book of Jubilees and 1 Enoch develop the guardian myth further. In
the Testament of Naphtali (one of the Testaments of the Twelve Patriarchs),
it is said that Sodom departed from the "order of nature" as the guardians did.
Here we may perhaps think of an interpretation of Sodom's sin as intercourse
between men, but the analogy with the guardians strongly suggests another
interpretation to be more likely: unlawful boundary crossing. Just like the an-
gelic guardians violated the boundary between angels and humans, the men
in Sodom attempted to do something similar, although in reverse.

The same association that we find in the Testament of Naphtali is also
found in the New Testament Epistle of Jude. This short text written near the
end of the first century CE warns of false teachers who live in debauchery. Here
the guardians and the Sodomites are explicitly compared:

JUDE 6–7

And the angels who did not watch over their position, but left their own
dwelling, he has kept in darkness with eternal fetters until the judgment on
the great day. Likewise, Sodom and Gomorrah and their surrounding towns
who committed sexually illicit acts in a similar manner as these [i.e., the
angels], and pursued different flesh, are displayed as an example, suffering
punishment of eternal fire.

The author clearly perceives Sodom's sin as sexual in nature but comparable to the guardians' unlawful boundary crossing. The Greek text literally reads: "in the same way as these [i.e., the angels], having committed sexually illicit acts (*ekporneusasai*) and having gone after foreign flesh (*apelthousai opisō sarkos heteras*)." It may be technically possible to interpret this as saying that by practicing sex against people of the same sex, the Sodomites transgressed a natural boundary and did something as alien to their human nature as the angels did in relation to their heavenly nature when lying with human women. But such an interpretation is both strained and far-fetched, since the text stresses the *otherness* of the bodies (*sarkos heteras*) with whom the perpetrators had sex, not the *likeness*. Besides being sexually immoral in general, the men of Sodom try to rape *divine* strangers. Second Peter, which dates still later than Jude, borrows the entire Epistle of Jude and modifies this section but does not develop this track at all.

In another of the Testaments of the Twelve Patriarchs, the Testament of Levi, pederasts and people who have sex with animals are condemned (T. Levi 17.11). But here the author does not take the opportunity to refer to Sodom. It seems that even when Sodom's sin began to be associated with sex, homoeroticism did not emerge as an obvious candidate for comparison.

It is with the Jewish philosopher Philo of Alexandria that we first find such an interpretation. Philo was contemporaneous with the apostle Paul and wrote in Greek. His aim was to show how the Jewish scriptures, when read as allegories, were in fact superior expositions of Hellenistic philosophy. The only thing required to interpret them correctly was, of course, the imagination of Philo. According to Philo's exposition of the story of Sodom in his *De Abrahamo* (133–166), the area teemed with tens of thousands of excesses based on pleasure, appetite, wealth, luxury, and desire. The people threw off the restraints of "natural law" to engage in gluttony, drunkenness, and forbidden sex.

Gluttony and drunkenness need no closer exposition, but forbidden sex is all the more gratifying to develop further, as does the philosopher in line with the Jewish-Hellenistic traditions we find attested in the Wisdom of Solomon and Paul's Epistle to the Romans—two texts that we will soon look at more closely. Philo continues:

ABR. 135–136

Not only did they ruin the marriages of others in their madness for women, but by mounting men, despite also being men, the doers (*hoi drōntes*) did not respect their common nature with the sufferers (*tous paschontas*). As a result, when they tried to breed children they were proved to breed only unfinished offspring, but this proof was of no use since they were defeated by much stronger desires. Then little by little they accustomed those who were born men to endure the woman's role and provided them with a feminine disease, hard to defeat. Not only did they feminize their bodies through softness and weakness, but they also degenerated their souls, and did what they could on their part to destroy the whole of humankind. Indeed, if Greeks and barbarians had joined forces together in bringing about such associations, then city by city would have been laid waste, emptied as if by a plague.

The philosopher continues to explain how God, the savior of humanity, out of love and compassion ensured that natural associations between men and women resulted in an increase in offspring, while the unnatural Sodomites were punished with fire from heaven. This is not Philo's main point though. Eventually he arrives at an allegorical moral sermon about the five cities on the plain representing the five senses. But that is another story.

We see that Philo on the one hand sees Sodom as the archetype for excessive pleasure both in terms of food and drink and in terms of sex. On the other hand, he focuses particularly on sex between men as the worst form of forbidden sex that he can imagine. The starting points are clear: intercourse between men is understood as an act of a man with unnatural desires who penetrates another man as if he were a woman. Thus, the penetrated man is feminized, and his body becomes weak and his soul degenerate. If everyone did this, humanity would become extinct.

The interesting thing is that at the time, Philo seems quite alone in interpreting Sodom's sin this way. Among the graffiti from the city of Pompeii, which was destroyed by a volcanic eruption in the year 79 CE, Sodom and Gomorrah are mentioned. Part of the graffiti is of a sexual nature, but it is difficult to draw any conclusions from a single occurrence of Sodom. The Jewish historian Josephus, who wrote his works a few decades after Philo, sees Sodom's sin primarily as inhumane and xenophobic behavior. The same applies to the rabbinic texts that we know from the first centuries of the Common Era. When they talk about Sodom, they focus on injustice, greed, xenophobia, and oppression, and this despite the fact that emerging Christianity is taking the story in a completely different direction.

It is the Christian tradition that, in the footsteps of Philo, develops an interpretation of Sodom as a symbol of sex against nature. It is not the only

Christian reading of Genesis 19 in the early church, but it gradually gains ground. It is possible that the author of Jude held this view, but for reasons already presented above such a reading is rather unlikely. Later, however, this interpretation is expressed by some of the church fathers, although neither Tertullian nor Origen in the early third century CE interprets Sodom's sin as sexual intercourse between men, despite the fact that they include sexual sins among the city's misdeeds. A homophobic reading only takes over during the fourth century CE, when John Chrysostom develops it systematically and more church fathers follow suit. But there is no room here for any further discussion of the history of interpretation.

Wisdom of Solomon

The Wisdom of Solomon, written during the first century BCE, belongs to the Old Testament Apocrypha, a collection of Greek Jewish texts that did not become part of the Hebrew Bible. But since these texts were used by Greek-speaking Jews, they naturally came to belong to the Christian Old Testament, although not all Protestant denominations today include them. Thus, the Wisdom of Solomon was known and used by several of the New Testament writers, including Paul.

The text depicts divine wisdom, which Solomon sought to find. Wisdom is almost personified as a woman. It is Wisdom who saved the righteous through Israel's history, and she also freed the people of Israel from Egypt. From chapter 11 onward, the author begins to ridicule the idolatry of the gentiles as foolish and associates them with an unrighteous life: "They had wandered so far on the paths of delusion that they accepted as gods even the most despised among shameless animals, being deceived as having the judgment of silly infants. Therefore, you judged them as ignorant children, to their scorn" (Wis 12:24–25). The text continues to describe how stupid someone is who carves a crooked piece of wood, paints it, and then believes it to be a god. This is a rhetoric we recognize from some of the prophets (Isa 40; Jer 10). Gentiles are simply stupid! The author continues to ridicule:

WIS 15:14–19
But most foolish and more pitiful than infants were your peoples' oppressing enemies, since they considered the idols of the peoples to be gods—those who have no functioning eyes to see with, nor noses to inhale air with, nor

ears to hear with, nor fingers on their hands to feel with and whose feet are useless for walking. A human being made them and one whose spirit was a loan formed them. For no human being has the power to form a god similar to himself. Being mortal, he makes something dead with lawless hands, for he is better than his objects of worship since he has come alive while they never have. They even worship the most hateful animals that in comparison to the others are the worst in their foolishness, animals that one does not desire like those whose appearance happens to be beautiful, but animals that have escaped God's praise as well as his blessing.

The bottom line for the author is that the Egyptians were punished with the same abominable animals that they themselves worshiped, while the people of Israel were saved.

As part of this long section on senseless idolatry—which both uses material from the prophets and reminds one of a kind of Greek rationalistic criticism of traditional religion—we also find vast lists of sins or moral shortcomings that idolatry by necessity is thought to induce:

WIS 14:22–29

But not only was it enough for them to be deluded about the knowledge of God, but living a life of ignorance in great strife, they call such evil things peace. Whether they engage in rituals of child-murder, secret mysteries, or mad, strange orgy rites, they no longer keep either their lives or their marriages pure, one lies in wait to murder another or cause him pain by adultery. Everywhere is a confusion of blood and murder, theft and deception, corruption, faithlessness, disorder, perjury, uproar against the good, forgetfulness of favors, defilement of souls, interchange in breeding (*geneseōs enallagē*), disorder in marriage, adultery, and promiscuity. For the worship of the unnamed idols is the origin and cause and limit of all evil, whether by becoming crazy through feasting, or prophesying lies, or living unrighteously, or rashly committing perjury. Because they believe in lifeless idols they do not expect to be harmed when they have sworn falsely.

The author thinks that because pagans do not believe in gods that can punish them, they live and behave in any way they like—but justice will eventually overtake them (Wis 14:30–31)!

Throughout human history it has been common to vilify and accuse "the other" of anything from child murder to secret rites and sexual orgies. We do not have to look far back in time to find precisely this kind of accusation against Jews in an anti-Semitic Europe. Prohibited sex is also a recurring feature of such vice lists. Pagans are suspected of violating everything that the Jewish law prohibits because they lack it: adultery and orgies because everyone knows that pagans act that way, unlawful or disorderly marriages because their incest rules are not identical to the Jewish laws, and unnatural intercourse. The phrase rendered "interchange in breeding" above is sometimes translated "unnatural intercourse" or "sexual perversion." The meaning is rather unclear: the Greek *geneseōs enallagē* can in theory mean change of birth, exchange between races, or perverse breeding. Here, it probably refers to deviating sexual behaviors in general.

Thus, the Wisdom of Solomon does not explicitly discuss sexual acts between people of the same sex, although the Greek original makes it possible to interpret the text in this way. As we shall soon see, this is what Paul does in Romans.

Paul's Letters

Paul was never a disciple of Jesus during his lifetime but, according to his own statement, he began his career as an enemy of the early Christians. A dramatic experience changed his course. Luke portrays the event as a kind of conversion in three, not entirely coherent, versions found in the book of Acts. Paul himself does not provide the same details and seems to have perceived what happened rather as a kind of calling: the resurrected Jesus revealed himself to him and commissioned him to proclaim the gospel to the "gentiles," that is, to "the peoples," the "others," those who were not Jews. For Paul, this gospel meant that non-Jewish males were not required to be circumcised and non-Jews did not need to follow Jewish practices regarding Sabbath or purity in order to become incorporated into the covenant community.

The communities we are talking about are the associations of early Christ followers, which both by themselves and by others were still considered a Jewish sect. Paul faced fierce opposition for his position both from Christ believers in Judea and from other Jews—Christ believers or not—in various parts of the Roman Empire. Many Jews found it threatening to their own social identity and to their relationships with the outside world when non-Jews became integrated into Jewish communities on what could be perceived as loose grounds without fully embracing Jewish practices.

Paul wrote his letters between 50 CE (or just before) and his death a few years into the 60s. Most scholars accept seven letters as having been genuinely penned, or rather dictated, by Paul. In addition, there are a number of later letters that came to be attributed to him. These letters modify and adapt Paul's image and further develop parts of his thinking, using his authority to control and influence developments in the early church occurring late in the first century CE and into the first half of the second century.

Paul's letters contain a couple of texts that explicitly mention sexual acts between men. One of these may also refer to sexual acts between women. The other also seems to find an echo in one of the letters written after Paul's death. In a discussion on legal disputes in 1 Corinthians, Paul lists a number of people who are considered unrighteous and thus cannot inherit the kingdom of God (1 Cor 6:9–10). The language is very specific, and the translation of a few words has occasionally caused vehement discussions. Many Bible translators have had problems translating the Greek words *malakoi* (singular *malakos*) and *arsenokoitai* (singular *arsenokoitēs*) that appear in this list. Some have merged them together and translated them as "homosexuals" (Swedish *NT81*; cf. NAS) or similar translations like "men who practice homosexuality" (ESV) or even "sexual perverts" (RSV). However, as consciousness about homosexuality has increased, such translations have become more and more untenable. Instead, some translations have looked for presumably more neutral expressions, like "men who have sex with men" (NIV; cf. Swedish *B2000*). This is hardly an improvement, however, since the Greek wording is quite precise and mentions two categories. In this regard, the old King James Version did better, as it distinguished between the "effeminate" and "abusers of themselves with mankind." Similarly, the NRSV distinguishes between "male prostitutes" and "sodomites," but the latter term is pejorative and the updated edition (NRSVUE) changed it to "men who engage in illicit sex," which is quite unspecific. In any case, prostitution has to be read into the text. Several translations have variations on this theme. Besides some translations perpetuating Philo's and the church fathers' understanding of the sin of Sodom, all reveal different interpretive biases as they rely on various historical reconstructions and interpretations of same-sex activity in the ancient world.

A fairly literal translation of the text we are discussing could look like this:

1 COR 6:9–10

Do you not know that unrighteous people will not inherit the kingdom of God? Do not be deluded: neither people engaging in shameful sex (*pornoi*), nor idolaters, nor adulterers (*moichoi*), nor "softies" (*malakoi*), nor "male-bedders" (*arsenokoitai*), nor thieves, nor the greedy, nor drunkards, nor abusers, nor robbers, will inherit the kingdom of God.

The meaning of *pornos* (m.) and *pornē* (f.) in Paul's time was no longer restricted to prostitution (as in classical Greek) but covered notions of illicit and shameful sex in general, and there are no simple equivalents to the words *malakoi* and *arsenokoitai*. *Malakos* simply means "soft" or "weak" and could be used disparagingly about men who, in one way or another, were perceived as effeminate or feminized. This included men who took on the "passive" role in a penetrative intercourse. *Arsenokoitēs*, on the other hand, is a rather odd word that means something like "male-bedder." When the Septuagint (LXX), the Greek version of the Hebrew Bible, translates the Holiness Code's condemnation of the man who lies "woman-lays" with another man, the word *arsēn* is used for "man, male" and *koitē* for "bed, lying" (in a sexual sense). For a Greek-speaking Jew with the Septuagint in mind, *arsenokoitēs* quite obviously refers to a man who, against the prohibition of the Holiness Code, lies "woman-lays" with another man and penetrates him. And the other man, who allows himself to be penetrated, or is forced to be so, could be termed a *malakos*.

One of the problems with translations like "men who practice homosexuality" or "men who have sex with men" is that based on our present understanding of sex, whether between people of the opposite or the same sex, we usually perceive such wordings as expressions of reciprocity when the text actually distinguishes between two roles: he who penetrates another man and he whose behavior is considered soft or effeminate because he is penetrated like a woman.

The word *arsenokoitēs* is also used by the author of 1 Timothy, who borrows the authority of Paul, in a similar list of the sins of the unrighteous. Here no *malakoi* are mentioned in the Greek, just *arsenokoitai*:

1 TIM 1:8–10

But we know that the law is good, if one uses it lawfully, considering this, that the law is not there for the righteous, but for the lawless and rebellious, for the ungodly and the sinful, the unholy and profane, for those who com-

mit patricide and matricide, for murderers, for adulterers, "male-bedders,"
kidnappers, liars, perjurers, and any other who oppose the sound teaching.

In both texts, same-sex activities belong to lists of how unrighteous pagans
typically behave, since they do not have access to the divine law. These vice lists
have their background in Jewish polemics against the idolatry of other nations,
and we recognize the means of expression from the Wisdom of Solomon.

The similarities with the Wisdom of Solomon become even clearer when
we look at the second Pauline text that mentions sexual acts between people
of the same sex. In the opening chapter of Romans, Paul argues that Jews and
other peoples (i.e., gentiles) share the same basic preconditions, even though
Jews have access to the law while other peoples live in ignorance. He claims
this because, in his view, it is behavior that counts and both groups act contrary
to the knowledge they actually have: the Jews break their law, and the peoples
act against the knowledge provided by creation itself. Therefore, there is no
defense for either Jews or others (Rom 1:10; 2:1). Everyone has sinned and
everyone must be judged in relation to the "law" to which they have access
(Rom 2:12–16). Paul's bottom line is that through Jesus all other peoples, as
well as Jews, can become "righteous" or "saved" into a single community, in
which no special features or distinguishing marks, such as circumcision or
certain ritual practices, play a role.

Paul's rhetorical strategy to catch the attention of his audience (the letters
were read aloud in the congregations) is to begin by painting a rather crude and
prejudiced caricature of the gentiles—something that was standard in Hellenistic Jewish polemics against "idolatry." Rhetorical tactics as well as contents
are borrowed from the Wisdom of Solomon. First, Paul portrays the origins
of foolish "idolatry":

ROM 1:18–23

For the wrath of God is revealed from heaven, over all human ungodliness
and injustice that have captured the truth, since that which can be known
about God is evident among them—God has revealed it to them. For his
invisible attributes are clearly visible through his works from the creation
of the world, his eternal power and divinity, so they are without excuse. Although they knew God, they did not give him glory and thanks as God,
but their thoughts became foolish and their hearts became darkened and

without understanding. Claiming to be wise they became stupid, and they exchanged the glory of the incorruptible God for corruptible idols in the form of humans, birds, quadrupeds, and reptiles.

Paul then continues, just like the Wisdom of Solomon, by spelling out the moral implications of the animistic and polytheistic misunderstandings that have victimized the gentiles:

ROM 1:24–32

Therefore, God handed them over through the desires (*epithymiais*) of their hearts to impurity (*akatharsia*) so as to dishonor (*atimazesthai*) their bodies with each other. They exchanged God's truth for falsehood and venerated and worshiped creation instead of the creator—he who is blessed forever, amen. Because of this, God handed them over to dishonorable passions (*pathē atimias*): Their females exchanged the natural "use" (*physikēn chrēsin*) for that [which is] against nature (*para physin*), and similarly males also abandoned the natural "use" (*physikēn chrēsin*) of females and were inflamed with a yearning for each other in that males practiced shamefulness (*aschēmosynēn*) with males and received in themselves the necessary payment for their error (*tēn antimisthian hēn edei tēs planēs autōn en heautois apolambanontes*). And as they did not consider keeping God in mind, God handed them over to an insufficient mind, to do that which is improper, filled with all kinds of injustice, wickedness, selfishness, and evil, filled with envy, murder, strife, deceit, and malice, becoming gossipers, slanderers, god haters, violent, arrogant, boastful, inventors of evil and disobedient to their parents. They became ignorant, unreliable, impassible, and merciless. Although they understand God's decree that those who do these things are worthy of death, they not only do them, but also approve of others performing them.

In this text we find some of the formulations that perhaps more than any others have served to justify homophobia in those parts of the world that are influenced by Christianity. These verses by Paul have often been invoked to condemn homosexuality and homosexual people and are still referred to today. As we can see, the verses about sex are part of a much longer vice list and not the climax of the passage. Compared to Wisdom of Solomon 14:22–29, cited earlier, Paul seems to turn the order around, concluding with a vice list. And he expands or interprets what is sometimes translated in Wisdom of Solomon 14:26 with "unnatural intercourse" to include sexual acts between people of the same sex. We need to look more closely at these verses.

First, Paul says that as a consequence of idol worship, God handed over, or surrendered, people to impurity (*akatharsia*) in, or through, their heart's desires (*epithymiais*), with the purpose or consequence that they dishonored (*atimazesthai*) their bodies with one another. So far, Paul basically says the same thing as Wisdom of Solomon 14:26 does regarding "unnatural intercourse," with the addition that he clearly associates unlawful sex with impurity, as in the summaries of the Holiness Code. But then, Paul becomes more specific with regard to the "dishonorable passions" (*pathē atimias*) to which God has surrendered human beings. Some of his formulations are difficult to translate, and I have chosen to translate them in a fairly literal way.

Paul talks of exchanging the natural "use" or "intimacy" (*chrēsis*) for an unnatural "use." This undoubtedly refers to sexual intercourse, which is conceptualized as being either natural (*physikē*) or against nature (*para physin*). Exactly what women's unnatural intercourses are supposed to consist of is not entirely clear. If we interpret the statement about women in analogy with what Paul then says about men, it is reasonable to infer that he is thinking of some kind of sexual act between women. But based on the dominant view in Paul's time of what would have been natural in a woman's sexual practice, this statement could also refer to women who took an overly active role in the intercourse, took pleasure themselves in the act, or possibly engaged in anal sex. We will return to ancient views of women's sexual roles in chapter 5. Here it must suffice to point out that Paul could very well be referring to sex between women, and there are some good arguments for it, but we cannot be entirely certain that he does so. None of the relevant texts from the Hebrew Bible says anything about sex between women. We already sense the reason for this, and we will discuss this issue further in later chapters too.

As for Paul's talk of unnatural intercourse between men, it clearly refers to same-sex sexual acts: males yearned for each other and acted shamefully with other males. However, what these shameful acts (*aschēmosynēn*) consisted of more precisely in Paul's mind is not as clear. Although the language seems precise, we do not know for sure how to interpret it, and scholars disagree concerning what this actually means. It is clear that Paul considers their behavior to be a delusion, and that by necessity there will be some payback for this (*tēn antimisthian hēn edei tēs planēs autōn*). This "reward" is something the men involved will receive (*apolambanontes*) in themselves (*en heautois*). Some people think that Paul is here referring to the wide anuses that some were considered to incur by allowing themselves to be penetrated by other men too often. This may at first sight seem far-fetched, but the fact is that several ancient Greek writers, in a derogatory manner typical for its time, ridicule men who allowed themselves to be feminized by taking on the role of a woman in intercourse between men and mock them for their large assholes. This, of course, does not mean that Paul must have thought along such paths, but it makes it quite possible.

Paul's negative attitude, especially to men who had anal sex with other men, is quite easy to explain in view of his background as a Hellenistic Jew. The Holiness Code came to play a major role in Second Temple Judaism and equally so for Christ believers. It contains several of the commandments about neighborly love and compassionate behavior that we encounter in the Jesus tradition, and it is referred to both now and then in early Christian texts. Therefore, it is no wonder that Paul and others took such rules regarding prohibited sexual acts for granted. In addition, sexual acts between men had been discussed in the Greek cultural sphere since the classical period. Despite all that is sometimes said about homosexuality among the ancient Greeks, sex between men was no simple matter for them either. But the reasons for this are not as obvious and easy to understand for people with modern mindsets. Hence, we need to investigate more closely the conceptual world within which ancient people lived. If we avoid doing this, their opinions and values will be impossible to understand.

$$\boxed{3}$$

IMPURITY, DISGUST, AND SEX

Jewish Conceptions of Purity

As we saw in the previous chapter, illicit sexual practices, including intercourse between men, are associated with impurity in both the Holiness Code (*ṭum'â*) and the letters of Paul (*akatharsia*). Paul views such practices as degrading and the Holiness Code calls them abhorrent or abominable (*tô'ēbâ*).

For Paul to use concepts of purity in this way may be thought to involve a contradiction, since he argues that gentiles are not to be pressured to follow Jewish purity laws. But such language is not unusual; indeed, it is very common in both the Hebrew Bible and the writings of neighboring cultures. As a matter of fact, terminology for purity is used very frequently by New Testament authors, and not the least by Paul, in discussions of morality and ways of life. So what is it about some sexual practices that is considered impure? What is purity all about in Israelite religion and ancient Judaism?

Impurity is first and foremost a ritual concept used in the book of Leviticus in its priestly laws. Impurity language is used concerning particular animals that should not be eaten or whose carcasses should not be touched, particular states of the body that were thought to defile and give rise to a form of contagion, and particular conduct or actions that were regarded as unacceptable. Unclean animals and states are dealt with in the purity laws of Leviticus 11–15. Certain birds and terrestrial and aquatic animals were not to be eaten, and one class of little crawling or swarming creatures (*šereṣ*) found on land, in the air, or in the water is explicitly described as disgusting or detestable (*šeqeṣ*). Not only should their carcasses not be eaten, but utensils, food, or drinking water must not come into contact with them either (Lev 11). Eating unclean animals was prohibited, and contact with their carcasses conveyed an impurity that required objects to be rinsed with water or discarded and people to wash their clothes and remain unclean until evening.

Similarly, impurity was seen as contracted through contact with people suffering from various unclean conditions (Lev 12–15). This applied in the case of a number of skin disorders (*ṣāraʿat*) in which the skin turned red, flaked, or cracked, and which, despite not being the disease we associate with the term, is often translated as "leprosy." It applied to men and women with discharges from their genital organs, not just those that resulted from illness (like gonorrhea or irregular uterine bleeding) but also ordinary menstruation and postnatal bleeding as well as the emission of semen (Lev 12; 15). Someone was also thought to become unclean through contact with a dead person. Detailed rules concerning corpse impurity were developed a little later (Num 19). Someone suffering from pathological discharges or a skin disorder was regarded as unclean as long as symptoms persisted. After the cessation of symptoms, a purification period of seven days was required, the same length of time as the purification period for a menstruating woman and for someone who had come into contact with a corpse. A person who was unclean like this for an extended period of time was thought to transmit impurity to other people, utensils, food, and so on—an impurity that lasted throughout the day, sometimes necessitating the washing of clothing.

The majority of impurities required a ritual of some sort involving water when the period was over. The most common was ritual bathing, first in running water and later, beginning in the Hasmonean period, in a pool of sufficient size. Corpse impurity involved the sprinkling of a special water of purification, and by the turn of the Common Era the different purification rituals had largely been synchronized and various methods had been invented for reducing the level of impurity during the purification period. Seven-day periods, at least after contracting corpse impurity, were begun with an additional bath. Instead of waiting until evening, lesser impurities, lasting for one day only, could partly be neutralized with an immediate ritual bath, at least according to certain groups. Men with penile discharges could wash their hands, and the practice of hand washing came to be extended to meals in order to avoid a chain reaction through which various lesser kinds of impurity might be spread via food and drink.

How, then, did illicit sexual practices relate to impurity? The way the Holiness Code speaks about impurity is both similar to and different from the priestly purity laws. According to the Holiness Code a person becomes unclean, explicitly, through having intercourse with a kinsman's wife (Lev 18:20) or with an animal (18:23), or by turning to mediums or diviners (19:31). According to the summary at 18:24–30, a person is defiled by any and all of the practices just listed. This ought to mean that, in addition to becoming unclean through the practices explicitly mentioned, a person also becomes unclean by violating any of the incest laws that were listed earlier by lying with a woman during menstruation, by sacrificing children to Molech, or by lying "woman-lays" with a man. The summary also states that the land is defiled by such practices and that the people become unclean by following the customs of its previous inhabitants.

Later on in the Holiness Code we learn that the temple, too, is defiled by child sacrifices to Molech (20:3). Priests become unclean from touching the dead (21:1–4, 11), and while they are unclean, they may not touch or eat sacred donations or sacrificial food (22:2–8).

Peculiar to the Holiness Code's talk of impurity is the use of the word tôʿēbâ, "abhorrent thing" or "abomination," not only to describe men's sexual intercourse with men, but also to sum up the various acts that are said to defile human beings and the land. In the Holiness Code, the term is used in parallel with "unclean" (ṭāmēʾ). There is a prior history to this word. In Deuteronomy its use to denote things that are utterly unacceptable is liberal and sweeping: other gods and their worship, child sacrifice, the sacrifice of defective animals, forbidden foods, women wearing men's clothing, interest on loans and fraud. The term simply indicates abhorrence at certain kinds of behavior, several of which are associated with the customs and practices of foreign peoples. The Holiness Code, which came about sometime later, takes up this usage to indicate disgust with a number of undesirable behaviors that, for the most part, are labeled unclean.

While the purity laws allocate rituals for effecting purification from the impurities the laws describe, purification rituals are nonetheless lacking for most of the conduct that the Holiness Code calls "unclean" and "disgusting." Rather, these are thought to provoke the disgust of God and the land to such an extent that the people must be thrown out. An interesting example that is found in both collections, and thereby serves to make this difference clear, is the prohibition against sexual intercourse during menstruation. According to the purity laws, a man who has intercourse with a menstruating woman is unclean for seven days (Lev 15:24). For impurity of this sort there are purification rituals. But in the Holiness Code, sex during menstruation is forbidden and counts among the practices that defile the land. For acts of this sort, be they illicit sexual practices or, say, child sacrifices, no purification rituals exist.

How, then, are we to understand the Holiness Code's habit of applying the labels "unclean" and "disgusting" to cultic and sexual behaviors that its priestly authors see as needing to be curbed? One common view is that the Holiness Code is talking metaphorically about moral impurity by analogy with the ritual impurity of the purity laws. But what we tend to refer to as ritual impurity is, in fact, just as metaphorical. At its heart is a notion, and a sense, of real dirt, dirt that defiles and needs to be removed. Menstrual blood and other genital discharges, secretions from skin disorders, and mold growing on textiles and buildings (see Lev 13–14) are all capable, one might think, of being wiped, scraped, or rinsed off. But ritual impurity is transmitted by touch, by contact, or by being in the same room, even when there is no physical substance that could soil anything or be transferred from one person to another. Rituals involving water are used even when there is no substance to rinse off. There is thus a level of metaphor involved here. In contrast, the impurities of the Holiness Code cannot be washed away by means of the purification rituals of the purity laws. The temple might become defiled and the land might vomit out the people because of these forbidden practices, but the impurity associated with these practices seems to be of a sort different from that found in the purity laws.

Disgust and Conceptual Metaphor Theory

What unites the different forms of impurity that we find in the Pentateuchal law codes is an underlying sense of disgust. Not everything described as unclean is of the kind that people naturally find disgusting. But the various types of impurity do appear to have certain common features that can be explained on the basis of emotional factors or of evolutionary biology or psychology. There is a great deal of research into disgust as an emotion, including its origins, evolution, and function. A number of the senses, not merely taste, are involved in disgust, which has evolved to prevent us from ingesting harmful substances. One of the most famous researchers into disgust, Paul Rozin, has identified nine "elicitors" or triggers that make people feel disgust. These are food, body products, particular animals, particular sexual practices, contact with death or corpses, body-envelope violations, poor hygiene, interpersonal contact (with unpleasant individuals), and particular moral infractions.

Feelings of disgust play a larger role in our moral compass than we would usually like to admit, and we sometimes use terms for disgust as value judgments. This is problematic as disgust sometimes "lags behind," eliciting emotional responses to behaviors and things that no longer represent a threat to the survival of either the species or the individual, similar to how fear or stress can sometimes be triggered by things that do not pose a danger or call for physical mobilization. Thus, our emotional responses, disgust among them, are at times dysfunctional and it may be dangerous to cite them as a basis for society's morals or laws. Even so, our emotions, including disgust, are evolution's way of developing the human species into a morally reflective being.

If we examine the various different conceptions of impurity mentioned earlier, we can easily see that Rozin's "elicitors" all fit. Little crawling, swarming, and slimy creatures, in particular their carcasses, readily provoke people's disgust across cultural boundaries. Where the lines are drawn is not entirely obvious—from the exceptions to the food laws, for example, we gather that the Israelites apparently learned to eat certain kinds of grasshopper in Babylonia— but we can discern some basic features. Genital discharges and corpses would have quickly acquired an unpleasant odor in a warm climate without access to modern sanitation. Male disgust at menstrual blood was widespread in ancient cultures. The skin disorders, too, that were regarded as unclean may readily have provoked disgust. Finally, research has shown that we find some moral and sexual infractions repugnant, and this is precisely what the Holiness Code exemplifies. At an evolutionary, biological, and psychological level, disgust can thus be understood as a common denominator behind the rather disparate phenomena that are described as unclean. This accords with the language that is used in the Pentateuchal legal material.

But here and there in the priestly purity laws we come across things that do not fit as well. Is a pig more disgusting than a goat? Why is a rabbit considered unclean? Why is a woman unclean for forty days if she gives birth to a boy, but for eighty days if it is a girl? Are girls more disgusting than boys or does the mother bleed for longer? And what precisely is disgusting about sexual practices?

Disgust may work as an underlying explanation for all of the different *categories* of impurity that we have identified, but it is not sufficient to explain every aspect and *detail*. We have to suppose that cultural and historical factors have led to new impurities being incorporated into preexisting basic structures. One model that can help us to understand this process and understand why certain illicit sexual practices were regarded as unclean is conceptual metaphor theory.

Conceptual metaphor theory rests upon the fundamental insight that our language is profoundly metaphorical. Consider the last sentence. What images do "rests," "fundamental," "insight," and "profoundly" evoke? We think and talk using language that derives from our experiences and the information gathered from our senses and from the movement of our bodies in time and space. A metaphor is said to come about when a word belonging to a specific source domain is used in a target domain where it is not initially at home. "Insight," for example, in its original source domain means to see into something (with one's eyes), but it is almost exclusively used metaphorically in a target domain concerned with understanding. Accordingly, we no longer think of the word as a metaphor.

Impurity is originally about pollution with some physical substance, and purification, in the word's original domain, has to do with wiping, scraping, or washing away that substance. When instead impurity is used in another target domain, it brings with it elements from the source domain and applies them to phenomena in the target domain. One such target domain is individuals who, for various reasons, elicit a sense of discomfort and disgust (Lev 13–15). Another is disgusting little creatures (Lev 11). A third is moldy textiles or buildings (Lev 13–14). A fourth is offensive behaviors (Holiness Code). Strategies for removing these impurities are, to a degree, carried across from the source domain. Mold can be scraped or washed away. Contact with people or dead animals might perhaps also be conceived of as capable of being washed away. But it's hardly possible to wash away the consumption of disgusting animals; for the digestive system, we find no purification ritual. And offensive behaviors, rather than being washed away, are removed otherwise. "Whoever commits any of these abominations (*hattô'ēbôt*) shall be cut off from their people" (Lev 18:29). And if nothing else, the land will vomit out those who behave abominably.

In this way the impurity metaphor can be expanded and used in many different areas and in many different target domains for things of which one disapproves. But to understand further how this happens, we can turn to theories of "conceptual blending." Conceptual blending describes how a new "blended space" arises out of two or more "input spaces" that have some things (though not everything) in common—a "generic space." One such generic space might be the avoidance of unpleasantness and disgust, which is shared by various input spaces. One input space might be the avoidance of contact with objectionable dirt known as impurity (*ṭum'â*); it is perceived as revolting and sticky but it can be washed off. Another input space might be the avoidance of contact with people who provoke offense, because they have certain skin disorders, for instance, or genital discharges. They elicit an unpleasant feeling that "sticks," but how can it be got rid of? In the blended space between these two, it becomes possible to think of such people as dirty or "unclean" and to take the unpleasant feeling that accompanies contact with them as "impurity," which allows the possibility that it can be washed away with water.

If we now add a third input space, the avoidance of people who behave in ways that elicit offense—whether it be spontaneous feelings of disgust or conduct that we have learnt is vile or forbidden—it likewise becomes possible to think of these people as unclean and of their impurity as something contagious. Yet it remains unclear what such impurity consists of and how it could be washed away, since the connection to a material substance is more tenuous than in the second input space. Interestingly, even though the Holiness Code does not go as far as this, in time certain Jewish groups nevertheless developed the view that other nations were more or less unclean by definition, so that contact with them or their wares necessitated rituals involving water.

A similar model may explain the status of pigs (and certain other animals). Taboos surrounding certain foods make up a comprehensive generic space. One input space is the little crawling and swarming creatures that should not be eaten, the carcasses of which defile, and which are perceived as disgusting. Another input space is pigs, which for a number of reasons simply were not reared in the Israelites' heartland in the Iron Age and hence did not serve as food, even though their meat was appetizing. It is quite possible that an older taboo about this did exist, but archaeologists and anthropologists have other explanations as to why people in the hill country tended not to keep pigs. In the blended space, pigs (along with certain other animals that did not form part of the diet or that resembled pigs) came to be both unclean and disgusting, like the little crawling and swarming creatures. This could be regarded as a rhetorical move on the part of priestly writers, but it need not be an especially conscious one. They are advancing and justifying cultural rules by transferring feelings of disgust to things they believe should generally be banned.

Spilling Seed and Mixing Bodily Discharges

We are now getting closer to the question of how and why sexual practices, and in particular sex between men, came to be regarded as unclean. But it is not an easy one to sort out, and the answer is not clear. First, a short digression will be necessary.

In the purity laws the emission of semen (*zera'*) is thought to give rise to a mild form of impurity, even during the intercourse of husband and wife. This can be explained as the result of conceptual blending in which the inputs are partly pathological discharges, for example gonorrhea (unpleasant and unclean), and partly the emission of semen (pleasant). Of course, these different phenomena had certain common denominators (a generic space) that made it easy for them to become linked. Thus, the normal emission of semen became something that defiled those who had intercourse. The connection between sexual activity and conceptions of impurity has some nasty consequences, both for how women's sexuality is presented in general in biblical literature and for the relative hostility toward sex in Christianity that developed later. But it does not explain the attitude toward sex between men.

One possible explanation has to do with the spilling of semen to no avail. The Holiness Code also condemns intercourse during menstruation and sex with animals. Is this chiefly because of a sense of disgust? Or is it also about the impossibility of begetting children by such means, even if this is never explicitly stated? Might the prohibition of sex between men have a similar explanation? One thing that might support such an interpretation is the observation that fertility and growth, God's promise of a great nation to Abraham, is a repeated theme in the Pentateuch. Child sacrifice, of course, which is condemned in the Holiness Code along with the other abominations, likewise hinders the growth of the people.

This explanation might receive support from the narrative about Judah, his sons, and his daughter-in-law Tamar in Genesis 38. Judah's eldest son, Er, is married to Tamar but he "was evil in the eyes of Yahweh" and Yahweh killed him. Tamar, who had not yet borne children, is then married to Onan, Er's brother, as was customary in this traditional culture. The crux of the matter was that in such levirate marriages the first child, or "seed" (*zera'*), would be accounted the dead brother's issue, which Onan was not prepared to allow. He therefore practices *coitus interruptus*, the withdrawal method. It so angers Yahweh that Onan "spoiled" his semen "on the ground" that he kills him as well. At this point Judah gets cold feet and dares not give Tamar to his third son. After going childless, and thus disgraced, for a long while, she dresses herself as a prostitute at the sheep-shearing festival, and Judah, who does not realize this, buys sex from her without noticing who she is. Then later, when she turns out to be pregnant and is about to be burned, Tamar produces the pledge she received from Judah three months earlier and the case is dismissed.

Onan has lent his name to onanism, though what he is engaging in is hardly masturbation. Yet the story suggests that spilling one's seed to no avail was regarded as worthy of punishment. Or is it rather the refusal to fulfill one's duty to a dead brother (which would result in a reduction of Onan's inheritance from Judah) that God punishes? If the main problem were with the semen, then masturbation ought to be regarded as just as great a sin as intercourse during menstruation and sex between men. But, by and large, the Bible says nothing about masturbation—the few hints that we do occasionally find are just as ambiguous as the tale of Judah and his sons. Both the emission of semen and intercourse during menstruation, according to the purity laws, lead to impurity, but the Holiness Code only cites intercourse during menstruation as abhorrent and worthy of punishment. In any case, if the emission of semen mentioned in the purity laws was understood to include masturbation, the authors of the Holiness Code saw no reason to remark upon the fact.

Another interpretation of the role of semen would take the prohibition as applying to illicit mixtures. In all of the illicit sexual practices mentioned, semen is, or risks being, mixed with the wrong things: blood, the semen of animals, the semen of other men, or feces. Traces of such interpretations are found in rabbinic literature. The upshot, of course, is that these sexual practices cannot result in any offspring, but that need not be the main issue. Rather, the point could be more to keep things in their proper place. Intercourse between a man and his daughter-in-law (Lev 20:12) and sexual activity involving a woman and an animal (18:23) are characterized as *tebel*, which, though often translated as "perversion," may mean "confusion" or "mixing." Perhaps it is the mixture of different sorts of unclean secretions that is the problem.

Could this work as an explanation for the prohibition of men's anal intercourse with men? One complicating factor is the fact that excrement is not regarded as ritually unclean in the purity laws. Excrement is, however, regarded as unclean in the book of Ezekiel, which is closely related to the Holiness Code. Thus, the authors of the Holiness Code may indeed have assumed that feces were unclean and that the problem in this case, too, was the mixture of two unclean secretions.

The question is what evidence we have that it was specifically the mixing of bodily fluids that constituted a problem for the Israelites. Examples of this in the biblical texts and in neighboring cultures are scant, rendering the theory less probable. We do, however, have evidence of prohibitions of other mixtures in the Holiness Code itself:

LEV 19:19
You shall keep my statutes. You shall not cause two kinds of your animals to breed; you shall not sow (*tizraʿ*) your field with two kinds; and you shall not put on clothes of two mixed materials.

This prohibition appears to be a modified version of a similar, earlier text from Deuteronomy:

DEUT 22:9–11
You shall not sow (*tizraʿ*) your vineyard with two kinds, or the whole yield you have sown and the produce of the vineyard will be set apart. You shall not plow with an ox and a donkey together. You shall not put on [clothes made of] wool and linen together.

What the Holiness Code states, more systematically, is roughly the same, but the command not to plow with two different beasts has been replaced by one about breeding. The notion that neither seed nor breeds should be mixed can be linked to the prohibitions against incest (seed/semen) and sex with animals (breeds). Yet the prohibitions against sex during menstruation and sex between men still fit rather loosely with this. Neither of those prohibitions can be traced to mixing seed and, in the case of sex between men, the problem is hardly difference but similarity.

Conceptual Blending as Rhetoric

We need, perhaps, to go back to models of conceptual blending and to consider the role of disgust once more. Some of the illicit sexual practices mentioned in the Holiness Code and looked upon with aversion correspond to the triggers that can, according to research, elicit disgust. One of these is bodily discharges. It is not hard to see why intercourse during menstruation could be regarded as disgusting, especially in societies with limited access to sanitation, where such bodily discharges would often end up acquiring a much stronger odor than those who live under affluent circumstances might imagine. Another stimulus that can be shown to easily elicit disgust is particular animals, or rather anything in animals perceived to threaten or compromise our humanity. This is a fairly subtle phenomenon but a clearly observable one. From this viewpoint, sex with animals can easily provoke an instinctual sense of disgust in a person. Conceptual blending can explain how such behaviors might similarly come to be regarded as unclean, just like certain other phenomena that provoke disgust. Disgust is the generic space that these share, which makes it possible for elements from the various input spaces to be blended. The resulting blend is a broadening of the concept of impurity.

Sex with another man's wife or with a close family member, however, is harder to link with one of the established elicitors of disgust. Similarly, none of Rozin's nine triggers explains why sexual intercourse between people of the same gender should be perceived as any more disgusting than other sexual practices. In these cases, it is more plausible to seek other factors. The disgust, and hence impurity, that is associated with these practices in the Holiness Code can hardly explain how these prohibitions came into being. To understand the *why* we need to investigate an entirely different set of ideas. Incest laws and prohibitions against sex with someone else's wife are widespread, being found in most cultures. There are a multitude of possible underlying reasons for this, which we shall not delve into here. Rather less evident throughout history are prohibitions against same-sex sexual relations. But these almost always appear to be associated with ideas about men and women, power and subordination, honor and shame. Investigating such ideas will be the task of subsequent chapters.

The prohibitions against sex between people of the same gender thus have other underlying explanations than an instinctual sense of disgust. Conceptual blending is able to explain *how* disgust and impurity have come to be ascribed to such acts. They share a generic space with other forbidden sexual practices that elicited feelings of disgust and that had been labeled unclean on account of the fact that they, in turn, shared spaces with other unclean and repugnant phenomena. In a blended space that develops over time, all illicit sexual activity is lumped together, and impurity and disgust come to mark all such practices, regardless of whether the individual acts themselves display features that trigger aversion.

Did the Holiness Code regard a man's lying "woman-lays" with another man as unclean because it was perceived as disgusting, or was it perceived as disgusting because the Holiness Code classified it as unclean? Probably both. Sexual relations between men were taken to be both disgusting and unclean because they were viewed as improper or forbidden, like other illicit sexual practices that were regarded as objectionable and unclean in a more immediate sense. And once the connection is made, the feelings may also appear. It seems that the priestly authors of the Holiness Code are modifying an older prohibition against the penetration of a free man or an equal (based on ancient notions of power and honor) in such a way that their audience should feel abhorrence at such acts and both parties receive the blame. Conceptual blending proves to be a rhetorical tool for deterring people from doing that which is forbidden and for feeling disgust at the impurity associated with such acts.

When Paul, then, in Romans 1:24, and before him the Wisdom of Solomon 14:24, talk of illicit sexual acts as impurity or the absence of purity, these authors are using language in a similar way. And even a non-Jewish audience ought to have understood such rhetoric. Greek and Roman cultures might not have had the same kind of ritual prescriptions for purity as the Jews did, but they, too, had their own ideas about "impurity," something they could talk about as if it were a quasi-material substance or in terms appropriate for moral value judgments. Thus, Paul's talk of impurity in connection with same-sex sexual relations can likewise be regarded as a rhetorical means of provoking or strengthening his listeners' aversion toward, and sense of disgust at, such practices.

POWER AND SUBORDINATION

Masculinity and Domination

The relationship between sex and power is extremely complicated. Sexual acts have often been used throughout history to mark status and exert power. We like to think that the link between sex and power confuses things that shouldn't be related—that some people misuse sexuality as one of several means of power to dominate and exploit others. The examples are many, from pedophilia to buying sex, trafficking, and rape.

If it were easy to separate sex and power, we could solve most of the problems where some people exploit others. But it's not quite as straightforward as we might like it to be. Throughout much of human history, people have exercised their sexuality in asymmetrical relationships, by which we mean relationships in which one partner has dominated or had the upper hand in some way.

In historical times, males have usually dominated the scene, at least in public life. As always, there are evolutionary and biological aspects to this, while the particular forms domination takes, and the ways in which it is enacted in human groups, are socially and culturally constructed. Male dominance is common in mammals and gives privileged access to food, reproduction, and other resources, but it is also often costly, as it increases stress and reduces fitness over time. Female dominance is less common but found in certain species, including the bonobo.

The social and cultural construction of male dominance in human societies is a field of study in its own right. In recent years, the study of masculinity has developed partly out of feminist studies. Hegemonic masculinity is a kind of prototypical male behavior within a particular society, a cultural ideal. Although it does not necessarily correspond to the practice of most males, it provides legitimacy to male dominance over other categories—including other men whose masculinity corresponds less to the hegemonic type but is more complicit or subordinate. When it results in aggressive and violent forms of behavior that are damaging to others—to subordinates as well as to society in general—the term "toxic masculinity" has been employed. This includes stereotypical attitudes and actions against women as well as violent and dominant types of sexual behavior. At the same time, hegemonic masculinity is not static and usually does not rest on raw violence and domination but on some sort of agreement. Power also needs legitimacy, the acceptance of others, in order to gain authority.

While power remains at the base, the construction and perception of masculinity is always context dependent. In ancient cultures, as today, masculinity could be manifested in various ways and shades. Besides a hegemonic ideal, which usually included a dominant and penetrative sexual behavior, there were other more subordinate roles, as relationships were hierarchically stratified. This explains why and how men could take on a number of sexual roles depending on their place in the hierarchical social structure. Dominance and subordination were relative to one's position on the social ladder, and sexual activities almost always assumed asymmetric relationships.

Asymmetric Sexuality

All the texts we have discussed so far show much the same pattern. The Holiness Code's prohibition against lying "woman-lays" (Lev 18:22; 20:13) assumes that one man penetrates another (i.e., anal intercourse) and is rooted in the notion of an active and a passive partner. This approach corresponds to some extent, as we have seen, to legislation in the Middle Assyrian laws, although the Israelite laws differ somewhat in that both the active and the passive partner are blamed and punished, which was not always the case among other peoples. This applies both to illicit sexual intercourse between men and women (for example adultery) and between males.

We have also noted that what caused "moral" problems in most ancient cultures was when a free man in a sexual act was subjected to an equal—in other words penetrated—either by force or by free will. A free man could, in principle, exercise his sexuality toward anyone, as long as the other person had a lower status and was not subordinated to another man of the same status. The laws were not nearly as strict with regard to sexual acts against slaves. This is also true in the Pentateuch. The Decalogue (Ten Commandments) does prohibit men from coveting their neighbor's wife, slave, or slavewoman (Exod 20:17; Deut 5:21), but only penetration of the neighbor or his wife was punishable by death. Sexual acts against someone else's slave were certainly considered inappropriate, but the abuse (against the neighbor who owned the slave!) was compensable. So, it was the slave owner who was considered to be violated, not the slave. And sexual acts toward one's own slaves were fairly uncontroversial in the ancient world. The special case of the promised slave woman in Leviticus 19 reveals the basic view:

> LEV 19:20
> And a man who has sexual intercourse with a woman and she is a slave woman acquired by another man to be ransomed but not yet ransomed or freed, he must pay damages for her. They must not be killed since she was not freed.

If the woman had already been ransomed, she would have been considered the wife of another free man and the assault would have been viewed as adultery, punishable by death under the law. But in the example above, the woman still has the status of a slave, and therefore damages are sufficient. The example implies that if a slave woman is *not* betrothed to a free man, no major problem arises—one can assume that some form of fine or compensation could be considered, although this is unclear.

A little worse, but still not unsolvable, was the case of a free man's daughter who had not yet been betrothed—in our view probably an underage girl, given that betrothal took place at a young age. During the royal period when the Covenant Code was composed, the Israelites seem to have solved the matter simply by paying the customary bridewealth, whether the man took the girl or not:

> EXOD 22:16–17(15–16)
> And when a man seduces a virgin who is not betrothed and lies with her, he must certainly pay the bridewealth for her to him. If her father absolutely

refuses to give her to him, he shall weigh up silver equal to the bridewealth for virgins.

However, the ability of the girl's father to receive the money but keep his daughter at home as formally "untouched" was curtailed over time, as the somewhat later Deuteronomistic law shows:

DEUT 22:28–29

When a man comes across a young virgin girl who is not betrothed, and he seizes her and lies with her, and they are found, then the man who has lain with her must pay the young girl's father fifty silver [shekels] and she must be his wife. Since he has humbled her, he will not be able to divorce her as long as he lives.

Based on an ancient understanding of sexuality and honor, this solves a moral problem. The man is forced to take responsibility for the girl whose virginity he has taken, and the father is spared the problem of having a raped daughter in the house who would be difficult or impossible to marry off. In fact, according to Deuteronomistic law, a woman whose husband could prove that she was not a virgin at the time of her marriage was subject to stoning. However, with today's sense of morality, the problem is exacerbated because we see not only the abuse of a minor girl but also a forced marriage resulting from the abuse.

We have previously discussed cult prostitution and its possible existence in ancient Israel. Whatever the case, prostitution was generally not considered a major problem in the ancient world, as long as the prostitute was a slave or had low status. This can be illustrated by the fact that the Holiness Code urges Israelites not to allow their daughters to prostitute themselves and forbids priests to take prostitutes as wives (Lev 19:29; 21:7–9, 14). At the same time, this is the same Holiness Code that also prescribes damages for sexual intercourse with a betrothed slave woman (Lev 19:20, see above). In the latter case, the problem is that another man has an options contract on her, so to speak, but this very circumstance reveals that the low social status of slavewomen normally made them sexually available. This is why Genesis 38 does not criticize Judah for the affair with Tamar, as we saw earlier. After all, he thought he was just buying sex from a prostitute, although he was misled.

A different type of text with similar implications can be found in the book of Amos, which in the midst of its criticism of social injustice condemns father and son for going to the same prostitute (Amos 2:7). A closer look at the text reveals that it is probably not criticizing sex purchase per se. What Amos is objecting to is that father and son would have sex with *the same* woman, which was considered unacceptable according to Israelite incest rules.

Prostitution was part of Israelite society. The attitude toward sex purchase is quite ambivalent both in texts from the Second Temple period and in later rabbinic texts. In some texts we find strong condemnations and in others acceptance, sometimes on condition that the prostitute is not an Israelite. A prostitute's status is, at any rate, low.

Almost all the texts we encounter assume that sex is practiced in asymmetrical relationships by a superior against a subordinate. This is seen as the natural framework for sexual acts: "active" acts aimed at penetration of a "passive" or "receptive" party. Within such a conceptual framework, it seems natural for a free male to exercise his sexuality toward various categories of people who are lower in status than himself and not subordinate to any other free male: his wife (or wives), his male and female slaves, and to a certain extent "unbound" (from our perspective usually underage) girls and prostitutes. As we shall see shortly, the Greeks also included underage boys.

Paul reflects a similar understanding, although he is much more critical of prostitution than the texts we have encountered so far (1 Cor 6:12–20) and grants the married woman what might be described as reciprocal sexual rights and obligations, which is more than one could expect from the historical context (7:1–5). But Paul is a child of a fundamentally patriarchal and hierarchical society in which sexuality is defined as an act performed by an active party toward a passive or receptive party. As we have seen, this is the starting point for his conventional description of sexual acts between men: between *arsenokoitai* and *malakoi*, between "male-bedders" and "softies." From Paul's point of view—which he had in common with many people in antiquity—it was perceived as unnatural for a free, adult man to assume a subordinate female role and subject himself to another man's penetration. At the same time, Paul's Jewish outlook was of the stricter kind. This made it quite impossible for him to imagine some of the asymmetrical solutions offered in the ancient world, such as prostitution and, in Greek culture, pederasty.

Thus, when sex was practiced between men who were supposed to be each other's equals on the social ladder, the logical effect was that the one penetrated was also disgraced or degraded by being subordinated to the active partner. This is what the stories of Sodom and Giva are all about. In both cases, the men of the city assert their superiority and mark their status by seeking to rape (in the sense of penetrating) and thus dominate and feminize the strangers or their women and daughters. The gender of the strangers does not matter; it is the asymmetrical nature of the act that counts. Through penetration, an asymmetrical power relationship is constructed.

This basic approach partly explains the age-old role of rape in conflict situations and wars, including the rape of male enemy soldiers. We sometimes say that rape is not really about sex but about power. But rape does involve a sexual act. Perhaps we mean that rape has nothing to do with what we today think sexuality is about—or should be about? But then we must also ask ourselves to what extent asymmetrical sexual acts between men in antiquity are related to what we today call homosexuality. The question becomes particularly clear when we consider the Greek so-called boy love. But to get there, we have to detour over human prehistory.

Indigenous Peoples and Initiation Rites

The notion that same-sex sexuality is a phenomenon that occurs in civilizations in decline has been proven to be completely wrong. As already mentioned in the introductory chapter, homoerotic attraction seems to have evolved and become part of the biologically rooted repertoire of the human species because it has been beneficial to human group interaction and is thus one of many components that contributed to human survival.

This applies not only to the general attraction to individuals of the same sex that facilitates cooperation and reduces tensions and competition, but also to the exclusive homoerotic attraction experienced by some people. It has been argued that small, family or clan-based groups where some individuals without offspring of their own could contribute to the livelihood and protection of others' children had greater potential for survival.

Homoerotic attraction occurs in most animal species, not least among mammals, and among both males and females. In some species where one male dominates and monopolizes many females, other males find an outlet for their sexuality with each other. But in several species, we find similar behaviors among females living together in groups. Among advanced social species, not least primates, same-sex sexual acts are common regardless of the availability of opposite-sex partners. It seems that sexual acts can, on the one hand, be used to dominate within social hierarchies, but on the other hand can also be reciprocal and counteract the social hierarchies. In baboon societies, which are relatively hierarchical, long-term same-sex pair relationships between males have been observed. And among the less hierarchical bonobos, which are probably most similar to the first prehistoric hominid, same-sex sexual behavior is even more important for social interaction, discouraging aggression and resolving conflicts. It is therefore not surprising that homoerotic attraction and same-sex sexual behaviors have been part of human social interaction since prehistoric times.

Virtually all scholars now agree that the earliest humans lived in relatively egalitarian social groups that in many ways resembled the family- or clan-based hunter-gatherer societies that still exist today. In many of the indigenous peoples studied by anthropologists over the past century, same-sex sexual acts occur in various forms. In other indigenous or clan-based societies, homoeroticism is unusual, but outright condemnation is rare.

If it is the case that homoerotic attraction has been part of the emotional and social repertoire of the human species since time immemorial, but that a unique or exclusive homoerotic "orientation" is not nearly as common, we might expect same-sex sexual acts to take different forms and occupy different amounts of space in different types of groups and societies depending on the social circumstances. This also seems to be the case.

Most hunter-gatherer societies we know today are mixed forms. The most "typical" ones, which could most closely resemble prehistoric societies, are very small and consist of no more than thirty to forty individuals. Since we can never prove to what extent their way of life represents prehistoric hunter-gatherer societies, the arguments unfortunately remain speculative. But if we do assume that small contemporary hunting and gathering communities, such as the San people of the Kalahari, may have retained prehistoric features, what can we reasonably surmise? The limited hunter-gatherer societies we know today usually show neither resistance to nor preference for homoerotic relationships.

There are those who conclude that the human predisposition to homoeroticism developed mainly during the transition from the hunter-gatherer stage to agricultural societies—women would have increasingly preferred less aggressive and more verbally competent men for practical reasons. Others point to the implausibility of human genetic predisposition to homoeroticism evolving in such a short time, especially as all closely related animal species exhibit distinct homoerotic traits. Considering the interaction between homoerotic potential and social circumstances helps us to understand why small, typical hunter-gatherer societies do not express homoeroticism between men to any great extent. The fact is that statistical studies using the large ethnographic database HRAF have shown that homoerotic expression between men seems to increase with the size of the community, the degree of farming, and women's lack of control over their own sexuality.

A number of indigenous peoples still living mainly as hunter-gatherers, but in larger units than the original prehistoric groups and moving toward a somewhat more complex stage of evolution, exhibit an interesting form of ritualized asymmetrical homoeroticism between men. The literature describes a variety of same-sex sexual initiation rites, particularly in tribes in New Guinea and Melanesia.

The context is usually that prepubescent boys move away from their mothers and live with the older boys and men to be trained as warriors. In the process, the younger boys are given the task of regularly pleasuring the older boys with oral sex or, from another point of view, it is the task of the older boys to provide the younger boys with semen. This is seen as a natural part of adulthood in the tribes that practice the custom, and beliefs revolve around the importance of sperm for growth, strength, and virility. How would the boy grow up to be a man if he was not allowed to swallow sperm? Some tribes say that sexual intercourse with women depletes the body of energy and that if men gave all their sperm to women, the women would gain too much power. It is common for these rituals to be kept secret from the women.

Among some tribes, these relationships last for a few months; among others these last longer, up to fifteen years. For some, it is ideal to be paired with their uncle or their sister's husband. After puberty, the boy switches roles and for a corresponding period is sucked off by a younger partner. The vast majority eventually marries and then lives exclusively, or at least predominantly, heterosexual lives, but in some tribes sexual relations between men continue for life alongside heterosexual marriage.

This type of initiation rite is thus based on cross-generational, same-sex sexual acts, and the age difference makes the relationships asymmetrical in a way that is difficult to imagine in smaller, more egalitarian hunter-gatherer societies. The same-sex sexual rites involve virtually the entire male population at certain stages of life and are enabled by the homoerotic potential that most people seem to carry, but they do not appear to be expressions of specifically homoerotic preferences. Rites ultimately aim to reinforce the male role as a powerful warrior and maintain the distinction between men and women. Depictions of similar initiation rites for women based on homoerotic behaviors are almost entirely absent.

Transgender Sexuality and Shamanism

A completely different pattern, also with ritual elements but focused on individuals, is found among indigenous tribes in both North and South America. When Europeans arrived in North America, they discovered that some Native American men dressed as women, identified with women, performed typically female chores, and could even marry men and assume a woman's traditional sexual role. Such a "two-spirit"—or *berdache* as Europeans came to call them, using a French loanword to denote the passive partner in male-male intercourse—was usually respected by the tribe and considered to have shamanistic abilities. Not all shamans were *berdaches*, of course, but some were.

Similarly, some women could take on a traditionally male role in society as brave warriors and even marry another woman, but they were rarer. In some contexts, these people dressed as the opposite sex; in others they did not. There were—and still are—different variations on the theme. In any case, these almost institutionalized roles seem to have provided opportunities for individuals whom we might today call transgender to find a respected place in society.

Compared to, for example, New Guinea's ritualized homoeroticism, indigenous Americans exhibit a much higher degree of individualism, but then again, North American indigenous societies were usually larger than New Guinean tribes and had room for more specialization and division of labor. From Latin America, too, Europeans described encounters with men who took female roles—in some cases as shamans—while female *berdaches* seem to have been rarer.

Over time, researchers have discovered similar phenomena among indigenous peoples in many parts of the world, particularly in shamanistic societies in the broad sense and in societies that may have been shamanistic further back in history. Evidence exists from East and Southeast Asia and Africa.

Shamanism has its roots in prehistoric times and is one of the oldest forms of human religion. Patterns of cross-gender identities do not seem to have emerged in the very oldest and numerically limited hunter-gatherer societies but probably developed in slightly larger clan societies. Nor do we encounter this type of cross-gender identity in societies where intergenerational and asymmetrical same-sex sexual rituals are widely practiced. In these societies, men's focus is often on consolidating and strengthening their position, and homoeroticism serves as a means of reinforcing male identity. In such a society, taking on what is perceived as a female role and exchanging male activities for female activities would be a loss of status. In contrast, in societies with room for cross-gender identities, such role change or identity shift does not imply a major loss of prestige but is perceived more as a choice of other tasks and different relationships. Obviously, attitudes vary in different contexts, but differences in gender relations and the hierarchy of social structures probably play an important role in the way same-sex sexual acts have been expressed and viewed throughout history.

Heroes, Warriors, and Comrades

Homoerotic motifs appear in a number of heroic tales from quite diverse settings, and some of these stories have been cited as possible examples of mutual homosexual relationships in attempts to find ancient models. This is not entirely straightforward, however, as we shall see. Three such heroic tales that are often discussed are the stories of Gilgamesh and Enkidu, of Achilles and Patroclus, and of David and Jonathan.

The earliest of these stories is about Gilgamesh. The oldest Sumerian text about Gilgamesh that we have is from around 2000 BCE, but the story is even older. The version most commonly cited—the Babylonian version—was recorded a few centuries later. Gilgamesh, king of Uruk, is described as a massive warrior, part god and part human. He is as immense and insatiable in his building activities as in his sexual desires, consuming young men and women on a regular basis until the gods implore the goddess Aruru to create someone he can match. Aruru creates Enkidu, a hairy primordial man, savage, and warrior.

Since the story exists in slightly different versions in Mesopotamian texts, we will not go into all the details here and instead focus on the relationship between Gilgamesh and Enkidu. Enkidu wants to meet Gilgamesh in single combat, and Gilgamesh, having heard of Enkidu, dreams of him in the form of the symbols of a meteorite and an axe, both of which are very similar to the names of certain worshipers of Ishtar who had sexual connotations. Gilgamesh tells his mother, Ninsun, about the dream, and she interprets it to mean that Gilgamesh will find a companion and love him like a woman.

After Enkidu is civilized by the harlot Shamhat, he sets off for Uruk, blocking the road for Gilgamesh who is on his way to a wedding. They fight but end up embracing each other as friends. The two then set off on various adventures, killing the monster Humbaba,* felling the cedar forest, and slaying the celestial bull. But then Enkidu falls ill and dies suddenly. Gilgamesh is heartbroken and laments him in a long dirge.

The epic is about two strong warriors and heroes who somehow find their match in each other and unite in a close relationship—so close that Gilgamesh turns down the goddess Ishtar's offer of marriage and sex. The story is hardly a prudish one: it describes Gilgamesh's sexual exploits before he meets Enkidu as well as Shamhat's lovemaking with Enkidu in order to tame and cultivate him. But despite the sexual allusions in Gilgamesh's dream, nothing is ever said about Gilgamesh's and Enkidu's sexual relationship. Admittedly, the relationship with Enkidu solves the problem of Gilgamesh's excessive and destructive sexuality. But it seems that the scholars who claim that the epic is not mainly about homoeroticism are right. Life, death, and sexuality are part of an overarching existential question about humankind's lot and place in life: what is it that makes humans into civilized cultural beings and distinguishes them from gods and animals?

At the same time, the epic is a tale of male courage, combat, and camaraderie. Two strong warriors find each other and love each other more than they love women. One dies and the other expresses his despair in a dirge. This motif is also found in other archaic heroic tales. Homer's epic work on the Trojan War and its aftermath is often dated to the eighth century BCE but is based on older oral traditions, and the story world probably belongs to the twelfth century BCE. In the *Iliad* we meet the protagonist Achilles and his companion Patroclus.** The story revolves around Achilles's anger at Agamemnon taking

---

* https://www.ehs.se/dss, figure 2, relief from King Kapara's temple palace, Syria, tenth century BCE; two heroes (Gilgamesh and Enkidu?) pin down a bearded foe (Humbaba?), while grabbing at his pronged headdress.

** https://www.ehs.se/dss, figure 3, red-figure kylix tondo (circled inside of a flat drinking cup), ca. 500 BCE; Achilles bandages the wounded Patroclus.

his booty, the slave girl Briseis, and his refusal to take part in the war up to the point when his friend and brother-in-arms Patroclus is killed by the Trojan Hector. Achilles mourns Patroclus violently and then returns to the battle, avenging Patroclus and killing Hector.

Achilles expresses very strong feelings for Patroclus in Homer's depiction, but as in the story of Gilgamesh and Enkidu, nothing is ever said about their possible homoerotic relationship. Many explanations for this have been proposed, and given the nature of Greek warrior culture, it is not impossible that even the earliest audience for the story assumed such a relationship. But we cannot be absolutely sure.

The origin of the story is Achilles's anger at being bereaved of his slave girl Briseis, and the *Iliad* describes in the ninth song how Achilles and Patroclus lie opposite each other with one girl each. Of course, this does not prevent the audience from perceiving Achilles and Patroclus's relationship as homoerotic. So did most Greek writers of the classical period (fifth century BCE onward) who treated Achilles and Patroclus, but their frame of reference, on the other hand, was the pederastic customs that we shall discuss shortly. Whether the roots of that tradition extended back to Homer's culture is a question on which scholars disagree.

The story of David and Jonathan in 1 Samuel is similar in many ways to the two preceding ones. Here, too, we have an archaic heroic tale, although in its present form it is part of a larger story of David's rise to the throne—a story that probably took shape in the seventh century BCE for propaganda purposes in support of King Josiah's Davidic claims. The heroic tale, however, has older roots, not least in that it appears to be woven together by several different traditions or layers.

In the story world, we find ourselves around 1000 BCE. Young David arrives at King Saul's court and at first becomes his favorite. But David's success in the wars against the Philistines leads to a problematic popularity. David marries Saul's daughter, and Saul's son Jonathan admires him greatly. Everyone loves David, but Saul becomes violently jealous, especially as Jonathan makes a covenant with David and is said to love him as his own life (1 Sam 18:1–5; 20:16–17).

Jonathan protects David from Saul's attempts to kill him, and when both Saul and Jonathan fall in battle against the Philistines, David mourns them both as violently as Achilles mourns Patroclus, lamenting, like Gilgamesh, in a despairing dirge. Of Jonathan he proclaims: "I'm devastated over you, my brother Jonathan. You were very delightful to me. Your love was more won-derful to me than the love of women" (2 Sam 1:26).

The story has erotic undertones. In the first scene, when Jonathan declares his love for David and enters into a covenant with him (1 Sam 18:1–5), he is described as taking off his cloak and giving it to David along with his clothes, sword, bow, and belt. The depiction is ambiguous: one of the words can be translated as Jonathan giving either the undergarments or the armor to David, and the sword as well as the bow may have sexual overtones. The scene can thus be understood as Jonathan undressing or as handing over his weapons.

In an outburst of anger, Saul later accuses his son of disgrace or infamy, using crude words that have sometimes been interpreted as alluding to a sexual relationship (1 Sam 20:30). In any case, derogatory language is used that aims to feminize Jonathan.

The ambiguities are probably deliberate. Relational and sexualized lan-guage could also be used for political purposes. Assyrian vassal treaties writ-ten during the time when the David and Jonathan story took on its propa-gandistic form use the phrase "love Assurbanipal as himself" to refer to the vassal's loyalty to the Assyrian king. The resemblance to the words of 1 Samuel about Jonathan's love for David is striking. Likewise, the eroticized undressing scene—whatever the exact interpretation—reinforces the claim and legiti-macy of the Davidic dynasty.

All three epic tales describe relationships between heroic warriors using language drawn from family relationships and the love of women. At the same time, there is no emphasis on, or even any explicit mention of, homoerotic relationships between the two heroes. All the stories describe a mutuality and deep emotional love, and in all three heroes' tales one party dies and is violently mourned by the other. At the same time, the relationships are not portrayed entirely symmetrically, and the stories play on clearly hierarchical models. Gilgamesh is the obvious protagonist of the Babylonian epic. Enkidu's role is to match him. But in the older Sumerian versions of the story, Enkidu is not a wild man but a servant of Gilgamesh (there called Bilgamesh), that is, subordinate to him and not his equal. Patroclus, though a little older than the stronger Achilles, is called upon to follow and exert influence over him for that very reason. In the *Iliad*, Patroclus acts partly as Achilles's sidekick. He often performs tasks that would normally be the responsibility of women and does whatever Achilles asks of him. Jonathan is the king's son and is expected to inherit the throne but renounces it in favor of David, whom he is repeatedly said to love—even as much as his own life. Jonathan also initiates a covenant with David, while David is not explicitly said to love Jonathan. Even in the emotional lament over the death of Saul and Jonathan, David speaks of Jonathan's love for him rather than his own love for Jonathan.

So, while they are about camaraderie and strong love between two warriors and heroes, there is an underlying asymmetry in all three stories. They are based on archaic motifs and contain partly eroticized language and sexual innuendo. Their literary and ideological purposes are rather different, but the underlying stories seem to reflect settings without any great fear of homoerotic feelings or actions. On the other hand, these stories can hardly be used to make any detailed claims about the place, function, or practical application of homoeroticism in the historical societies in which these heroic tales have their roots. In order to say anything about homoerotic relations in actual societies in antiquity, we need to study other texts. One of the questions that then arises is the extent to which ancient expressions of homoeroticism are reciprocal or asymmetrical, that is, what kinds of power relations they reflect.

Initiation, Mentoring, and Aesthetics

Homosexuality has sometimes been called "Greek love," which is quite misleading. It is true that same-sex sexual acts were widely accepted in ancient Greece, but within a certain framework: sexual relations between men were mainly of an asymmetrical nature. This was true both in the Spartan military context and in the refined educational ideals of Athens.

Greek homoeroticism is mainly about pederasty: relationships between adult men and young boys from about the age of twelve upward. In today's West, most pederastic relationships would legally be classified as pedophilia, but it would be misleading and confusing to use that term for the phenomenon we are talking about here, partly because pederasty was institutionalized in significant parts of ancient Greek society, and partly because sexual acts with children under the age of twelve were also regarded as completely out of place in ancient Greece.

Thus, Greek culture did not regard same-sex sexual acts as problematic in themselves, but the overarching issue was how power was exercised within the framework of prevailing hierarchies. Our knowledge of the origins and development of Greek pederasty is highly uncertain—scholars have debated this back and forth for more than a hundred years—but despite elements of speculation, there are at least three circumstances that appear to be crucial. One concerns the relationship between archaic initiation rites and the male warrior role with roots in a dim ancient past. The second is the Greek sense of aesthetics with its emphasis on the beauty of the body, which came to play a major role in the Olympic Games as well as in the local gymnasia as Greek urban cultures emerged. The third circumstance is the refined idealization of "boy love" with educational ideals, which was developed and cultivated in Athens in particular during the classical period. We shall deal with them briefly in turn.

Manhood Rites

Many examples suggesting homoerotic relationships between men are about male courage, fighting, and camaraderie. We have also noted intergenerational sexual acts between men in clan-based cultures around the world, mainly in the form of ritual acts and initiation rites. Same-sex sexual initiation rites are often linked to notions of male strength in war and of sperm as a life force. Among some of the tribes that practice such rites, we also find the idea that this life force originates in the brain, which explains headhunting and the consumption of enemy brains. Some prehistoric findings of skulls could suggest that similar beliefs and behaviors have existed for a very long time. This kind of reasoning is based on weak chains of evidence and is necessarily highly speculative. But apart from the possible link to headhunters, it seems quite plausible that since ancient times some form of ritualized homoeroticism was linked to young men's initiation into an adult hunter-warrior role.

The question is how far back we can trace historical trajectories. Scholars who want to see connections between prehistoric initiation rites and more recent homosexual practices in the West like to point to various traditions about "blood brothers" in literature. Such "warrior couples" appear in many Indo-European cultures—among the Scythians, Celts, Germanic tribes, and Nordic peoples, to name a few—from the Archaic period to the Middle Ages. On the one hand, it is quite plausible that men in aristocratic warrior cultures engaged in same-sex sexual acts, such as in ancient and feudal Germanic, Norse, and Celtic warrior societies, where men drifted about and made their living by hunting and raiding because they lacked their own farmland. On the other hand, the source material does not provide enough information; the gaps remain large and the conclusions unreliable.

The long trajectories are therefore uncertain. But if we confine ourselves to looking at homoerotic expressions in ancient Greece, the evidence at least suggests that archaic initiation rites and male hunter-warrior roles may have been important background factors.

When we look at aristocratic warrior societies from antiquity, asymmetrical relationships seem to have been the rule. Presumably there is a logic to this, since the role of the fighter largely involves courage, competition, and honor. Slightly younger boys or youths could serve as partners without compromising the status of the fighter. Xenophon describes how Greeks in the service of Cyrus the Younger brought boys into their service or bought slave boys for the purpose. Thebes was famous for its Sacred Band (*hieros lochos*) of elite soldiers: three hundred warriors with horse and chariot, each with a partner. The latter was a younger subordinate who protected the chariot soldier. In Sparta, where the free minority population was in many ways organized as a military training camp, young boys were taught by adult men who were also their lovers.

The Greeks themselves seem to have believed that pederasty originated in Crete. Others pointed to Sparta, Elis (where the Olympic Games were organized), and Boiotia (where Thebes was the capital). One theory that has been discussed for a couple hundred years but especially since the early twentieth century points to the Dorian tribes that invaded central Greece in the twelfth and eleventh centuries BCE and, among other things, conquered most of the Peloponnese (where Sparta was located) and Crete. It is difficult to form an objective view because much of our information comes from ancient texts by biased writers. Plato complains about the attitude to same-sex sexual acts in the laws of both Crete and Sparta. Aristotle claims that the Cretans separated men and women to keep the population growth in check. Such claims must be taken with a pinch of salt. But Strabo's statement that the Cretans practiced a form of initiation of young boys is probably based on reality.

Strabo—who borrowed his account from Ephorus (fourth century BCE)—describes how men in Crete, unlike the Athenians, kidnapped their young boys. The abduction took place in a socially ordered fashion, with the boy's friends (relatives?) knowing about it in advance. The man then lived with the boy in the countryside for two months and taught him to hunt. In the meantime, they had a sexual relationship. At the end, the boy was given armor

and weapons, an ox to sacrifice to Zeus, and a drinking cup. The context is boys
living and being raised in age groups with adult leaders, where, in addition to
learning to write, they engaged in activities including music and martial arts.
We do not know how widespread this custom was. However, a drinking cup
from Crete's Minoan period, dated to around 1500 BCE, depicts an older youth
and a boy in military dress, which is consistent with Strabo's account.*

In Sparta, the warrior ideal was highly valued because all free men were
needed to dominate the enslaved majority population, the Helots. The free population was raised mainly in gender- and age-segregated groups. No depiction of
this closed society comes from within, making it difficult to separate fact from
prejudice, and the Athenians liked to speak ill of the Spartans. But overall, the
texts of Aristotle, Xenophon, and Plutarch paint a picture of a society in which
boys of different age groups had casual sexual relationships with each other, on
the one hand, and fairly permanent and intense relationships with a lover from
one of the older age groups, on the other. Plutarch says that at the age of twelve, a
boy was assigned an adult soldier who was responsible for his military education
and acted as a lover. This role could continue well into his twenties, when the
boy himself took on the role of lover in relation to another young boy. The lover
(Greek: *erastēs*) was spurred on by the love of his beloved (*erōmenos*) to show
his utmost courage in battle, and as the boy grew older and fought alongside his
lover, he was naturally spurred on to prove himself equally worthy and brave.

Xenophon says similar things about Elis and Boiotia: the lover and the
beloved fought together. The core of the Boiotian army was Thebes's Sacred
Band, which consisted entirely of warrior couples united in homoerotic relationships. These examples are not Doric, and scholars disagree on the extent
to which the link between warrior culture and same-sex sexual initiation rites
really originated in Sparta and Crete. In any case, it is in Crete that a bronze
statuette from the seventh century BCE has been found depicting two warriors
hand in hand, one older and one younger, both with erect penises.**

One indication of a broader background is the role of the abduction in
Greek mythology. The most famous example is Zeus's abduction of the beau-

---

* https://www.ehs.se/dss, figure 4, Minoan drinking cup ("Chieftain Cup"), sixteenth
century BCE; youth and boy in military attire. Cf. Strabo's (Ephorus's) description of
abductions in Crete.

** https://www.ehs.se/dss, figure 5, archaic bronze figurine from Kato Syme in Crete,
seventh century BCE; two ithyphallic men (warriors, hunters?) of somewhat different
height (age?).

tiful youth Ganymede,* but the literature contains many more similar myths in which gods or heroes kidnap beautiful boys. These myths seem to reflect an ancient practice akin to same-sex sexual initiation rites of a kind that was neither confined to Greece nor to the Indo-European cultural sphere. At the same time, Doric culture displays one of the clearest links between initiation, homoeroticism, and warrior cult in antiquity.

On a rock face near the temple of Apollo Karneios in the Spartan colony of Thera (present-day Santorini), a number of inscriptions have been found, probably dating from the sixth century BCE, some with homoerotic or possibly pederastic contents.** The most famous reads: "By [Apollo] Delphinius, here Krimon fucked a boy, Bathycles's brother." Krimon appears a few more times: "Krimon fucked Amotion" and a line about him pleasing Simias with dancing. Some other inscriptions also seem to be about dancing. Against the background of Doric warrior cult and ritual, some have been tempted to see here evidence of some form of ritualized same-sex sexual initiation in connection with the temple. However, the placement and character of the texts, and especially the informal depictions carved next to them, suggest that the context is not ritual but graffiti. Old Thera is spectacularly located at the top of a mountain peak.*** The erotic inscriptions are to be found in a relatively secluded spot at the far end, where the habitable surface ends. Remains of a gymnasium nearby suggest that the area was probably used for sports and competitions when the texts were inscribed, although the building itself would be of later date than the inscriptions. Perhaps the inscriptions are more akin to schoolyard graffiti. In any case, they do not hold up as evidence of any formal initiation rite. At most, they may indicate a connection between homoerotic acts and athletic exercises in a Doric culture similar to Sparta and Crete.

Beauty of the Body

This brings us to the second of the three factors that are important for the emergence of Greek pederasty: the worship of the beauty of the body. Greek

* https://www.ehs.se/dss, figure 6, Zeus pursuing Ganymede by the Athens painter 470–460 BCE.

** https://www.ehs.se/dss, figures 7–9, inscriptions (graffiti) on the rocks near the temple of Apollo Karneios in ancient Thera (Santorini), sixth century BCE.

*** https://www.ehs.se/dss, figure 10, view of ancient Thera, rocks with inscriptions in distant background.

aesthetics is strongly linked to sports, the Olympic Games, and the local gymnasia of the cities. According to tradition, the Olympic Games were founded in 776 BCE. Whatever the historical veracity of this dating, it is clear that athletic competitions played an important role already in archaic times. The *Iliad* depicts soldiers passing the time with various games and sports. The Spartan military regime attached great importance to sports.

It is not entirely clear why boys and men exercised and competed naked in the gymnasia emerging in the Greek urban cultures that developed from classical times onward. According to legend—which is hardly historically credible—it began with a runner from Megara who lost his loincloth at the Olympics in 720 BCE. Elis, the city that organized the Olympics, is mentioned by both Plato and Xenophon as a place for homoerotic relationships. Among other things, a male beauty contest was organized there with a suit of armor as the prize. In Megara near Corinth, a similar contest, Diokleia, was organized in memory of a soldier who died in battle while protecting his lover. We see how sports, war, and hero cult were intimately linked.

Greek art relies heavily on the aesthetics of the naked body.* This is true not only of all the sculptures that today often come to symbolize ancient Greece, but also of the thousands of painted ceramic objects that have survived to the present day. For example, over five hundred vases from various sites have been found dedicated to beautiful, usually young people—perhaps akin to the celebrities or cultural idols of our time. They are often mentioned by name together with the adjective *kalos*, "beautiful."** Over two hundred young men are mentioned in this way but only about thirty women. There are plenty of motifs from the sixth and fifth centuries BCE with sexual scenes of various kinds, not least same-sex ones.

Gymnasia and wrestling schools were places where young, strong boys were trained and admired.*** Aristophanes jokes around 400 BCE in several of his comedies about how men used to hang around the wrestling school in order to seduce boys or follow beautiful boys from the gymnasium and the

* https://www.ehs.se/dss, figure 11, front face of base for funerary kouros showing athletic youth wrestling, ca. 510 BCE.

** https://www.ehs.se/dss, figure 12, terracotta bobbin in Attic white-ground technique by the Penthesilea painter, ca. 450 BCE; Nike, the goddess of victory, hands the victory ribbon to a young athlete. The text reads: "The boy is beautiful (*ho pais kalos*)."

*** https://www.ehs.se/dss, figure 13, red-figure kylix with motifs from the gymnasium and wrestling arena, ca. 500–450 BCE.

baths. Eros statues at some of these buildings suggest the link between beautiful youths and erotic feelings.

Many philosophical texts concern the balancing act between aesthetics and sexual desires. Plato's *Symposium* from around 380 BCE is one of the best examples. Plato constructs a number of fictional dialogues between Socrates and various interlocutors. During the *Symposium*, Socrates recounts a conversation with a woman, Diotima, who has been teaching him about the nature of love. Love (*erōs*) is in itself neither ugly nor beautiful, neither good nor evil, but loves what is beautiful, and since the objects of love are changeable and perishable, love is ultimately a desire for offspring, for eternity. Plato describes, through the words of Diotima, a development in which a man seeks physical beauty by first being attracted to his beloved, but in time learns to see the beauty of all bodies as one and the same, and thus becomes less compulsively obsessed with a single individual. The next step is to value mental beauty more than physical beauty, then discover the beauty of knowledge, and finally understand Beauty as divine essence. Eroticism is thus interpreted as the first rung on a ladder where, by starting with the "right kind of pederasty," a man eventually approaches absolute Beauty:

PLATO, *SYMP.* 211B–C

This, then, is the right way to go, or to be led by another, in matters of love: beginning from these beautiful things, for the sake of Beauty, to keep climbing as if on a ladder, from one to two and from two to all beautiful bodies, and from beautiful bodies to beautiful practices and from practices to beautiful teachings, and from teachings he finally arrives at the teaching that is nothing but the teaching of Beauty Itself, that he may finally know what Beauty is.

The one who thus comes to know Beauty will no longer be seduced by boys and young men, but the desire for Beauty itself will transcend the desire for physical love and result in real virtue, says Diotima. Plato then has Socrates agree, explaining to the other participants in the symposium that this is why he praises Love (Eros) as the best helper of human nature.

Pedagogical and Pederastic Ideals

This kind of philosophical rationalization of pederastic customs in terms of education and aesthetics may seem strained from the perspective of our time.

But the maneuver is made possible by the very specific background we have sketched for ancient Greece, where pederasty had long existed, at least in ritualized form, and where the beauty of the naked body was worshiped in mythology and warrior cult as well as in the Olympic Games and the local gymnasia. The third factor that not only enables but also necessitates philosophical rationalizations and problematizations of pederastic practices is the educational framework around pederasty, especially in upper-class Athens during the classical period.

According to the pattern that emerges in classical times, and that we know above all from Athens, pederasty was a natural part of the education of boys. But the framework was no longer one of initiation rites but one of education and training. Adult men fell in love with young boys and wooed them with praise and gifts until they "gave in." It was considered appropriate for the boys to resist but only for a time. To say no to a man of good standing in the long run was considered snobbery. In a way, courting boys was similar to the game between men and women that we know from urban environments in later Europe.* It probably served a similar function in ancient urban culture, where girls were married off early and decent women were not very visible in the public sphere.

In the social game of institutionalized pederasty, a form of reciprocity emerged that many men do not seem to have experienced in relation to women, at least not with their wives or, for that matter, prostitutes. The exception was the *hetaira*, a woman who was partly outside the regulated family system and who could act as a companion. Unlike wives or daughters, *hetairai* were able to participate in social life with symposia, conversations, and various kinds of entertainment. Such women were considered to possess, at least in part, mental and spiritual capacities on a par with those of men. This was also true of boys during the period when they began to develop into men. Love for boys was therefore also perceived to contain an intellectual reciprocity not usually considered possible in relationships with women.

The mutual relationships we are talking about were, of course, asymmetrical, similar to the relationships between men and women or free men and slaves but in slightly different ways. As we have already seen, beautiful boys could be

* https://www.ehs.se/dss, figures 14–17, attic red-figure pottery, fifth century BCE, showing courtship scenes between men or youth and boys.

admired and courted like the movie stars or celebrities of our time. Many texts, not least poetic ones, express a high degree of objectification. In poetry from the Archaic to the Hellenistic period, the smooth cheeks of boys and the poet's longing for their thighs and sweet mouths are praised. Boys are described as elusive, capricious, and unfaithful. Their lovers desire them, are captivated by their gazes, and feel themselves to be slaves to love. The way they objectify the objects of their desire and love is similar to men's love poetry directed at women throughout the ages. Often the lover portrays himself as inferior to the object of love while the social power relationship was the reverse.

Like married women, boys were also not expected to be active sexual partners but rather passive recipients who provided and granted satisfaction to men. The boy was not expected to enjoy the sexual act in the same way as the man did.

Usually, pederastic relationships lasted for a few years. Young men often had to wait for marriage—at times there was a shortage of girls in the ancient Mediterranean—and in the meantime they had one or more homoerotic relationship with boys. But many continued with pederastic relationships even as married fathers of families, and in some cases such relationships could continue for life. The latter could be perceived as problematic, as we will return to shortly.

Pederastic practices were naturally integrated into the hierarchical and authoritarian social framework that prevailed. Even at the beginning of the second century CE, in a context where romantic love between men and women was much more valued, Plutarch describes love relationships within the framework of a clear power order:

PLUTARCH, *AMAT.* 754D

If the nurse rules the infant and the teacher the child, the gymnasiarch the youth, and the lover the boy, who when he grows up is ruled by the law and by the commander—since no one is his own master or independent—what would be so strange if a sensible older woman governed a young man's life?

Plutarch here argues for the possibility of an opposite kind of asymmetrical relationship between a man and a woman, which is interesting in itself and says something about the changes in traditional views that were discussed during the imperial period. But at the same time, the passage makes clear the traditional hierarchy within which pederastic practices had their place.

In the classical period, pederasty was thus intellectualized and idealized. It has sometimes been argued that Greek pederasty in general, and Athenian pederasty in particular, was the product of elite upper-class culture. How else do we explain the fact that men could find time to loiter around gymnasia, wrestling arenas, or baths during daytime to woo young boys? However, it is probably not the phenomenon of pederasty as such but the specific philosophical-pedagogical superstructure that reflects an elite culture.

Pausanias's speech in Plato's *Symposium* is quite revealing. Plato has Pausanias defend Athens's "refined" version of pederasty as "complicated" or "multifaceted" (*poikilos*) in contrast to pederasty in other places, such as Elis or Boiotia, where it is applied in a simple way: "it is simply legislated as something good to please lovers, and no one, young or old, would call it shameful" (*Symp.* 182b). But foreigners and many in Ionia do call it shameful, says Pausanias, blaming the latter's rulers for being uninterested in the development of magnanimous thoughts and strong friendship ties among their subjects. The peoples of Elis and Boiotia, on the other hand, are so poor at oratory that they cannot be bothered to engage in the kind of courtship that is part of Athens's "complicated" exercise of pederasty. Apart from the prejudices about others—we must reasonably assume that pederasty was culturally regulated in other states as well—Plato's Pausanias says something about the Athenians' self-image.

Pausanias distinguishes between *Aphrodite Pandemos*, the general, popular Aphrodite (the love or rather the sexual behaviors that people in general engage in) and *Aphrodite Ourania*, the heavenly love. The popular Aphrodite thus represents the "ugly sex" of ordinary people:

PLATO, *SYMP.* 181B

This is the way the simple people love. Such, in the first place, love women at least as much as boys. Moreover, they love their bodies rather than their souls. Further, they go for the stupidest because they have eyes only for the "accomplishment" (*pros to diapraxasthai monon blepontes*) and do not care whether it is aesthetic or not.

After this contemptuous description of the hetero- and homoerotic behavior of the mob, in which "accomplishment" is a euphemism for the sexual act, Pausanias's view of the delights of the heavenly Aphrodite follows:

PLATO, *SYMP.* 181C–D

But heavenly love, in the first place, has no part in the feminine but only in the masculine—and this is the love of boys. Moreover, it is older and free from hubris. Therefore, those who are inspired by this love turn to the male, because they love that which is stronger in nature and has more reason (*nous*). And one can also know those who, in their love of boys (*paiderastia*), strive entirely for this [heavenly] love: they do not love boys until these begin to possess reason (*nous*), which is when they begin to grow beards.

Love for boys at this age, says Pausanias, leads to lifelong, responsible relationships and prevents abuse. The appropriate age for pederasty is thus said to be when the boy is just beginning to get a fuzzy chin. Various sources point to prepubescence as the "right" age to start, while courting or having sex with boys younger than twelve was considered immoral and illegal. One such source is Strato of Sardis, who probably lived during the first century and was almost contemporary with Paul. In a poem included in his homoerotic collection, *Musa puerilis*, he describes at length the ages and advantages of boys:

STRATO, ANTH. PAL. 12.4

I delight in the climax of a twelve-year-old. But a thirteen-year-old is even more desirable than this one. He who provides twice seven is a sweeter love flower yet. And the one who begins three times five is lovelier still. The sixteenth year is for the gods. But to seek the seventeenth is not for me but for Zeus. And if anyone has desire for still older ones, he no longer plays (*paizei*), but seeks him who "replies."

The last line contains a play on words—the verb for joking or playing, *paizō*, has the same root as the word for boy, *pais*. Thus, according to Strato, the man who seeks sex with eighteen-year-olds and older is no longer engaging in pederasty but wants a full sexual response from a grown man.

The Problem of Penetration

The quote from Strato raises the question of how the Greeks conceived of pederastic sex as different from other sexual acts. The ideal is both described in texts and depicted in vase paintings, especially on Athenian ceramics from the sixth and fifth centuries BCE. Later paintings are rarely as "permissive" or pornographic if you like. This probably coincides with increasing criticism of pederastic practices.

Some of the paintings depict orgies of various kinds,* with men and women engaging in various forms of masturbation, oral sex, and anal sex. There are also depictions of young people of the same age engaging in anal group sex. To what extent such images reflect common social behavior or the artist's sexual fantasies is difficult to know. But when pederastic relationships are depicted, much is consistent with the descriptions in the texts. The ceramic paintings mostly show men or slightly older youths— with beards—courting beardless youths or boys. Often, they come with a gift.** Sometimes the boy looks away, sometimes he is completely dismissive or shies away from the man. Sometimes he is "receptive." Some paintings depict sexual advances. The man often holds one hand around the boy or touches his face while touching the boy's genitals with the other hand.*** The next step in these paintings is for the man and the boy to embrace and for the man to pleasure himself between the boy's thighs.**** This is just about where the limits of a pederastic relationship should stay, according to the ideal.

Some scholars argue that this was how the custom was usually practiced, while others question whether pederastic relations in reality were limited to such intercrural intercourse. Would the vase painters—who at this time seem to have had no qualms whatsoever about sexual motifs—have been so delicate about pederasty? Well, maybe. Partly because the motifs were adapted to the use of the objects, and partly because pederasty was a delicate and "complicated" custom, at least for the Athenians. At the same time, much of the "com-

---

* https://www.ehs.se/dss, figure 18, part of a black-figure amphora from Vulci (Etruria), sixth century BCE; orgy scene with nonsense script.

** https://www.ehs.se/dss, figures 14–16, attic red-figure pottery, fifth century BCE, showing courtship scenes between men or youth and boys.

*** https://www.ehs.se/dss, figures 19–22, pottery or drinking cups showing sexual activity between two males and pederastic scenes.

**** https://www.ehs.se/dss, figure 23, image 2, three male same-sex couples at various stages of courtship and sex.

plication" was precisely about regulating pederastic behavior in accordance with overarching cultural values.

As we have seen in previous chapters, the penetration of a free man by another free man has been regarded as highly problematic in many cultures. This was also the case among the Greeks, as such an act constituted an infringement and disrupted the existing hierarchical order. A free man could practice his sexuality against women and slaves, or rather against women and men, as long as they were inferior in rank. But to penetrate a man of equal rank was almost always tantamount to subordinating or dishonoring him. This, of course, was used to shame defeated enemy soldiers or punish people by raping them. Penetrating a free man outside this framework was punishable in many cultures, although same-sex sexual acts of other kinds could occur without much problem. The Greeks included such an act within the concept of hubris.

Ritual "insemination" of boys, however, complicates this picture. As we have noted, our knowledge of such customs is fragmentary, but it is entirely conceivable that, in some contexts, initiation rites included anal intercourse between a man and a boy. Thus, with a caveat for the weak chain of evidence, it is possible that such customs created a gray area outside the ritual context. Be that as it may, the Athenians' self-image was that they tried to regulate customs in line with their other cultural beliefs, while other peoples could engage in same-sex sexual behavior without such considerations.

While girls were often married off or at least promised off early, boys at puberty constituted an intermediate category. They were no longer considered children—with whom sexual acts were not permitted—but they were not yet men. They could therefore, from one point of view, play the "passive" or "receptive" role of a woman in relation to adult men, and yet they could offer some resistance. They could thus assume a role that, due to social conventions and hierarchies, was not available to most free women but was appreciated by many adult men. Indeed, from another point of view, they were not seen as "passive" or feminized at all—they were on the threshold of becoming active, free men, and the sexual play had to do with coming of age. Even if sexual penetration of boys had occurred in archaic initiation rites, such practice did not sit well with the cultural self-understanding of the pederastic game that developed around the gymnasia and the educational system in a Greek urban culture. Therein lies the "complexity" of pederasty in Athens—and probably in several other urban cultures as well. The pedagogical and philosophical su-perstructure could interpret pederastic practices either as steps on the road to friendship, maturity, and understanding or—in what many see as Plato's version—as a kind of cipher for a thoroughly mental, spiritual love, a desire for beauty and knowledge.

No matter how "Platonic" Plato actually imagined relationships between men and boys, the practice was quite physical. Unfortunately, it seems impos-sible to get an unambiguous picture of where the boundaries of this type of asymmetrical sexual relationship went. Scholars simply disagree on whether the ancient Greeks penetrated their boys anally or only engaged in intercrural intercourse according to the ideal.

One piece of evidence supporting the latter is that in the many poems of pederastic love that have survived, a recurring theme is the short time during which a boy is attractive. As soon as the boy becomes too hairy, it's all over. Therefore, the boy should "yield" to the lover while there is still time. All too soon there comes a time when the boy is no longer attractive. The poems sometimes plead, sometimes threaten. The boy seems to be attractive as long as he is smooth like a woman. If he becomes hairy, intercrural intercourse ceases to be as satisfying. This theme recurs throughout the centuries. Theognis, a poet from the sixth century BCE, writes in one of his elegies:

THEOGNIS, ELEGIES, 1327–1330
O boy, as long as your chin is smooth, I will not cease to praise you, not even if I have to die. For you it is a good thing to give, and for me who loves it is not shameful to ask.

And Alcaeus of Messene, from about 200 BCE, is attributed the following lines in Strato's *Musa puerilis*:

ANTH. PAL. 12.30 (GOW AND PAGE 44–47)
Your leg, Nikandros, is getting hairy. But take care
so that your ass (*pygē*) doesn't undergo this unnoticed.
Then you will experience the lack of lovers.
Consider already now how irreversible age is.

An anonymous poem in the *Musa puerilis* also reads:

ANTH. PAL. 12.39 (GOW AND PAGE 3782–3785)

Nikandros is extinguished! Every flower has flown away from
   his complexion
and of his charms not even the name remains—
he whom we formerly used to count among the immortals!
So don't think higher thoughts than mortals, young men.
There are hairs!

Strato himself addresses the issue of hair in several ambivalent poems in the *Musa puerilis*. On the one hand, he says that a single hair ends beauty (Anth. pal. 12.195). On the other hand, he does not intend to abandon his beloved just because he is getting hairy and growing a beard—or marries (Anth. pal. 12.9, 10). But as we read more of Strato, we get the feeling that it's probably only a matter of time before he changes the object of his attraction.

Thus, as long as the boy was without pubic hair, it was not considered shameful for him to "give" and for the lover to demand. The question is what the boy is expected to provide that then becomes problematic in adulthood. Alcaeus of Messene speaks of *pygē*, the buttocks or ass. It is perhaps possible to still see a reference to sex between the thighs, since the word for anus is a different one (*proktos*). The verb *pygizein* is, however, not limited to sex between the thighs but is often used of anal intercourse. Strato, who provides coarse and crude poetry in a never-ending stream, says:

ANTH. PAL. 12.245

Every unreasonable animal just screws (*binei*). But we who are rational have this advantage over other creatures: we have invented anal sex (*pygizein*). All those who are ruled by women have no advantage over unreasonable animals.

It would be more than a stretch to suggest that Strato is talking about anything other than anal intercourse here. Given the interest many erotic poems take in boys' anuses, the constant jokes about anal sex by classical comedy writers, and how often anal intercourse with women (slaves and *hetairai*) is depicted in ceramic paintings, it is quite unreasonable to think that men in their pederastic relationships with boys, at least eventually, would not have expanded the repertoire, even if they initially followed the protocol. It seems evident that socially accepted pederasty in ancient Greece was surrounded by a framework that was clear in theory but flexible in practice. Young boys could sexually satisfy adult men according to certain rules and within certain limits, but when they became adults, they could not occupy the same sexual role as during puberty.

Ancient Criticism

The regulation of pederasty, as well as its philosophical and pedagogical idealization and superstructure, can be seen as the result of a centuries-long process of transformation in which a rite of initiation evolved into a social convention established over time. Less speculatively, it can be seen as a defense against the growing criticism of a practice that was, on the one hand, readily idealized and, on the other, easily derailed. It was certainly criticized. The interesting question, however, is what the subject of the critique actually was.

Some of the clearest examples of criticism can be found in the ancient comedy writers of classical times. Euboulos says of the Greeks' ten-year siege of Troy that there was not a single *hetaira* there, so they had to satisfy each other and came home with asses wider than the gates of the city they conquered. Aristophanes's plays poke fun at Athenian elites with a sundry of crude jokes. In his play *The Acharnians*, Aristophanes lists pederasty and adultery among various immoral behaviors (*Ach.* 263–279). Athens's upper classes and politicians are mocked as arse-fucked (*katapygoi*) and broad-assed (*europrōktoi*).

But the question is what this criticism was really about. On closer examination, it is easy to see that a comedy writer like Aristophanes had no moral qualms about men exercising their sexuality on other people of any gender. The criticism was rather one of contempt for politicians. Men of power are ridiculed through crude invective and portrayed as feminized by being assigned a sexually passive role. The criticism may also concern the practice of selling sex for money. Is it not the case that boys, like whores, also sell themselves for money? This is the question asked by one of Aristophanes's characters in his comedy *The Rich Man* (*Plut.* 149–159), and the answer is that this does not apply to noble boys. So, what do *they* want, then? A horse or a hunting dog, perhaps? Maybe they are ashamed to ask for money and hide a dirty craft behind a fine facade?

In a famous speech from the fourth century BCE entitled *Against Timarchos*, Aeschines accuses his opponent Timarchos in a trial of prostitution by trying to prove his bad character. He is said to have assumed the role of a woman in various same-sex sexual relationships, and he is alleged to have done so primarily for money. Interestingly, Aeschines himself has no moral qualms about either prostitution or pederasty. It is clear from the speech that female prostitution is socially accepted and that Aeschines himself has been both the boy (*erōmenos*) of a lover and has taken on the role of lover (*erastēs*) himself. Timarchos, on the other hand, according to Aeschines, has taken on the role of a woman as an *adult* and has done so for *profit*.

Nor does Plato's criticism of pederastic relationships exhibit moral misgivings of the kind we would expect from a modern perspective. In the *Symposium*, as we have already seen, pederastic love is portrayed as the first step in an evolution toward the love of forms and Beauty—an abstract desire for virtue that in the end seems to render physical eroticism superfluous. But neither sexuality in general nor pederastic relationships are criticized as such. They are rather phenomena or experiences that can serve as analogies to Plato's idealized goals.

In the dialogue *Phaedrus*, it becomes perhaps even clearer that Plato's ideal is asexual. Self-control is a paramount virtue, and the problem of sexuality is precisely the lack of self-control. The human soul is like a coachman with two horses, one white and one black, where the black one is unruly and must be held in tightly until it gets habituated. Plato here delineates through Socrates's speech a type of pederasty that stays with great effort within the boundaries of the ideal—whatever these boundaries were exactly. When the lover has been received (*dexamenou*) by the boy, both in conversation (*logon*) and in company (*homilian*), and granted the privilege (*eunoia*), then the beloved discovers how superior this friendship is to all other friendships. Plato describes how the friendship continues to develop through the lover's physical proximity: he touches the boy in the gymnasia and in their other interactions (*homiliais*), which leads to an unspecified love filling the boy, a reflection of the lover's love, which makes the boy want to see the lover, touch him, kiss him,* and lie down with him—which does happen (*Phaedr.* 255). And now Plato's Socrates becomes rather explicit:

---

* https://www.ehs.se/dss, figures 24–25, attic red-figure kylix tondos (circled inside of a flat drinking cup) by the Briseis painter, ca. 480 BCE, and by the Carpenter painter 515–500 BCE; kiss between lover (*erastēs*) and boy (*erōmenos*).

PLATO, *PHAEDR.* 255E–256A

So, when they lie down together, the lover's troublesome horse has something to say to the coachman and feels he deserves a little pleasure for his
hard work, while the boy's [troublesome horse] has nothing to say to him
but swelling and confused he embraces the lover and kisses him, welcoming
him as being very kind. When they thus lie down together, surely, he would
not refuse to grant (*charisasthai*) the lover his share if he were to ask for it.
But at that point, the yokefellow [i.e., other horse] and the coachman resist,
out of a sense of shame (*met' aidous*) and reason.

The text continues: if the better faculties of the mind prevail in favor of a well-
organized life of philosophy, the couple will live happily ever after and then soar on
wings because they have won one of the three truly Olympic sports. If on the other
hand they should live more laboriously and without philosophy, still usually behaving honorably, but under the influence of intoxication or some other imprudent
circumstance yielding to the two troublesome horses and doing what is considered
by many to be the greatest bliss, continuing in this now and then, though not so
often because the entire mind does not quite approve of it—then these, too, will win
eternal friendship. Perhaps not as strong, but still! And when they leave the body,
they may not have real wings yet, but at least they have begun to grow a little and
will grow out in time (*Phaedr.* 256).

This can hardly be called a criticism of pederasty as such but is rather an
argument for the noble art of self-restraint. At the same time, however, Plato
seems to know that such extreme self-restraint is reserved for a few philosophers only. He therefore makes room for a "working-class morality" that is also
described as praiseworthy—and here the physical expressions of pederasty
have a natural place.

In Plato's unfinished and very utopian work *The Laws* we see examples of
the same ambiguity. Here he experiments with the idea of a law that either forbids men all sexual relations at all, except within marriage, or at least does not
allow men sexual relations with other men but only with women belonging to
the home (including "bought" women?)—that is, sexual relations sanctioned
by the gods and legitimized by marriage (*Leg.* 841c–e).

It is sometimes claimed that Plato in *The Laws* has taken a further step in
his criticism of pederastic relations. This is possible, but the work consists of

utopian speculation, self-restraint is still the overriding virtue, and pederasty is part of the "unrestrained" reality he is trying to navigate. But the traditional pederasty serves mainly as a springboard for Plato's discussion (836b–c). What really poses the problem is men who in their lust for pleasure give in to feminine impulses and assume a woman's role in the sexual act (837c). Such behaviors are described by Plato (841d; 839a) as "men's exercises against nature" (*agona arrenōn para physin*) as opposed to sex in accordance with nature (*kata physin*)—a usage of language we also find in Paul.

Aristotle, a pupil of Plato but in some respects his opposite, attempts in book 7 of his *Nicomachean Ethics* to distinguish between natural pleasures and those that are pleasurable without being so by nature. Pleasures that are not natural can be bestial, they can be explained by defects in those who experience them—like diseases—or by people having learned to enjoy certain things. Examples of sickly or habitual behaviors are:

ARISTOTLE, *ETH. NIC.* 1148B

pulling up hairs, biting nails, eating coal and earth, and in addition to these, sexual pleasure through men (*hē tōn aphrodisiōn tois arresin*). Some are due to nature, others result from habit, as with those violated from childhood (*hybrizomenois ek paidōn*). In cases where nature is the cause, no one can say that they are unrestrained, just as no one can say that about women just because they do not mount (*ouk opyousin*) but are mounted (*all' opyontai*)—nor of those who are habitually sick.

Aristotle's explanation is not quite transparent, and it seems that he uses "nature" and "natural" in several different senses. In our time, it would be easy to think that he distinguishes between homosexuality as an orientation and as a result of social circumstances. But this is not even half true. What Aristotle is saying is that those who do unnatural things by nature cannot be accused of lack of self-control any more than women can be accused for not taking an active but a passive role in the sexual act. These unnatural behaviors that people engage in by nature include nail-biting, earth-eating, and—for a man, since the male perspective is always assumed in these texts—finding sexual pleasure through other men. The Greek wording (*hē tōn aphrodisiōn tois arresin*) shows that Aristotle is not talking about men who penetrate other men, but about men who find satisfaction in the "passive" or receptive role in anal sex. This is one of several examples that, according to Aristotle, can be explained as either a "natural" unnaturalness, that is, as a deviance, or a result of what one subjected and accustomed to as a child. But notice that Aristotle is thinking in terms of various "abuses" (*hybrizomenois ek paidōn*). He does not claim that boys in "normal" pederastic circumstances will assume the role of a woman as adults. After all, in the Greek imagination it was just the opposite—boys in "decent" pederastic relationships were expected to become active men—and the verb *hybrizein* in sexual contexts *does not* denote what a lover is normally expected to do with his *erōmenos* but characterizes abuse and assault. Here it indicates cases in which boys were *not* treated according to the rules of the pederastic game. Thus, according to Aristotle, pederasty does not create feminized men. This is due to "natural" variations and in some cases childhood injuries.

Aristotle's psychology, as well as his notions of active and passive sexuality, are, of course, outdated in relation to our current state of knowledge. This is even more true of the explanation of the distinction between passive and active men offered in the subsequent Aristotelian tradition. The author of *Problems*, a writing attributed to Aristotle but largely of a much later date, attempts to sort out why some men enjoy being subordinated in the sex act and why certain men sometimes want to be on top while others don't want it at all. This is explained by the existence of a defect in feminine men: seminal fluid accumulates around the anus instead of in the penis, creating a craving to be penetrated instead of penetrating ([*Probl.*] 879a–880a). The defect is not total—had it been so the person in question would have become a woman.

Wherever we turn, then, we find—despite the differences—a similar picture. The main problem for the Greeks was grown men behaving like women in bed. A free man who allowed himself to be penetrated was seen as unnatural, immoral, and shameful. Being attracted to boys, on the other hand, was not seen as a defect.

Power and Subordination in Rome

The early Christian movement reflected in the New Testament texts emerged mainly in areas steeped in Hellenistic culture. However, at the same time when Paul was writing his letters, the entire Mediterranean region was part of the Roman Empire, and Roman customs and traditions were mixed with Greek ones. Therefore, it is reasonable to ask how the Romans viewed same-sex sexual relations and whether we can find crucial differences between the Roman and Greek approaches.

One such difference, at least if we allow for some simplification, is the degree to which traditional Roman ideals of masculinity emphasized virility and dominance. This does not mean that masculinity equaled "heterosexuality." The gender of the person toward whom a man directed his sexuality did not really matter as long as he was the "active" partner, that is, as long as he penetrated his counterpart and did not allow himself to be penetrated. It was the assumption of the "passive," "female" role that damaged his reputation as a free man and Roman citizen.

An illicit sexual act—with or without coercion—in Latin was called *stuprum*. Having sex with another free Roman man, or with a free Roman man's wife, daughter, or son (or mother, for that matter) was deemed *stuprum*: it led to dishonor and was punished. The most serious case of *stuprum*, of course, was sex with another man's wife. Sex with another free man led to punishment, but in practice the "perpetrator" could get away with saving his masculinity as long as he was demonstrably the "active" party. The lack of self-control was, of course, no merit. Sex with prostitutes and slaves, on the other hand, was not seen as a problem.

An older argument that the Romans would not have accepted homoerotic relationships is the so-called *Lex Scatinia* (also spelled *Lex Scantinia*), which is sometimes claimed to have been a law against same-sex sexual acts. However, as the text has not survived, it is very uncertain what this law actually contained or how old it was. The *Lex Scatinia* may have originally regulated *stuprum* in general, but after Augustus's *Lex Iulia* regarding adultery was introduced, the *Lex Scatinia* may have only been referred to in cases of hubris against a boy (*puer*), and possibly also in cases of adult men who took a passive role. All the Roman material we have suggests that men's active sexual acts were almost never considered problematic as long as they were not directed at freeborns.

The difference between free and slave was thus crucial. But the dividing lines were not quite as clear as they first appear. Freed slaves constituted an intermediate category. They were often dependent on the person who had freed or redeemed them, both of whom existed in a client-patron relationship that could sometimes resemble serfdom. In his *Controversies*, Seneca the Elder describes how a famous orator, Haterius, defended a freedman who was accused of having acted as a passive partner (*concubinus*) to his patron:

SENECA THE ELDER, *CONTROV.* 4.PRAEF.10

inpudicitia in ingenuo crimen est, in servo necessitas, in liberto officium
Shamelessness for a freeborn is a crime, for a slave a necessity, and for a freedman a duty

A free man could thus in practice have sexual relations with both slaves and freedmen who were dependent on him, whether they were men or women.

What the Romans had difficulty understanding about the Greeks, at least initially, was their pederastic practices. After all, the "Greek vice," as they called it, subjected freeborn boys who were Roman citizens to something that was usually only legal to do with slaves and freedmen. Pederasty, then, was *stuprum*. It is important to note that the Romans were not objecting to homoeroticism as such, or to the boys' young age, but precisely to the fact that they were the children of free citizens.

The upper age of the objects did not play as important a role in Rome either. It is difficult to find in Roman texts the same obsession with hair growth as among the Greeks. At the risk of sounding a bit stereotypical, the Romans were not as subtle. Why would a beautiful slave be less attractive in his twenties? The Greeks could certainly express themselves crudely in both erotic poetry and other literary depictions, but the Romans were at least as good at it. In particular, Greek pederasty required some form of reciprocity—even if very asymmetrical—where the lover devoted much energy to flattering, wooing, and coaching his erotic object, sometimes to the point where he is described in poetry as despairing, trapped and enslaved by his beloved. Such a role did not sit well with the Roman ideal of masculinity.

But as the eastern Mediterranean fell into Roman hands, Greek culture came to influence the way of Roman life, especially among elites. This was often interpreted in the past as meaning that Roman homoerotic behavior generally arose under the influence of the Greeks, but this is incorrect. What did happen, however, is that a variety of cultural behaviors of the kind we know from the Greeks became increasingly common in Rome over time. This includes pederasty, which in practice became more and more accepted from the mid-second century BCE onward. At the same time, there was growing criticism of the "softness" of the Greeks, which was not suited for raising good, disciplined soldiers but beautiful athletes who hang around the gymnasia and wrestling arenas (Plutarch, *Quaest. rom.* 274d). Pederasty is part of what is being criticized, but the criticism is broader than this and concerns a number of Greek customs and habits that were seen as weak and self-indulgent and testify to a lack of self-discipline.

In the first century CE, we thus find a situation where pederasty was quite common also in Rome, even if sex with freeborn boys was in theory punishable. Sex between adult men was partially accepted, but the passive partner was regarded with contempt and his status as a Roman citizen could be questioned. This created some problems for the law and many situations of double standards. Texts by Roman satirists such as Martial and Juvenal show that sex with boys was common, that sex with prostituted men was accepted, but taking a passive role, and in some cases even paying to be penetrated by another man, was seen as decadent.

Nevertheless, several of the Roman emperors seem to have had homoerotic relationships and even to have taken the passive role. Caesar was rumored to have been the lover of King Nicomedes of Bithynia in his youth. Augustus was reviled by his opponents, Pompey and Mark Antony, for having previously had Caesar as a lover and being forced into the passive role and also for having sold sex to a Spanish man for a huge sum of money. Tiberius spent his last years on Capri with a harem of men. Both Caligula and Nero were known for their orgies and for willingly taking the passive role in sex with men. Titus and Domitian were also alleged to have had lovers, and Hadrian's partner Antinous is well known.

Some, but hardly all, of what ancient sources claim about these emperors is, of course, slander. In part, these stories may have served to excuse the fact that the general population did not live according to theoretical norms either. But in any case, most of the evidence points to a certain discrepancy between reality and traditional ideals of masculinity.

Self-Control and Unnatural Behaviors

The most serious moral criticism came from Stoics like Seneca the Younger and Musonius Rufus, both active under the emperor Nero in the 60s CE and thus contemporaries with Paul. For the Stoics, self-control was one of the most important virtues and this included sexual restraint. Sex was considered legitimate mainly for procreation within marriage. Self-control was also emphasized by many other philosophical approaches and in time became the basis of Christian asceticism, which became influential from the second century CE onward.

Seneca was exiled by Emperor Claudius to Corsica for a time in the 40s but was recalled and became Nero's teacher and political advisor. In 65 CE, he was ordered by Nero to commit suicide. As a Stoic, Seneca advocated sexual moderation even within marriage. In his moral epistles or tracts, he complains about behavior that goes against "nature." In Seneca, too, the criticism concerns sexual excesses in general, where sex with men, including taking the passive role, is part of a larger context. This is evident in the long description of the orgies of Hostius Quadra, which includes virtually every conceivable act, and in which Hostius also sets up systems of mirrors to view the whole thing from all sides. Hostius's behavior is seen as deviant or impure (*impurus*) in relation to both men and women: he is not content to sin according to nature (*ad naturae modum*) but seeks to deliberately go against it (*Nat.* 1.16).

For Seneca the Younger, nature served as a moral yardstick, but "nature" means less so biological conditions than cultural and social norms. In one of his moral treatises, he lists a variety of behaviors that are to be considered vices against nature (*vitia contra naturam*), such as turning the clock, drinking wine before taking solid food, growing fruit trees on top of a wall or trees on a roof, or making artificial swimming pools (*Ep.* 122.7–8). The right and natural is the simple. In this context, Seneca also mentions what he considers to be unnatural sexual behaviors:

SENECA THE YOUNGER, *EP.* 122.7

Do you not think they are living against nature (*contra naturam*) who exchange clothes with women? Are they not living against nature (*contra naturam*) who try to gleam boyishly (*qui spectant, ut pueritia splendeat*) at the wrong time [in life]? What could be more cruel or vile? Will a person ever be a man as long as he is passivized by men? (*Numquam vir erit, ut diu virum pati possit?*) [Alternative translation: Will he never become a man just to continue as the passive partner with another man?] And though his sex should have spared him such disgrace (*contumelia*), shall not even his age spare him this?

Here Seneca links men who dress as women and men who try to resemble boys even though they are adults with men who take the sexually passive role in relation to another man. Seneca assumes that the latter is something that should really be considered unnatural and dishonorable (*contumelia*) even for a boy, and even more so for a man of adult age. In Seneca's imagination, the passive role is unacceptable even for a minor, although he knows that in reality boys are often forced to take on this role. For an adult man, the role should be completely unthinkable.

Men who behave and act "femininely" are thus one of several examples of "unnatural" behavior. The criticism is directed mainly at people who live in luxury and opulence. Seneca's focus is on the sweet and "soft" life in general.

Musonius Rufus similarly criticizes a life of luxury and opulence, which for him is often linked to sexual excesses or deviance:

MUSONIUS RUFUS, *DIATR.* 12

A not inconsiderable part of extravagant luxury (*tryphē*) is accounted for by sexual pleasures (*aphrodisiois*), as those who live extravagantly (*hoi tryphōntes*) demand a plethora of not only legal but also illegal "sweethearts" (*paidikōn*), not only female but male as well. They pursue one kind of beloved (*erōmenous*) after another, and they do not settle for the available ones but go for the rare ones as well in search of shameful sexual acts (*symplokas*), all of which are major human defects. Those who are not extravagant or wicked must consider sexual intercourse (*aphrodisia*) proper only within marriage and for the purpose of procreating children, which is also legal. But the pursuits of love for pleasure only are wrong and illegal even within marriage. Of other sexual acts, adultery is the most unlawful, and not a bit more acceptable are those between men and men, as this is a challenge to nature (*para physin to tolmēma*). But besides adultery, all sexual intercourse with women that has no legal basis is shameful because it is done out of intemperance. So, one who is moderate (*meta ge sōphrosynēs*) does not hold on to intercourse with either a *hetaira* or a free woman outside of marriage, no—by Zeus—not even with his own slave girl.

Musonius Rufus goes on to describe all such relationships as shameful, taking on the traditional notion that a man can have sex with a *hetaira* or another unmarried woman without a problem, because he is not spoiling another man's hope of having children. Musonius Rufus argues that even if such a man does not harm another (man), he behaves like a pig through his lack of self-control. Musonius Rufus makes a daring thought experiment for his time and environment: why is it considered by many to be self-evident that a master can sexually exploit his slave as he pleases, while it is appalling if a free woman has a sexual relationship with a male slave? Men should be better than women at self-control, says Musonius Rufus, especially if they want to exercise power over them (*Diatr.* 12).

Musonius Rufus's reasoning is of course based on a hierarchical and paternalistic view, but the interesting thing is that in several of his texts he argues that women have the same abilities and reason as men. Therefore, daughters should receive the same education as sons and women should study philosophy. At the same time, Musonius is not a feminist—that would be an anachronism. He assumes a fairly traditional division of roles but for practical and partly biological reasons rather than principled ones and without value judgment. From today's perspective, his view of the family is certainly conservative—sex is for childbearing within marriage—but his emphasis on reciprocity in marriage is nevertheless striking in context.

For Musonius Rufus, as for Seneca the Younger, the overarching criticism in this context is one of lack of self-control and sexual excess. Sex between men is seen as part of a larger complex. In the quoted text above, two words are used for pleasure-seeking men's sexual objects: *paidika* and *erōmenoi*. Both bring to mind pederastic relationships with boys, although here they seem to be used in a broader sense. In any case, they indicate asymmetrical sexual relationships.

The Stoic arguments against sexual acts between men place great emphasis on issues of self-control and often refer to nature. One of the consequences of this is that the active partner is criticized as harshly as the passive one. The imagination is still largely characterized by a traditional asymmetrical view of the sexual act in which one party takes an active role while the other is passive. Sexuality is understood mainly within the framework of a system of superiority and subordination. But as Epictetus puts it a generation after Seneca and Paul, it is not only the passive partner who loses his masculinity but also the active one:

EPICTETUS, *DIATR.* 2.10.17

What does the one who endures the passive role (*ho ta tou kinaidou paschōn*) lose? Masculinity (*ton andra*)! And the one who performs the act? Besides many other things, [he loses] masculinity (*ton andra*) no less than the other!

Both parties are thus condemned, but the premise for criticizing the active party is that the passive role is traditionally associated with lack of masculinity, unnaturalness, lack of self-control, and shame.

Power and Homoeroticism in Paul

It is quite clear that the criticism of sexual acts between men that we encounter in some biblical texts has the same basic power perspective that seems to have been taken for granted throughout the period we are discussing. This view of sexual acts as an essentially asymmetrical activity of domination and subordination has carried over into modern times.

We can also see some similarities between the views of the Stoic philosophers of the early Roman Empire and the Jewish tradition as expressed in the Holiness Code as well as in Paul. Already the Holiness Code seems to condemn not only the one who is penetrated but also the one who performs the act. In Paul, it is clear that the passive party is not singled out specifically, but his criticism applies to both parties. Although Paul rarely refers to manliness, he is critical of lack of self-control and pleasure seeking in general.

Above all, Paul resembles the Roman Stoics in his conception of what is "natural" and in the moral guiding role he attributes to "nature." When Paul in Romans 1:26–27 speaks of women and men exchanging what was natural (*physikēn*) for behaviors against nature (*para physin*), he sounds quite a lot like Seneca, who was also his contemporary. This becomes even clearer when we look at the other context in which Paul similarly refers to nature as normative, namely in a discussion of men's and women's headgear during prophecy and prayer, where he bases one of his arguments on customs regarding hair length:

> 1 COR 11:14–16
> Does not nature (*physis*) itself teach you that if a man grows long hair, it is a disgrace to him, but if a woman grows long hair, it is a honor to her? Since she has been given the hair for a covering. If anyone intends to quarrel, we have no such custom, nor has [any of] God's congregations.

Paul is hardly suggesting that congregations are not in the habit of quarreling in general, but rather that their practice is to follow cultural conventions regarding male and female hairstyles. The "nature" to which Paul refers is demonstrably not biological, since hair grows on more or less all heads regardless of gender. True, men are more likely to go bald than women, but Paul is not making any such argument against men having long hair. It is simply a matter of a cultural understanding of nature in the Stoic spirit. According to such a view, long hair is disgraceful to men while an honor to women. We will return to issues of shame and honor in the next chapter.

Paul's criticism of same-sex sexual acts is thus based on an understanding of what is natural, that is, cultural, normative, and moral. It was simply not considered appropriate for a man to subordinate himself like a woman. On the other hand, Paul does not go quite as far as Musonius Rufus, who is skeptical of sexual pleasure for its own sake without the purpose of procreating children within marriage. Although Paul would like everyone to be like himself—which seems to have meant some kind of celibacy (1 Cor 7:7)—he speaks of mutual obligations between a man and a woman and seems quite skeptical about abstinence in general (7:2–5). Paul is probably too much of a Jewish realist to be enthused by any generally and strongly ascetic philosophy, but in this very respect he is similar to Musonius Rufus, who valued family and children highly and argued that philosophers should also marry.

It has sometimes been suggested that the homoeroticism that Paul knew and criticized was mainly about pederastic relationships. However, the texts we have examined earlier do not use specifically pederastic language but point to sexual acts between men in which one is assumed to take the active role and penetrate the other, who is passive. Some then try to turn the argument around and claim that Paul both knew about and condemned same-sex relations between consenting adults.

Both ways of reasoning are deeply problematic, especially if the starting point is that Paul should somehow be normative for our time. The result is a serious anachronism, in which ancient beliefs and values are conflated with our understanding and knowledge today. Given what we have found about homoerotic relationships and same-sex sexual acts in ancient Greece and Rome, there is no doubt that Paul must have known about pederastic practices as well as sexual acts between men of every conceivable kind. His criticism applies to all of them.

For most people in modern times, it is the asymmetry, the superiority and subordination, that is most disturbing. Our view of equality and human dignity makes it hard to imagine pederastic practices, but we usually have no objection to consenting adults, as long as people show mutual respect and do not harm each other. But the perceptions and descriptions of sexual acts between adult males in antiquity are, just like in pederastic relationships, also asymmetrical and framed in a social hierarchy, a social pattern of superiority and subordination.

For those who from a religious point of view see Paul as somehow normative but still want to defend same-sex relationships, it may be tempting to think that Paul is addressing the very pattern of subordination and exploitation. But this is just wishful thinking because Paul belongs to a different time. In reality, he repeatedly uses hierarchical models and assumes a social structure of superiority and subordination not only in society but also, to some extent, in the church (for example, in 1 Cor 11; Rom 13). On the other hand, in Paul, as in Musonius Rufus, there is an incipient understanding of human relationships as essentially reciprocal. From a modern point of view, these approaches are inadequate and inconsistently implemented. But in their ancient context they should have been challenging.

It becomes equally problematic for those who seek Paul's support against same-sex sexuality on the grounds that his criticism would have been directed at consenting adults. The fact is that very little of the pressing issues of our time—sexual orientation, discrimination, same-sex marriage, and so on—would have made any sense at all in Paul's day. For Paul, as for almost all people in antiquity, sexual relations were part of the hierarchical structures on which the whole of society rested. For Paul, as for some contemporary Stoic philosophers, sexual acts belonged within marriage and were accorded at least some degree of reciprocity. For Paul, as for some other critics, same-sex sexual acts were contrary to "nature" not primarily in the biological sense, but because they went against either the custom of one's own group or the ideal social order that the critics advocated.

Paul, like many of his contemporaries, thus sees "nature" as essentially a matter of culture. And at the heart of a culture that sees sex as an exercise of power and condemns "passive" men are deeply rooted notions of what constitutes masculinity and femininity, that is, what is honorable and shameful behavior in relation to a person's gender and status.

HONOR AND SHAME

Anthropological Concepts

In recent years, the concept of honor has been used in various contexts but rarely has been explained. We are expected to understand the meaning of "honor" in phenomena such as honor killings, honor violence, and honor culture. In historical research, not least in biblical studies, the opposing pair of honor and shame has come to be used as an analytical tool. From a cultural anthropological perspective, honor and shame are seen as key concepts for understanding and interpreting various kinds of human behavior and human interaction in ancient societies as reflected in historical texts.

Cultural anthropological methods are usually developed for the study of contemporary societies, and it is always debatable to what extent they are suitable for historical studies and textual analysis. In the case of honor and shame, many scholars used to talk about a general Mediterranean or Middle Eastern culture where the concept of honor is the focus in a way that is very similar to what we can learn from antiquity.

There are a number of risks associated with such an approach: among others, it may lead to anachronistic conclusions. Contemporary attitudes are assumed to have prevailed in the ancient world or, vice versa, contemporary people from these areas are attributed historical tendencies and values from ancient West Asia, Greece, and Rome. There is also a risk for Western observers to put on blinders and perceive honor and shame as notions typical of "the other"—

people from the South or the East—even though both notions and behaviors live and thrive just as well in Northern Europe or America as elsewhere.

"A day of shame for Sweden—even the girls did it better!" That's how a Swedish tabloid put it around twenty-five years ago when the men's national team lost while its women's team was doing well. It might just as well have been in ancient Mesopotamia or Greece, except for the football as the only anachronism (or was it hockey?—my grasp of elite sports is minimal). Here, all the ingredients are at least hinted at: an agonistic (competitive) culture and a patriarchal set of values where honor is a male virtue manifested in winning points, and where shame is associated with the feminine. In other words, for a man it is shameful to be associated with the feminine, to be feminized, by others taking his honor (points) from him. For a woman, on the other hand, it is honorable to assume the role that, for a man, would be associated with shame, but it is shameful to adopt a behavior that would mark power and virility for a man. The latter is not apparent from the tabloid's contents but finds many expressions in Western societies still today. In this chapter we will try to understand these contradictory relationships and how they have influenced views of sexual acts between men and between women in ancient societies.

Winning Glory

In all human cultures through history, people have desired honor and avoided shame. Notions of honor and shame, like many other things, are socially constructed and may therefore differ in different societies. At the same time, these beliefs are rooted in biologically based physical reactions—they have to do with our emotions. Feelings of honor and shame are felt and manifested in the body. How we feel is linked to self-esteem and self-image as well as to how other people relate to us and respond.

Psychologists and therapists sometimes talk about different types of shame, how they affect us as people, and what function they have. There is a shame that has to do with a fundamental lack of self-respect and trust—a disproportionate shame on the verge of darkness and self-loathing. But this is not the form of shame we are discussing when we examine ancient conceptions and texts with honor and shame as analytical tools. Rather, we are talking about shame and honor in relation to the judgments, values, and acknowledgments of others.

Honor has to do with reputation and status. A person can be born to high repute or be ascribed status in some other way. But honor is also something that can be acquired. It is not enough to claim honor for oneself. Reputation is something that a person gains in the eyes of others. Without social recognition, there is no honor. And in certain circumstances, honor needs to be defended in order not to be lost or tarnished. In most ancient societies, a social game was constantly going on in which people won or lost "honor points" so that their "honor capital" increased or decreased. In this game, shame can be likened to minus points or debt.

The ancient game of honor and shame took place on several different planes, but in a way these formed a coherent arena. Honor and shame were intimately linked to prevailing hierarchies, the social structures that people were part of, born into, or moved up or down in. Honor and shame meant different things and were acquired in partly different ways depending on where in the hierarchical social fabric people found themselves. This was particularly true in relation to gender roles. Honor for a man and honor for a woman were partly different things. In the area of sexuality this becomes particularly clear, as certain actions and attitudes that brought honor to a man were considered shameful for a woman and vice versa. At the same time, self-control or self-restraint became a paramount virtue in the Hellenistic cultural sphere, as we already witnessed for Plato's Socrates and even more so for the Stoic philosophers.

Male Honor

Greek culture saw honor (*timē*) primarily as a male attribute, which occurred quite naturally since reputation (*doxa*) was linked to social recognition and thus depended on public life, which was mainly reserved for men. The basic attitude does not differ significantly from other ancient cultures, but Greek literature clearly articulates it. A man was supposed to be active, powerful, and courageous—courage and manliness (*tharsos* and *andreia*) were even synonyms in Greek—while a woman was supposed to be reserved and withdrawn. Men's space was the public sphere, while women's was the private sphere: above all the home, but also the well and the market where many women spent their time. In other contexts, an honorable woman was not supposed to appear without her husband or engage in conversation and socialize with other men. Of course, the whole of the ancient world over many centuries cannot be lumped together, and there are examples of both variations and exceptions. The extent to which such ideals were upheld was also a matter of class. But most of the texts we have referred to so far fit this picture quite well.

To maintain and strengthen his honor, a man needed to assert himself well in social circles. Some scholars use the fencing terms *challenge* and *riposte* to describe the competition in word combat depicted in many ancient texts, including the New Testament Gospels ("Honor as well as dishonor follows from words"; Sir 5:13). One person challenges another to a verbal duel, so to speak, and one of them comes out on top. One imagines that such literary depictions reflect or represent a rather common approach to social interaction in general. A man defends his reputation and refuses to be humiliated.

The consequences of such an agonistic approach are that a man asserts his honor and prestige by appearing strong and virile, by mastering others, and also through his sexual relations, controlling his family and defending his women and children against other men. As in most other cases of human behavior, it is easy to imagine an evolutionary biological backdrop, in which genes and offspring play a role (compare the phrase "a woman who leaves her husband and presents him with an heir by another man"; Sir 23:22).

What all this meant in practice we have seen in several examples from the previous chapter. For example, a man did not lose his honor by sexual penetration of people of lower status. In some cases, it could be a way of gaining honor or at least degrading another person, especially if the person in question was not subordinate or was an enemy. On the other hand, a free man lost honor by being penetrated himself, at least by someone of equal or lower status. Everything depended on where on the hierarchical ladder a man was situated.

From this vantage point, women and children thus represented part of a man's honor that he needed to protect and defend. A woman could certainly gain her own honor by showing bravery. Plutarch wrote a text on women's courage at the beginning of the second century CE. But the point then was to challenge men with examples that even women could be "manly"—"even the girls did better." We need to understand stories of brave women in the Israelite tradition, such as Deborah, Jael, Judith, and the mother of the seven brothers in 4 Maccabees, from a similar perspective. When it comes to sexuality, however, women did not gain honor by behaving like men, but rather the opposite was the case. Women were a constant source of concern for men, a potential threat to their honor. That is why men must control women. The book of Sirach (also known as the Wisdom of Ben Sira), a second-century

BCE Jewish writing translated into Greek from a Hebrew original, contains many clear examples of this:

SIR 42:9–14
A daughter is her father's secret sleeplessness and his worry for her takes sleep away: while she is young, lest she be overaged; and when she is married, lest she be hated; while she is unmarried, lest she be defiled and pregnant in the parental home; when she lives with her husband, lest she transgresses; and being married, lest she be childless. Watch strictly over a headstrong daughter, lest she bring upon you the ridicule of enemies, the gossip of the city, the accusations of the people, and disgrace (*kataischynē*) you before all people. Do not look at the beauty of anyone and do not sit in the company of women. For out of clothing creeps a moth and out of a woman female evil. A man's evil is preferable to a woman doing good, and a shameless (*kataischynousa*) woman renders insult.

The book of Sirach is probably the most misogynistic of all biblical writings, but precisely because of this the whole paradigm becomes overtly clear in his texts. At the same time, Sirach is influenced by Hellenistic and Stoic values and considers it shameful for a man to cast his eyes not only on other men's wives but also on prostitutes and even to take an interest in his own slave girl (Sir 41:20–22).

Female Shame

If honor was a male trait, shame (*aischynē*) was associated with women. In fact, one could say that shame was considered a female virtue, while shamefulness or shamelessness was a negative thing. Here, too, Sirach provides clues:

SIR 4:21
For there is shame (*aischynē*) leading to sin (*hamartian*), and there is shame (*aischynē*) [leading to] honor (*doxa*) and praise (*charis*).

The Greek *aischynē* can be translated as "shyness" or "timidity," even though it is more often translated as "shame." Sirach seems to be talking about two meanings of shame: on the one hand a shamefulness (or we might perhaps rather say shamelessness) that engages in norm breaking, on the other hand a sense of shame that prevents people from shameful (*aischros*) behaviors and makes them act in an honorable way, which brings them honor in return.

These two sides of shame become even clearer when we examine another, almost synonymous, Greek word. The noun *aidōs* is described in Greek texts from Homer onward as an emotion, an affect, a feeling of avoidance, timidity, withdrawal, or inferiority in relation to another, often more significant person. Sometimes it works to translate *aidōs* as "shame," sometimes as "modesty," sometimes as "respect." Interestingly, psychological research shows that people's bodily reactions when they feel shy, embarrassed, or ashamed are similar or identical. Typical reactions include blushing, slumping shoulders, bowed head, and shying away. I may have done something that I am ashamed of in front of another person, something that affects my self-image and other people's image of me—my status. Our feelings of shame depend a lot on the people we have before us. We feel more ashamed if they are significant "others" in relation to us, in the sense that we relate to them and that we recognize their status. Before such people we feel somehow inferior and experience a lowering of our own status, if we have done something worthy of blame.

Now, it is not necessary to have done anything in particular to experience an embarrassing difference in status. In a hierarchical society, it may be enough for me to belong to a subordinate category for it to be embarrassing to meet a person of a different social class. I have internalized other people's image of me—not necessarily of me personally but of people belonging to my group— into my self-image, so that I am embarrassed to meet people of higher status. In relation to such people, I feel inferior, shy, ashamed.

From this perspective, we can understand why *aidōs* can be perceived as something good, a fitting emotion or a virtue—especially for those who are supposed to be subordinate to other people. This "embarrassment" or "sense of shame" prevents me from violating society's norms. This is the underlying mindset behind calling a person who does not respect norms "shameless." Again, we can illustrate this with Sirach, except that here the verb *aischynomai* is used for feeling shame:

SIR 41:17–20, 27

Be ashamed (*aischynesthe*) before your father and mother for adultery, and before the leader and regent for lying, before the judge and the ruler for wrongdoing, and before the congregation and people for lawlessness, before companion and friend for dishonesty, and before the place where you live for theft, for breaking oath and covenant, and for placing your elbow in the food, for cursing receiving and giving, and for meeting with silence those who

greet, for looking after a loose woman (*hetairas*) . . . Then you will be truly
modest (*esē aischyntēros alēthinōs*) and find grace before every human being.

Embarrassment also prevents one from challenging people of higher status
and instead prompts one to show them the deference, respect, and modesty that
a hierarchical culture expects from a person of subordinate status. Sirach again:

> SIR 4:7
> Make yourself pleasing in the community,
> and humble your head before the mighty.

It is precisely this aspect of "shame" that makes it a typically—if not exclusively—female virtue. After all, women were usually seen as subordinate to
men in the social hierarchy, just as slaves were subordinate to free men, and free
citizens were subordinate to the ruling elite. To put it a little more bluntly, in
relation to those above a human being was a "woman," but in relation to those
below a human being was a "man" regardless of biological sex. Toward superi-
ors one was expected to display female virtues, and toward subordinates one
claimed male ones. Gender constructions and the social hierarchy were thus
very closely interwoven. This is expressed, among other things, in the texts in
which the people of Israel are constructed as women in relation to Yahweh,
God (Hos 1–3; Jer 2–3; Ezek 16; 23).

Ancient literature is replete with examples of what is considered appropriate for a woman, from King Alcinous's young daughter Nausicaa in book 6
of Homer's *Odyssey*, who despite her initiative and quest for freedom exhibits
a demureness and modesty (*aidōs*) appropriate for women, to 1 Peter's description of Sarah as an example of how virtuous women behaved, "subjecting
themselves to their own men, just as Sarah obeyed Abraham, calling him Lord"
(1 Pet 3:5–6). The tragedian Euripides (fourth century BCE) succinctly but
clearly articulates how virtue, a sense of shame, and honor or decency are
thought to relate to the different roles of men and women in social relations:

EURIPIDES, *IPH. AUL.* 558–572
Different are the natures of mortals, different are their ways, but the real good is
always plain. Well-educated nurturing leads to great virtue (*aretan*). For [a sense
of] shame (*to te gar aideisthai*) is wisdom and brings the gift of well-founded
insight into what is decent (*to deon*), and then good repute leads to timeless

fame in life. Chasing virtue is great: for women according to the hidden *Kypris* [= Aphrodite; i.e., by a discrete erotic life] and for men, on the other hand, innumerable forms of order (*kosmos*) lead to the growth (*auxei*) of a greater city.

Men rule and women are prudish, at least if they are properly brought up.

Sex and Shame in a Social Hierarchy

Notions of honor and shame in sexual relationships were consequently guided by prevailing hierarchies and gender roles. We have seen in the previous chapter how views on penetration depended on where on the hierarchical social scale the persons in question were located. The constant play of honor and shame in antiquity adds a further dimension to the problem.

What was honorable or shameful in an erotic relationship was therefore related to differences in status and the position of the people involved on the social scale, especially in relation to each other. We have previously quoted the phrase attributed by Seneca the Elder to the orator Haterius, but it bears repeating:

SENECA THE ELDER, *CONTROV.* 4.PRAEF.10
Shamelessness for a freeborn is a crime, for a slave a necessity, and for a freedman a duty.

In its context, the statement is about a man being penetrated by another man. For a free man this was considered shameful but not for a slave. The slave was already a "woman" in relation to his master. A free man was feminized by taking on a "female" role. In the case of a freedman, however, it became trickier. He occupied an intermediate position and was dependent on his former owner. Haterius defends the freedman's honor by arguing that it is not inappropriate for him to still provide, in relation to his former owner, what a slave was expected to do, only now as a service. Everyone agrees on the starting point: sex in accordance with the hierarchical structures is honorable, while sex in conflict with the hierarchical structures is shameful. Problems arise when the structures are not clear-cut or when they conflict with each other.

It is precisely this ambiguity—this conflict between different hierarchies—that forms the basis of the whole discussion of pederastic practices in Greek and Roman cultures with which we have become familiar. What, in fact, is honorable or shameful in relationships that are, on the one hand, clearly asym-

metrical (adult-child) and, on the other, not (both freeborn)? There are other
examples of situations where hierarchical structures are unclear. We have previously quoted Plutarch's questioning of the inappropriateness of a sensible
older woman controlling a young man. Could age and experience, as well as
the common sense that Plutarch generously imagines an older woman might
possess, possibly balance the asymmetry of gender roles? We have also seen
how Musonius Rufus, in a display of Stoic moderation, provokes his audience
with the image of sex between a free woman and a male slave as an argument
against free men allowing themselves to have sex with their slave women. Now,
most people in antiquity would probably argue that when it comes to sex between a free woman and a slave, it is the asymmetry between free and slave
that counts. Thus, such a relationship is shameful for the free woman. And the
case of a man and his slave woman would be seen by most as unproblematic
from a hierarchical perspective. For Musonius to stand a chance, he must rely
on a growing acceptance of Stoic virtues like restraint and self-control.

Here, at the intersection of hierarchical values and the emergence of ideals
of moderation, we can find keys to ancient judgments about and reactions to
lesbian relationships, that is, erotic acts between women. To simplify: sex between free women did not give rise to the asymmetry of sex between free men
or the conflict between hierarchies that pederasty caused, because according
to the prevailing view women were already subordinate in the social hierarchy.
In theory, none of the women should lose any honor because none of them
was degraded by penetration. And even if some form of penetration between
women was supposed to occur, the question is whether a woman—or her husband—would lose any honor through it, as long as no other man was involved.
In practice, however, many Greek and Roman texts exhibit a negative attitude.
After all, women who took an active role threatened the hierarchical pattern. And
a woman who was not content with her husband was often seen as lecherous and
shameless. A man who had no control over his wife's sexuality lost honor.

Eroticism between Women

Despite the death penalty for sexual intercourse between men, neither the
Hebrew Bible nor other ancient West Asian texts say anything about erotic
acts between women. How to interpret this fact is not self-evident, but it is reasonable to think that sex between two women was not considered particularly
serious, at least in social terms, since no known legal collections or other texts

address such relationships. It is highly unlikely that the phenomenon was un-known.* The question is whether ancient West Asian cultures regarded erotic relations between women as relatively unproblematic (no undue penetration) or as private rather than public (jurisdiction in the home belonged to the hus-band) or both. In any case, there was no other man involved, and perhaps the issue was therefore considered irrelevant to the interaction of free men in the public sphere. In that case, women's erotic relationships need not have affected their men's honor to any great extent and thus would not have been consid-ered particularly shameful. Such a development would require some form of cultural ideals of moderation of the kind that developed in classical Greece.

Reasoning in the absence of evidence to the contrary is, of course, specula-tive. Moreover, it would be naive to assume one and the same attitude to sexual relations between women throughout ancient West Asia and throughout the long period of time from which various types of source material are available. At the same time, however, it is not an unreasonable generalization, not least in view of the fact that early texts on eroticism between women from preclassical Greece lack shame-imposing tendencies. Such values appear only later.

A plate from ancient Thera (present-day Santorini), which depicts two women with wreaths facing each other, dates from the Archaic period (c. 625 BCE). One touches the other's chin, a well-known erotic motif. They are the same height, and the image does not give the impression of any age asymmetry.**

Dating from about the same time are the most famous archaic texts reflect-ing eroticism between women. They were written by Sappho of Lesbos, who lived at the end of the sixth and beginning of the fifth century BCE.*** (A date of birth around 630 or 620 BCE is a common guess.) In the oldest portrait we have of her (around 500–475 BCE) she is depicted holding a lyre (*barbitos*). Sappho's poetry was once collected but is now mostly preserved as fragments, many in the form of quotations given by later Greek writers or grammarians. Despite this, there is enough available to give us a fairly good picture of Sap-pho's poetry. However, it is very difficult to reconstruct her life. The sources

* https://www.ehs.se/dss, figure 23, image 1, two women facing each other sharing a cloak (a common symbol of marriage); and image 4, bride and men, probably illustrating a heterosexual relationship/marriage (?).

** https://www.ehs.se/dss, figure 26, two women with garlands, one making a court-ship gesture; archaic painting from Thera (Santorini), seventh century BCE.

*** https://www.ehs.se/dss, figure 27, Roman bust from Smyrna, portraying Sappho, second century CE; copy of older Greek original.

we have were written long after her death, and many of them are polemical and negative to Sappho's erotic writings about other women. Often, hints in the poems have been interpreted and overinterpreted much later by writers who had no access to any historical information about Sappho. This includes information about her family circumstances—a mother and a daughter both named Kleis, a husband named Kerkylas from Andros ("Dick from Isle of Man")—as well as the legend that she committed suicide because of unhappy love for a ferryman. In later texts about Sappho, two tendencies can be seen: either she is portrayed as "heterosexual," or she is vilified for her love of women.

According to a Greek inscription from Paros, dated to 260 BCE, Sappho was exiled to Sicily, and a rather unclear line in Sappho's fragment 98 could possibly allude to exile as well. We do not know why, but perhaps it was caused by the same political circumstances that also forced Sappho's contemporary compatriot Alcaeus from Lesbos for a time, although Sappho's poems have very little political content. Alcaeus (not the Alcaeus of Messene we previously encountered) describes her in fragment 384 as the "violet-haired (violet-weaving?), pure, honey-smiling Sappho" (*ioplok' agna melichomeide Sapphoi*).

In modern times, Sappho has sometimes been anachronistically portrayed as the director of a girls' school, but nothing in the source material suggests teaching or education in the conventional sense. One interpretation is that she was the leader of a *thiasos*, a ritual society of girls or young women who engaged in singing, poetry, and dancing. And she does not seem to have been the only leader of such a group; two other women who probably had a similar function for other groups are mentioned (Andromeda and Gorgo; Sappho frag. 130; here and in the following, Voigt's numbering is used).

Sappho's Association

What was the role of such an association? Some have suggested that it was of a distinctly cultic, religious nature; an Aphroditic cult, in analogy with male *thiasoi*, that could be associated with the cult of Dionysus, for example. But clear evidence is lacking—in fact, Sappho's own texts never use the term *thiasos*. A fragment attributed to either Alcaeus or Sappho speaks of women from Crete dancing around an altar while treading on the soft flowers of the grass (frag. S/A 16).* It has

---

* https://www.ehs.se/dss, figure 28, attic red-figure kalathos by the Brygos painter, ca. 470 BCE; the painting probably portrays Alcaeus and Sappho.

sometimes been linked to another fragment (frag. 154): "The full moon appeared and as they [feminine plural demonstrative pronoun, referring to women] stood around the altar. . . ." Novelists may allow themselves to use such loose threads for free speculation, but this hardly improves the evidence. Many of Sappho's songs turn to Aphrodite—naturally enough since she was the goddess of love. But Sappho's group does not seem to have been a specifically cultic society.

The choral lyricist Alcman of Sparta was contemporary with Sappho. He is mainly known for his *partheneia*, "girl songs." In the aristocratic and highly organized Spartan society, boys and girls were brought up separately. The system included societies, choirs (*choroi*), where girls were taught songs and dances to be performed at parties of various kinds.* In one such *partheneion* (no. 1), Alcman depicts the girls admiring each other's looks and clothes, and above all their leaders. The texts are very sensual, and the perspective is meant to be that of a woman, although the author was a man. In another *partheneion* (no. 3), more fragmentarily preserved, one of the girls sings about how another pretty (*glyk[ea]*) girl, Astymeloisa, looks at her so that she melts, and about a feeling of her limbs dissolving (*lysimelei te posōi*). The girl hopes she will love her and wishes she would come closer and take her soft hand (*idoim' ai pōs me . . . on philoi [as]son [io]is' hapalas chēros laboi*).

The Spartan organization of boys' and girls' upbringing and education was known to follow strict patterns. What Alcman describes in his *partheneia* probably reflects part of the coming of age for all Spartan girls who belonged to the free elite in the Archaic period. The "choirs" thus seem to have had an initiatory function. But it is interesting that Alcman describes the girls' relationships with their peers. When Plutarch, toward the end of the first century CE, gives his picture of Sparta and pederasty there, he says that the women did the same as the men—they took girls as their lovers. That Plutarch interpreted the culture of early Sparta in accordance with the common view of pederasty as an age-asymmetrical relationship is not difficult to understand. The question remains to what extent this was representative of the society Alcman describes.

Thus, there were more associations like Sappho's in ancient Greek societies, and it is reasonable that such groups had a kind of initiatory function in preparation for the transition to adulthood and marriage. However, unlike Sparta's

---

* https://www.ehs.se/dss, figure 29, bronze figurine in Peloponnesian style, perhaps originally from Sparta, ca. 500 BCE; girl running and dressed according to ancient descriptions of girls' attire at the Hera festival at Olympia.

"girls' choirs," such groups in Lesbos seem not to have been something that everyone participated in but voluntary associations for the daughters of the aristocracy, where they learned singing and dancing and were prepared for their sexual role and life as married women. One of the group's tasks was singing and dancing at weddings; some of the poems seem to be intended for wedding feasts, and these wedding songs (*epithalamia*) often sing of the strength of the groom and, above all, the beauty and attractiveness of the bride:

> FRAG. 30
> Virgins . . .
> all night . . .
> sing of your and the purple-clad bride's love.

> FRAG. 105A
> As the sweet apple blushes high on the branch
> high on the highest since the apple pickers have forgotten it—
> no, they have not forgotten, but they cannot reach it.

> FRAG. 112
> Happy bridegroom, for you the marriage you asked for
> has been fulfilled, and you have the virgin you asked for.
> (Her) appearance is pleasing to you, and (her) eyes . . .
> gentle, and love (*eros*) flows over your beautiful face.

Some of these poems say goodbye to the bride and to virginity:

> FRAG. 114
> Bride: virginity, virginity, where have you gone and left me?
> Virginity: I will never come again to you, I will never come again

> FRAG. 117
> Farewell, bride and farewell, groom

Other poems describe the loss of the girls who have left the group—we may assume precisely because of marriage:

FRAG. 94

I certainly would like to be dead!
She left me crying
and told me this:
Oh, what a misfortune has befallen us, Sappho!
I am really leaving you involuntarily.
I answered her this:
Farewell! Go and remember me,
for you know how we took care of you.
If not, I want to remind you . . .
and the beautiful (things) we experienced (*epaschomen*).
Many wreaths of violets, roses and crocuses
you wrapped around you by my side,
and many braided garlands of flowers . . .
around your narrow neck
and . . . with precious myrrh . . .
you anointed even in a royal manner
and on a soft bed, tender . . .
you satisfied your desire (*pothon*)

(The last lines become more and more damaged, but probably mention a cult place, a grove, and dancing.)

Eroticism in Sappho

The poem quoted above contains unmistakable allusions to erotic relationships between Sappho and the participants in her society. More fragments make this clear. In one song (frag. 22), Abanthis is asked to sing of Gongula while desire flutters around her. Gongula is referred to as "the beautiful" (*ta kalan*), and the sight of her attire arouses desire. This desire can be almost unbearable when it takes possession of the body:

FRAG. 130

Eros, the dissolver of limbs (*lysimelēs*), shakes me again,
bittersweet, untamable reptile.

But it can also be satisfied:

> FRAG. 48
> You came, you did [it], and I wanted you (*s' emaioman*),
> you cooled my heart (*phrena*) that was burning with desire (*pothōi*).

Erotic relationships between the girls (or women) in Sappho's group are thus mentioned without reservations. What is interesting is that they are described as relatively symmetrical. Some of these poems depict erotic feelings between the participants in a way that has no counterpart in the texts on pederastic relationships that we have examined in previous chapters. As in Alcman's texts from Sparta, there is a relative reciprocity here that is difficult to find in texts about erotic relationships between men. Sappho's fragments also contain very little of the objectifying and coarse expressions of hierarchical power found in many texts on male homoeroticism.

It would be an exaggeration to say that objectification is lacking. The examining and evaluating gaze plays an important role in relation to desire. But in the poem about the girl who has to leave the group (frag. 94), a "we" is mixed with Sappho's own relationship to her, and the satisfaction referred to is not Sappho's desire but the girl's.

There are two famous poems in particular, which depict the desiring subject most clearly. First, in the Hymn to Aphrodite below it is Sappho herself who asks for help with her love troubles. Here, the goddess addresses Sappho by name:

> FRAG. 1
> . . . you asked what I have again suffered and why
> I have again invoked,
>
> and what I most wanted to happen to me,
> my troubled heart. "Whom shall I again convince
> to bring you into her love? Who,
> O Sappho, offends you?
>
> For even if she flees, she will soon pursue,
> and if she does not accept gifts, she will give them,
> and if she does not love, she will soon love
> albeit reluctantly.

The tone here is quite different from the poems that describe the beauty and grace of the girls in Sappho's group and how they admire and long for each other. The Hymn to Aphrodite is a strong description of unrequited love, but the context is never explained in detail. The situation is in some ways similar to that behind a much later text from the second century CE, an incantation from Fayyum in Egypt in which a woman asks the spirit of the deceased Evangelos and the gods of the underworld for help in binding a woman she desires.

The second poem of Sappho, in which the desiring subject similarly comes to the fore, was already the most famous in antiquity.

FRAG. 31
As fortunate as the gods to me it seems
is the man who beside you
sits, and close by hears you
pleasantly speaking,

temptingly laughing. Certainly my
heart does tremble in my breast
when I briefly look at you—then it seems
I can no longer say a thing

but my tongue is broken and suddenly a
subtle fire has rushed under my skin,
with my eyes I see nothing, my
hearing is roaring,

sweat pours from me and trembling
grips my whole being. I am greener
than grass, coming close to dying
it seems to myself.

But all must be borne, since . . .

This poem has been subject to varied and contradictory interpretations. One older view saw it as a wedding song about the bride and groom, and even suggested that the focus was on the man and that Sappho was describing her envy of the woman in question. This type of interpretation was often linked to a desire to clear Sappho of accusations of "immorality." But the poem certainly expresses erotic feelings for the woman in question, and the bodily reactions Sappho describes speak for themselves. The man is definitely a side character. However, it is not impossible that the situation the poem describes has to do with a woman moving out of the community and into marriage, including the role of a wife and the love of a man. In what contexts such a song could be sung is an open question. Our imaginations easily limit what we think of as possible, but if erotic feelings and relationships between women, especially before or in preparation for marriage, were considered legitimate in Sappho's culture, the poem need not have been startling.

Although the poem expresses a desiring subject, Sappho herself does not emerge in the same way as in the hymn to Aphrodite. Nevertheless, it is easy to interpret this poem autobiographically as well. At the same time, it is unreasonable to try to reconstruct Sappho's life on the basis of individual poems. Poetry such as this has become immortal precisely because of the way it expresses experiences with which many people can identify.

Regardless of the extent to which Sappho's poems can be read autobiographically, at least some of them are formulated from the perspective of an examining eye and a desiring subject. If Sappho's poems represent her personal experiences, and if the group consisted of girls or young women, which is a likely reconstruction of the historical situation, we can speak of an actual age asymmetry in the attraction, desires, and erotic acts that Sappho describes. Fragment 58, which describes grief or anguish over old age, supports this. The poem seems to be addressed to the girls and can now be reconstructed almost in its entirety after additional fragments were found in 2004 in old mummy wrappings (used papyrus were at times recycled for this purpose, much as we make papier-mâché from newsprint). Sappho describes here how her skin and hair color are changing with age and how her knees are unable to dance. But "it is impossible for a human being not to grow old" (*agēraon anthrōpon eont' ou dynaton genesthai*).

The reflections on the increasing age gap, however, seem to reflect more of a grief over the loss of the community the group provided—a community of girls on their path to adulthood and marriage where erotic expression and relationships were part of existence.* Although historical reconstruction based on

* https://www.ehs.se/dss, figure 30, attic red-figure hydria (water vessel) from Barē

the poems is hazardous, the relationships between the members of the group are never depicted as expressions of hierarchical or asymmetrical relationships, which makes the picture we get here markedly different from the whole pederastic tradition. The age asymmetry that we reasonably assume between Sappho and her group has no special function in the context and is not a prerequisite for the same-sex erotic relationships described. There is little in Sappho's texts to suggest that these relationships are part of a hierarchical or asymmetrical game of superiority and subordination. Notions of honor and shame are conspicuous by their absence. We simply find no evidence of feelings of shame or embarrassment in the face of same-sex eroticism in Sappho's context.

Shameful Tribades

Lesbos came from classical times onward to be associated with "irregular" erotic behaviors, but it is unclear how early this transpired. Anacreon, a Ionian poet who usually wrote about relationships between men and was active nearly half a century after Sappho, has left a poem (frag. 358) about how Eros makes a man play with a girl wearing pretty sandals.* She turns out to be from beautiful Lesbos. The poem ends: "my hair—it is white!—she dislikes, and gapes/stares for another." The last line is difficult to translate because *allēn tina* (feminine) can refer either to another hair (feminine) or to another person, a girl. Does the sandal-wearing hottie turn the poet down because he is too old—there are other black-haired men, after all—or does she prefer another *girl*? The latter interpretation is common, but more or less assumes that Lesbos was already associated with women who preferred same-sex eroticism to sex with men in the sixth century BCE.

That assumption is questionable. It is only another century later that we have unequivocal evidence that Lesbos was associated with particular erotic behaviors, and then it is a matter of ridicule. The comedy writer Aristophanes uses the verb *lesbiazein* and the adjective *lesbios* in several of his plays to refer

---

(Vari), by the Polygnotos group, early fourth century BCE; Sappho (?) reads poetry for three other women, one of whom holds a lyre.

* https://www.ehs.se/dss, figure 31, pottery model from Crete, 575–550 BCE, woman's foot with painted nails and luxury sandal; and figure 32, votive offering from the Sanctuary of the Mother of Gods (Cybele) and Aphrodite, Pella, terracotta figurine of Aphrodite removing her sandal.

to oral sex (*Vesp.* 1346; *Ran.* 1308; *Eccl.* 920). We are now at the late fifth and early fourth centuries BCE, and it is clear that Aristophanes is using a stereotype common at the time: the inhabitants of Lesbos are behaving indecently. But this is still not about sex between women—it is about women having sex with men. During the classical period in Athens, a number of comedies were written in which Sappho figures, but in the few fragments that have survived there is nothing about her love for women. One fragment claims that she had two (male) lovers. It is only from Roman times that we find the beginnings of a vilification of Sappho for her desire for other women. A case in point is Tatian (second century CE) who, in a defense of Christian women studying, calls Sappho "a sex-crazed whore who sings of her own promiscuity" (*Or. Graec.* 33).

Women who love women were not an unknown phenomenon in classical Athens. Plato's *Symposium* contains a speech by Plato's character Aristophanes (perhaps molded on the comedian), in which he lays out the myth of the three original sexes: human beings were originally spherical with a double set of faces, arms, legs, and genitals. Some were male, others female, and the third kind was male on one side and female on the other. Because they posed a threat to the gods by making so much noise, Zeus cut them in half. Ever since, the two halves look for each other: men have sought women, but some men and women seek members of their own sex (*Symp.* 189c–193d). Women who seek their own sex are called *hetairistriai* by Plato's character. The term is a variant of *hetaira*, but the exact meaning is disputed, and it only reappears half a millennium later in Lucian (see below). While *hetairai* were women who were available to free men as "companions," a *hetairistria* seems to have been a woman who sought her own companionship with women.

However, the idea of women satisfying their sexual needs without any form of penetration was a rather remote thought in classical times. The comedy writer Aristophanes gives an example of this when he depicts in *Lysistrata* how the Athenian women stop the war with Sparta by refusing sex: "Since the Milesians betrayed us, I have not even seen [the glimpse of] an eight-inch leather dildo (*olisbon oktōdaktylon*), which could serve as an aid," says Lysistrata (*Lys.* 109–110). And a little later, when the women hesitate, fearing that the men will give up on them altogether—after all, they cannot bear to be without sex—she replies (158), "Then we shall skin a skinned dog" (*kyna derein dedarmenēn*), which in context simply means, "then we shall make/use a leather dildo," known in Greek as an *olisbos*.

Such *olisboi* are also depicted on the occasional less scrupulous vase paint-ing from classical times. Who such paintings were intended for is debatable, but it is highly doubtful that the context is homoerotic. Of further interest is Herondas's third-century BCE *Mimiambs* (no. 6), where Metro and Koritto are depicted discussing a very popular purple leather dildo, which seems to be circulating in their circle of friends and was made by the shoemaker Kerdon. The purpose of the text is, of course, to portray the upper-class women as frivolous and rather shameless, but it is hardly about homoeroticism. Female homoeroticism is, however, the topic in some later texts. When Seneca the Elder around the year 30 CE lets the participants in his *Controversies* discuss accusations of sexual misconduct, he mentions a man who caught his wife in bed with another woman and beat them both to death, defending himself by saying that "first I looked at the man to see if he was natural or stitched on" (*Controv.* 1.2.23). Sex between two women is thus assumed to require an active penetrating partner.

Some vase paintings, mainly from the early classical period, depict erotic touching between women.* Here too, hierarchical relationships or age asym-metry do not seem to be expressed, but over time, especially in the Roman period, a patriarchal understanding of sex as penetration within the framework of prevailing hierarchies became dominant. The inability to perceive sex be-tween women as anything other than an imitation of the prevailing hierarchical paradigm of male sexuality becomes overtly clear in, for example, Martial's *Epi-grams*, written around 90 CE. In one of the poems, he mocks Bassa (*Epigr.* 1.90) who fucks women (*fututor eras*) with her monstrous clitoris (*venus*), which she believes to be a penis (*mentiturque virum*). This is described as adultery (*adulterium*) even though no man is involved. Similarly, Martial describes the strong Philanis (7.67) who eats, drinks, and exercises like a man, raping both boys and girls and performing oral sex on women (*cunnum lingere*) instead of men (*non fellat*)—the most unmanly thing of which Martial can think.

This critique of "male" women continues to be articulated both by Chris-tians, such as Tatian (see above) and Tertullian, and by non-Christians. Lu-cian (second century CE) is an example of the latter. In his *Dialogues of the*

---

* https://www.ehs.se/dss, figure 33, red-figure kylix tondo (circled inside of a flat drink-ing cup) by Apollodorus, ca. 500 BCE; two nude women, one touching the other's vulva (or probably epilating pubic hair).

Courtesans, we find a group of women discussing sex. Clonarion questions
Leaina about the rumors that she is sleeping with a rich woman, Megilla, from
Lesbos. Leaina explains that this woman is terribly like a man (*deinōs andrikē*).
Clonarion does not understand what she means:

LUCIAN, *DIAL. MERETR.* 5.2

I do not understand what you are saying, unless you mean she is a type
of *hetairistria*? For they say that in Lesbos there are such male-like women
who do not want to do it (*auto paschein*) with men (*hyp' andrōn*) but lie
(*plēsiazousas*) with women as if they themselves were men (*hōsper andras*).

"Yes, that is right," Leaina confirms, whereupon Clonarion immediately wants
to know how Megilla seduced her. We can leave the details, but when Leaina
divulges about the circumstances and the erotic foreplay and gets to what
Clonarion (or rather Lucian's male readers and listeners, we may assume!)
would prefer to hear, she interrupts herself and says: "Do not ask me the details, for they are shameful (*aischra*), I will by the heavenly [i.e., Aphrodite]
not tell!" (*Dial. meretr.* 5.3).

Lucian's text contains a number of important clues and is extremely revealing. It shows how erotic acts between women were perceived at the time.
Above all, they were interpreted by analogy with prevailing pederastic customs
and entirely within the framework of a hierarchical view of sex as an affair between a superior, active, penetrating party and a subordinate, passive one. The
wealthy Megilla from Lesbos is described as such an active, "terribly manly"
(*deinōs andrikē*) woman who, in a sexual sense, associates with or comes close
to (*plēsiazousas*), that is, has sex with other women as if she were a man (*hōsper
andras*). Such a woman is called *hetairistria*—the same term from Plato half a
millennium earlier—and Lucian characterizes her as a woman who does not
want to submit herself to the sexual act (*auto paschein*) subject to men (*hyp'
andrōn*). In plain language, she does not want to assume the passive female role
and the subordination that was considered normative in sexual intercourse
between men and women. In Lucian's context, this is considered so obviously
shameful that he has his character Leaina say so herself.

The ensuing shame must reasonably be understood as a consequence of
several factors. First, it is considered shameful for a woman to go beyond her
given role and act as an active partner by penetrating another woman, which is

assumed from the prevailing hierarchical view of sexual acts. Second, it seems to be considered shameful for a woman to engage in sexual pleasure without a man being involved. It is not only the "active" role that is shameful but also the "passive" one. A woman's lewdness and lack of moderation does not promote a man's honor.

Lecherous Rubbers

In Roman times, the term *tribas* (pl. *tribades*) came to be applied to women who had erotic relationships with other women. The word is Greek and can best be translated as "rubbers" but came to be used mainly as a Latin loanword. Seneca the Elder calls the two slain women *tribades* (*Controv.* 1.2.23; see above), and Martial uses the same term for Philanis (*Epigr.* 7.67, 70; see above). Martial accuses other women of being *tribades* in his writings as well.

In Soranos of Ephesus's medical texts from the second century CE (some of which only exist in Latin translation in Caelius Aurelianus's *Chronic Diseases*, probably from the fifth century), *tribades* are described as sick (*Chron. pass.* 4.9.132–133): "They practice both kinds of sex but are more eager to have sex with women than with men and chase after them with almost male jealousy." Such things, Soranos explains, are nourished by shameful customs (*consuetudine turpi nutritas*). Soranos thus describes *tribades* as almost bisexual, but what makes them sickly is their masculinity, that is, their taking an active role. Although Seneca calls both women in his example above *tribades*, there is much evidence to suggest that the term was used primarily for "active" women in same-sex erotic acts—those that Lucian calls *hetairistriai*.

A seemingly corrupted phrase in Caelius Aurelianus's Latin translation (*iuvamini humilitate duplici sexu confectam*) can be interpreted as "a humiliating device was made for their dual sexuality." This interpretation is disputed, but possibly here, too, is an example of the hierarchical notion that sex between women required a dildo. And this was considered humiliating (*humilitate*) and shameful (*turpi*).

In the centuries that follow, the condemnation of sex between women increases further in Christian literature. We have space for only a few examples. Tertullian (*Pall.* 4.9) is outraged that elite women appear in the streets in the wrong kind of clothes, as do the *frictrices* (Latin equivalent of *tribades*), and calls this shameful behavior (*propudiis*). Clement of Alexandria around 200

CE describes homoeroticism, both between men and between women, as "against nature" (*para physin*). He condemns women who marry other women and thus behave like men, but probably also those women who adopt the passive role:

CLEMENT OF ALEXANDRIA, PAED. 3.3.21.3
Men have endured the lot of women (*ta gynaikōn hoi andres peponthasin*) and women behave like men (*andrizontai*), by against nature (*para physin*) both being married off with (*gamoumenai*), and marrying (*gamousai*) other women.

Whether Clement means that some women are "active" and others "passive" is not entirely clear. In any case, none of them stick to their female role. Both fail to do what for Clement is the woman's task: to receive her husband's seed (*Paed.* 3.3.19.1). Not taking care of the seed is shameful (*kataischynein*; 2.10.83.3). Shamefulness applies to women even more so than to men, as John Chrysostom (later part of the fourth century CE) makes very clear when he compares the homoerotic relationships of women and men in one of his homilies on the Epistle to the Romans:

PG 60:417
and more shameful (*atimoteron*) than this [sex between men] is when women also seek these associations (*mixeis*, i.e., sexual encounters), because they should display shame (*aideisthai*) more than men.

Embarrassment or shame (*aidōs*) was, as we have seen, a suitable emotion, especially for women, and deterred them from shamelessness. According to such thinking, women should have more of such inhibitions (*aideisthai*) than men, and therefore their same-sex sexual behavior becomes even more shameful and a greater harm to honor (*atimoteron*) than men's.

It seems symptomatic that Christian texts condemn both women in homoerotic relationships. The Apocalypse of Peter from the second century CE describes the eternal punishments and how different categories of sinners are to be tortured. These include "women ... who slept with each other (*synkoimētheisai allēlais*) as a man with a woman" (Apoc. Pet. 32 [Akhmim]).

Rabbinic texts from the first centuries CE are also disapproving but not as condemning. There are occasional disapproving references to marriage between women, such as Sifra Aḥare Mot 9.8 where this is considered an Egyptian custom. A woman who wears an artificial penis is condemned in the Babylonian Talmud (b. ʿAbod. Zar. 44a). But when the Talmuds (fifth to sixth century CE) discuss which women a priest can marry, the rabbis disagree. According to Leviticus 21, a priest may not marry a prostitute (*zônâ*), a woman who has been raped by someone, or someone who has been disowned by her husband. So far, everyone agrees. The question is how to count a "rubber." Can she be married to a priest and eat holy food? It turns out that this is a borderline case. As for two women "rubbing" with each other, according to the Palestinian Talmud the Hillel school says they can be accepted for marriage to a priest, while the Shammai school says no (y. Giṭ. 8:8, 49c). The Babylonian Talmud depicts the same exchange, but puts it in the mouths of two later rabbis, Rabbi Eleazar and Rav Huna (b. Yebam. 76a). According to Eleazar, the woman is merely loose, lewd, or indecent (*pərîṣûtāʾ*), but it is not adultery (*zənût*). So, there is a certain difference here compared to Christian texts from the same era.

At the core, however, we find the same basic view of women's sexuality: it should not take up space or make claims but be modest. Women need to have enough sense of shame not to behave shamelessly and compromise the honor of men. An important background factor for the development we have traced is to be found in the ancient view of moderation and self-control and is linked to the emergence of an explicit view of the human self, an increased self-awareness.

Moderation and Self-Control

Questions of self-control and the human ability or inability to act in accordance with beliefs and convictions are a recurring theme in many of the tragedies of classical drama. In Plato and Aristotle, the relationship between self-control (*enkrateia*) and lack of self-control (*akrasia*) takes the form of explicit philosophical and ethical discussions. The main problem concerns the relationship between human reason and emotion, and explanations for why human beings do not always act according to their convictions. In Xenophon's picture of Socrates (c. 370 BCE), *enkrateia* is the basis for a virtuous life.

For the Stoic philosophers from Zeno's successor Cleanthes (c. 330–230 BCE) onward, *enkrateia* became one of the cardinal virtues. Another cardinal virtue already in Plato was *sōphrosynē*, moderation. In the ancient dramas, this is a fitting virtue for women, not least in Euripides, where *sōphrosynē* characterizes the traditional female role: quiet, modest, chaste, and obedient. In the Stoics, *sōphrosynē* came to be one of the most important qualities for men as well in their struggle against the passions.

A Stoically modified Platonism (or possibly Platonically modified Stoicism) came in many ways to characterize the more popular philosophical thought from the Hellenistic period onward. By Roman times, self-control and moderation had become important and highly valued qualities, even if their concrete meanings were different for men and women. A man with sufficient self-control (*enkrateia*) did not risk falling prey to weakness (*akrasia*) and did not allow passions to override action based on knowledge and reason. The result was a life of moderation (*sōphrosynē*).

This thinking also characterized the Greek-speaking Jewish culture to which Paul belonged and in which the early Christian texts developed. The Wisdom of Solomon 8:7, on which we have seen earlier that Paul leans, describes wisdom (*sophia*) as the source of (the four Platonic) virtues (*arētai*): moderation (*sōphrosynē*), understanding (*phronēsis*), justice (*dikaiosynē*), and courage (*andreia*). Living virtuously by means of wisdom leads to honor (*doxa*) before the people, and esteem (*timē*) among the elders, even while one is young (Wis 8:10). Fourth Maccabees is even clearer in its very Stoic exposition:

4 MACC 1:13–19

So now we are investigating whether reason (*logismos*) is the ruler of the emotions (*pathōn*). We must define what reason is and what emotion is and how many forms emotions can take and whether reason can rule over them all. Reason, then, is the mind that consciously chooses (*meta orthou logou protimōn*) the wise life. Wisdom, then, is knowledge of divine and human things and their causes. This, then, is the guidance of the law, by which we learn divine things reverently and human things for our own good. The forms of wisdom consist of understanding (*phronēsis*) and justice (*dikaiosynē*) and courage (*andreia*) and moderation (*sōphrosynē*). But supreme power over them all has understanding (*phronēsis*), through which reason (*logismos*) rules the emotions.

4 MACC 1:30–32

For reason (*logismos*) is the leader of virtues and the ruler of emotions. Observe, then, in the first place, through the actions which moderation (*sōphrosynē*) prevents, that reason is the absolute master over the emotions. Moderation, then, is the ruler over the desires (*tōn epithymiōn*), but some of the desires are of the soul and others of the body, and over both of these, reason is shown to rule.

Philo, the Jewish-Alexandrian philosopher and contemporary of Paul, also discusses these four cardinal virtues (*phronēsis, sōphrosynē, andreia,* and *dikaiosynē*) alongside a number of other, more Jewish virtues (*Leg.* 1.63). Philo's thought is in many ways Platonic, but since he is also strongly influenced by Stoicism, he elsewhere includes self-control (*enkrateia*) among the virtues and treats it as almost synonymous with *sōphrosynē* (*Agr.* 98). Philo thus speaks of moderation and self-control in the same breath and sees the Jewish law as the best guarantor of these virtues (*Spec.* 4.55). By means of moderation and self-control, the law keeps the emotions or passions in check, and in particular desire (*epithymia*), which Philo sees as an enemy and the source of all sin (*Virt.* 100). Desire is in many ways the worst emotion, the one that never listens to the voice of reason and betrays humans. The law contains an explicit commandment against desire (Exod 20:17). In one of his allegorical expositions of Moses, Philo says that

PHILO, SPEC. 4.95

the holy Moses put off passion (*pathos*) and abhorred it as most shameful (*aischiston*), and as the cause of everything most shameful he declared above all desire (*epithymian*) as something corrupting the soul, which must be removed or subjected to the helmsman of reason (*logismō*).

For Philo, the law of Moses becomes a superior expression of contemporary philosophy, according to which reason rules over the emotional life.

Self-Control and Shame in Paul

Paul broadly shares Philo's Jewish interpretation of a Stoic-Platonic view of reason and emotion, self-control and incapacity, moderation, and desire, with the difference that for Paul it is not the law but the spirit that provides a solution to the problem. Self-control or self-restraint (*enkrateia*) is the last in Paul's list of "fruits of the Spirit" (Gal 5:23). In a passage with sports metaphors, Paul says that "everyone who competes must exercise self-control (*enkrateuetai*) in everything" (1 Cor 9:25). Self-control is particularly difficult when it comes to sexuality, and Paul, despite his ascetic tendencies, is far more realistic than many give him credit for, even if his realism is rather crass.

In 1 Corinthians, Paul discusses sexual relations on the basis of the Corinthians' explicit questions to him; the passage begins with "concerning the things of which you have written" (1 Cor 7:1). Yet it is impossible to determine whether the subsequent clause, "it is good for a man not to touch a woman," represents the congregation's assertion, is a direct question (i.e., "is it good for a man . . . ?"), or is actually Paul's own assertion. If the latter is the case, the question remains whether he is being rhetorical, ironic, or actually means what he writes. The exposition that follows shows ascetic ideals mixed with pragmatic realism, including a perspective that is relatively reciprocal for the context. Because of the immorality or promiscuity (*porneia*) of the time, Paul believes that every man in the congregation at Corinth should have a woman and every woman a man of her own, and that both owe each other intercourse. In this regard, Paul believes that neither of them determines or has sole power over (*exousiazei*) their own bodies (7:2–4). Temporary abstinence by mutual agreement is allowed for prayer, but then they must have sex again lest they be tempted by Satan "because of their *akrasia*" (7:5).

This, Paul says, is a concession, not a command, because he would really like everyone to live like him, but they cannot (7:8–9). Unmarried people and widows would do best to remain single, but if they cannot live abstinently (*enkrateuontai*) they must marry—marriage is better than "burning" (*kreitton gar estin gamēsai ē pyrousthai*). "To burn" was a common Greek metaphor for sexual desire.

A little further on, Paul sets out his basic position: each person should remain in the situation in which they find themselves. This is best because of the "impending distress" (7:26, *tēn enestōsan anankēn*). Time is shrinking (7:29) and the world is perishing (7:31). Here Paul alludes to Jewish notions of apocalyptic "tribulation," hard times, and violent upheavals. Such a worldview partly explains his attitude. But apocalypticism notwithstanding, the ascetic trait is firmly rooted in a Platonic-Stoic understanding of moderation and self-control as supreme virtues and necessary aids for reason to keep passions and desires in check.

Control over the body is therefore important to Paul. "Nothing shall have dominion over me" (lit. "I shall not be mastered under anything"), he writes in 1 Corinthians 6:12 just after the list of those who may not inherit the kingdom of God, which includes prostitutes (*pornoi*) and adulterers (*moichoi*) as well as "softies" (*malakoi*) and "male-bedders" (*arsenokoitai*) (6:9). In the first chapter of Romans, discussed earlier, the connection between self-control and what is perceived as sexual licentiousness is even clearer. The root of all evil, in Paul's view, is of course idolatry. But what idolatry leads to, and what in turn gives rise to what Paul perceives as unnatural sexual behaviors, is desire or lust (*epithymia*):

ROM 1:24, 26–27

Therefore, God handed them over through the desires (*epithymiais*) of their hearts to impurity so as to dishonor (*atimazesthai*) their bodies with each other. . . . Because of this, God handed them over to dishonorable passions (*pathē atimias*): Their females exchanged the natural "use" (*chrēsin*) for that (which is) against nature (*para physin*), and similarly males also abandoned the natural "use" of females and were inflamed with a yearning for each other in that males practiced shamefulness (*aschēmosynēn*) with males and received in themselves the necessary payment for their error.

Desire thus leads to passions and sexual behaviors that are considered dishonorable (*atimazesthai, atimia*) and shameful (*aschēmosynē*). Shamefulness consists largely of the lack of control over the body, that is, the inability of the mind to master the body's desires. This is the same line of thought that Paul expresses later in Romans, when he discusses sin:

ROM 6:12–13, 20–21

Sin, then, must not rule in your mortal body so that you obey its desires (*epithymiais*). Nor must you present your members as weapons of iniquity for sin, but present yourselves to God. . . . For when you were slaves to sin, you were free in relation to justice. What fruit did you use to get then? Such as you are now ashamed of (*epaischynesthe*) for the end of that is death!

Desire and lack of self-control, according to this thinking, lead to immoral actions, not least in the area of sexuality, and this is intimately linked to shame. Moderation, on the other hand, is associated with honor. But in Romans 1 the shamefulness also includes the violation of gender roles. Both women and men are said to act "against nature" (*para physin*). We have seen in previous chapters how Paul in 1 Corinthians discusses headgear and hair length for men and women respectively (1 Cor 11:2–16), referring to "nature" (*physis*) in the sense of "cultural custom." For a woman to violate gender roles by praying *without* something on her head is to shame (*kataischynei*) her head (11:5). To cut or shave off one's hair is shameful (*aischron*) for a woman (11:6), and to have long hair is a dishonor (*atimia*) for a man (11:14) but an honor (*doxa*) for a woman (11:16).

Honor and shame are thus clearly associated with cultural gender roles, but in the field of sexuality also (and especially) with the ideals of self-restraint and moderation that developed from classical times onward and had come to flourish among Stoics and Stoically influenced thinkers around Paul's time. The combination of cultural role expectations perceived as "natural" with the view of *enkrateia* and *sōphrosynē* as weapons in the fight against irrational passions and desires thus explains why shame came to be associated over time not only with sexual promiscuity but also with all sexual expression outside roles and norms. The evolution from the "passive" sexual role being seen as primarily shameful for men to all homoeroticism, including sex between women, being perceived as dishonorable is quite logical from this perspective. Despite the relative lack of violation of the prevailing hierarchical power order, women's erotic relationships came to be shamed. The inability of many men to conceive of female homoeroticism in any way other than the traditional pattern of male asymmetrical pederasty—a superior, active partner penetrating a subordinate, passive one—helped, of course. Since the pattern often did not correspond to reality, many men found it easy to regard such women as alternating between the active and passive role, and hence both were seen as equally shameful. From the archaic texts of Sappho, which are devoid of any hint of shame, to the ridicule of women's shameless sex drive in the comedies of the classical period, to the condemnation and shaming of eroticism between women in Roman times, we find a long trajectory stretching over seven centuries. The increasing negativity is really just a consequence of a view of women as loose and lecherous, lacking in self-control and moderation. The Pauline disciple who wrote 1 Timothy in Paul's name toward the end of the first century CE points out the direction:

1 TIM 2:9, 11
Similarly, women are to adorn themselves in appropriate attire with modesty/shame (*aidous*) and moderation (*sōphrosynēs*). . . . A woman is to learn in quietness and in complete subordination (*en pasē hypotagē*).

For such women, sexual initiative is hardly an option at all. That would be shameful. They can only "be saved by childbearing, provided they remain in faithfulness and love and sanctification with moderation (*sōphrosynēs*)" (1 Tim 2:15).

HOMOEROTICISM THEN AND NOW

Understanding Antiquity

In the previous chapters, we have tried to understand homoeroticism from an ancient point of view. We have examined ancient texts that describe sexual acts between people of the same sex and associate them with impurity and disgust. We have discussed sexual behavior in relation to social structures and patterns in ancient settings. We have analyzed social and cultural constructions shaped by notions of power and status, of superiority and subordination, and of honor and shame. We have seen how ideals such as moderation and self-restraint emerge and reinforce hierarchical tendencies.

Antiquity does not exhibit *one* view of homoeroticism and sexual behavior. Ancient beliefs differ over time and between societies. Nevertheless, we can generalize enough to say clearly that ancient views differ from contemporary understandings in some crucial ways. Certainly, modern societies do not have an *unambiguous* understanding, and certainly there are similarities between ancient and contemporary beliefs and behaviors. But the differences are there, and they are fundamental.

The differences relate mainly to how we view people's right to their own sexuality and the right of each person to decide over their own body. Based on today's democratic values and view of human rights—which we often praise but do not always follow—no human being should force another into sexual acts or sexual relations. Not only that, but we regard all forms of pressure as equally inappropriate, any exercise of power, any asymmetry in sexual relations. Sex is for consenting adults. Sexual acts with minors are punishable. Sexual exploitation of dependent people is usually considered immoral, even in cases where there is no formal offense.

Reality, of course, differs from these fine ideals. But the differences remain. In the ancient world, sexual acts were not expected to take place in equal relationships but, as we have seen, as an affair between a superior and a subordinate, an active and a passive one, one who penetrates and one who allows himself or herself (or is forced) to be penetrated. This is not to say that ancient societies lacked reciprocal relationships, but reciprocity looked different—it differed from our ideals. And while our reality is sometimes similar to the ancient one in that it is, in practice, more hierarchical and more patriarchal than we like to admit, there is still a difference in terms of the ideals we advocate.

The same relationship applies to our view of honor and shame. In the Western world, we often talk about foreign cultures of honor but do not consider our own cultures as part of that paradigm. But in fact, Western societies have many honor-related behaviors and traditions. Yet there is a fundamental difference from ancient cultures, where notions of honor and shame shaped official morality, and people in subordinate positions were expected to show the submissiveness, deference, and obedience that their relatively low status demanded. What this meant for sexuality we have seen. Women's initiative and freedom were severely restricted in many contexts. Men's behaviors were also restricted to those considered compatible with their role and status. It was considered shameful for a free man to take on a woman's role, and to force a free man to do so was to degrade him. Acceptable sex was to penetrate a subordinate, not an equal. Although such attitudes and behaviors occur in our time and culture more often than we would like to admit, the fundamental difference is that we do not generally affirm such values.

Can we then ever understand ancient ideals, values, and behaviors? Not entirely, but at least to some extent. Perhaps the secret is not to deny or suppress all the similarities that actually exist between people in the Western world today and the peoples of the past—or, for that matter, contemporary people from places and cultures that do not affirm what many of us perceive as democratic and humanistic values. Indeed, if we scratch the surface, we may recognize ourselves in ancient texts more than we would like to admit. The psychological resistance is, of course, strong. It is easier and safer to affirm our beliefs in the equal value of all people and in the freedom and rights of the individual. The problems and threats we sense lie elsewhere, among different people and in the past that we have left behind. But in fact, they are in the midst of our own culture and our own communities. We ourselves are part of them. When we accept and face that stark reality, we may not only gain a better understanding of antiquity, but *through* our understanding of antiquity we may also understand ourselves and the world of which we are a part.

Preference, Orientation, and Status

A major difference between our time and antiquity is, of course, our level of knowledge, particularly in the field of biology. None of the ancient West Asian texts we have examined, including texts from the Hebrew Bible, suggest any understanding or notion of sexual preference or sexual orientation. Same-sex sexual acts are entirely related to questions of human status and roles.

However, the difference is not absolute. As we have seen, the Greek philosophers could reason in terms of something at least similar to sexual orientation. The jocular myth of Zeus cleaving spherical protohumans provided by Plato's character Aristophanes can be interpreted as an awareness that people do not always choose their sexual preferences freely but are guided by underlying factors beyond their control. At the same time, we encounter an understanding of "nature" and "natural" that many times was really about culture or custom. Therefore, as we have seen, Aristotle can speak of same-sex sexual behavior as "unnatural" acts that are due either to "nature" or to habit and harm.

For most people, however, this kind of distinction seems not to have been part of their conscious understanding even in Greco-Roman culture. Sexual acts were not perceived to any great extent as a matter of orientation but, as in ancient West Asia, mainly as behaviors in accordance with a person's role and status in society.

In Hellenistic Judaism, including the New Testament epistolary texts we have discussed, same-sex sexual acts are understood in part as expressions of human choice. From the Wisdom of Solomon onward, deviant sexual acts are seen as the result of human ignorance and idolatry. Philo sees sex between men as the ultimate consequence of unbridled desire that is so strong that it transcends the limits of nature. In a way, Paul combines these lines of thought when he describes in Romans the human desire for sex against nature, with persons of the same sex, as a consequence of the worship of other gods. But it is doubtful whether we can interpret these texts in terms of orientation. Desire for people of the same sex is indeed described, but as a "punishment," a consequence of worshiping false gods. There seems to be no question of a biologically based orientation.

In our time, there is no consensus on the relationship between biological factors and social or cultural constructs. The reasoning in the first chapter is that both models are correct and necessary but answer slightly different questions. Sexuality has evolved because it is biologically functional, but sexual behaviors, sexual categories, and how we perceive sexual identity are very much social and cultural constructs. This is also true of same-sex sexuality. How sexuality has been socially constructed over time is not independent of biological conditions, but at the same time the relationships are not simple or straightforward. In particular, there is no straight path from biological factors to social norms.

Sexuality, Power, and Violence

We have seen numerous examples of how sexual acts are used to mark status and are constructed as expressions of power, sometimes under violent circumstances. The Holiness Code's prohibition against a man sleeping with another man "as with a woman" need not refer to coercive sex but may well do so. Under the Middle Assyrian laws, as we have seen, the man who spread rumors about another man would be punished by rape and castration. In the stories of Sodom and Giva, sexual violence is portrayed as an expression of xenophobia. Rape of enemy soldiers (in addition to civilians) has been a means of shaming defeated opponents in many cultures and periods of history. The practice is even depicted in Greek vase paintings.*

In ancient West Asian and Greco-Roman settings, sexual acts, including same-sex ones, were seen primarily as a matter of penetration. Such acts marked superior status and were thus something not to be inflicted on a person

---

* https://www.ehs.se/dss, figures 34–35, the Eurymedon vase; attic red-figure oinochoe (wine jug) by the Triptolemos painter, symbolizing the victory of the Greeks over the Persians at the river Eurymedon in the 460s BCE. The Greek soldier is just about to rape the Persian who bends down. The text says: "I am Eurymedon, I stand bowed down."

of equal status. From such a perspective, it is quite logical that sex, even in family relationships and in other civil situations, was also about the exercise of power and could involve violence and coercion to a greater or lesser extent. Slaves in particular were in a vulnerable position, as mentioned earlier.

The biological and psychological links between sex and violence are a subject in their own right to which more attention should be paid than is possible in this book. Sexual arousal can take violent forms in both humans and animals. Male chimpanzees often abuse females who do not yield to sexual advances. The reactions activated by sexual arousal are related to other strong affects. One example among many is case studies of how soldiers in combat experience sexual arousal and erection. Another is research on sexual serial killers. It is commonly believed that feelings of anger and rage or the need for power and control play a major role in the relationship between sex and violence. But at least in the case of serial killers, most evidence suggests that their motivation and aggression have more to do with arousal and desire. There is much evidence of a type of sexual aggression that is akin to the arousal that both hunters and predators can feel. Several studies show that a small minority of men are aroused by sexual aggression in thought or action.

This can be perceived as a rather inconvenient fact for those who would like to see sexuality itself as something completely separate from human hierarchies and social power structures. But such idealism is naive. The many sexual behaviors that human beings engage in may all be socially constructed, but the biological raw material contains what it contains, for better or worse. It need not be normative or guiding, but it must be managed and navigated.

Today, in much of the world and based on something like a human rights consensus, we choose to manage and navigate humanity's many and sometimes violent sexual behaviors in ways that are partly different from what the ancients did. With regard to homoeroticism, this means that, contrary to ancient beliefs, we reject asymmetrical sexual relationships and acts that exploit or dominate people who find themselves in a position of dependency or disadvantage. That is why pederasty, like sex trafficking, falls under public prosecution. We also reject ancient notions of sex as being essentially about penetration, that men who are penetrated thereby lose their masculinity, honor, and status, or that lesbians are lewd and indecent because they behave like men and step outside their role as women. Contrary to the common view in antiquity, we understand sexual acts, whether between people of different or the same sex, as legitimate *precisely when* they take place between consenting adults, without violence, coercion, or the exercise of power.

That is how we think in theory. In practice, the reality is not quite so pretty. People are sexually exploited, and in many parts of the world homosexuals are persecuted and killed. Even more are threatened, discriminated against, and maltreated even in superficially tolerant societies. Perhaps a better understanding of the ancient view of sexuality in general, and homoeroticism in particular, can help us to deal with a complex world? Perhaps a greater awareness of the interplay between social and cultural patterns and the biological conditions of human beings can be useful? And in this context, it becomes important to remember that the values from which we critique hierarchical and violent patterns—justice, empathy, freedom—are also grounded in the biological conditions of human beings as a social species.

The Role of Religion

What role does religion play in all this? Much of the discussion in this book revolves around biblical texts, that is, religious texts. But along the way we have seen that the same or similar views and values have been expressed in legal texts, philosophical texts, and various literary works. Which texts are to be considered "religious" is a matter of definition. For most of human history, religion has not been a concept because a secular culture, distinct from what we now perceive as religious aspects, was something unknown. What we call religion has been an integral part of all societies and cultures until modern times, and still is in many parts of the world.

What makes, for example, the Holiness Code's prohibition of lying "woman-lays" with a man a more religious text than the Middle Assyrian laws is the framework for the Israelites' precepts (God's word at Sinai, through Moses) and the status as sacred Scripture that the collections of laws in which the Holiness Code is integrated have acquired, not only in Judaism but also in Christianity. Something similar is true of Paul's (and others') letters, which were originally situational texts intended for specific contexts. No religious community today reads Philo or Seneca with the same reverence and sense of authority. But the texts contain much the same presuppositions and ideas. In this respect, religion mirrors culture, or, rather, they are two sides of the same coin.

On the other hand, religion as such (if one can express it that way) plays a small role in the values and judgments about homoerotic relationships or same-sex sexual acts mentioned in the texts we have read. Religion matters to the extent that religion is a function of the culture to which religion belongs. There was little tension between Israelite religion and culture, Hellenistic Jewish religion and culture, or Greek religion and culture.

Rather, the tensions belong to the modern era, when religion and culture have become at least partially separated, and ancient texts have acquired normative status for some but not for others. Modern fundamentalism is at least part of the problem, if not all of it. When sacred texts—that is, ancient texts that carry meaning and identity for an entire religion and culture—are regarded as an absolute norm, they become unmanageable. Throughout history, religious traditions have found many ways to negotiate their sacred writings so that they can be used and remain relevant in new times and contexts: reworkings, allegorical and symbolic interpretations, historical and contextual interpretations, and prioritization of different texts and traditions, to name a few. This is part of each religion's interpretation of its own scriptures. In actual fact, religious texts have rarely been treated as entirely normative but rather as *formative*. With this comes the possibility to discuss and negotiate with the texts and their world— and sometimes to reject their views and values as obsolete.

But religion is not just about texts; it is very much a matter of practice. In practice, religious representatives have many times, even today, condemned both homosexual lifestyles and homosexual people. In practice, religion in its various forms has contributed to the persecution and killing of people considered to be deviating from the "norm." The question is, however, whether this is due to religion as religion, or due to the fact that some forms of religion that lean toward fundamentalist ideas have lost the ability to deal with, interpret, and negotiate with their historical tradition, which naturally includes a number of texts with hierarchical, patriarchal, and homophobic features.

The latter is a rather reasonable conclusion, not least because other forms of religion have retained and expanded their toolbox for dealing and negotiating with history and tradition. In this respect, religion is no different from the rest of society, which includes people of the most diverse kinds. Some have the tools to interpret and develop their historical heritage and tradition of ideas in the light of new knowledge and humanistic values. Others find it much more difficult to accept and affirm that which seems foreign to their tradition because it goes beyond inherited notions and norms. They do not need a sacred text to adopt such a stance; they carry it with them anyway.

In all cases, then, knowledge is the key. And it is also knowledge—of history and of our own times, of human beings and their biological and social conditions, of texts, traditions, and values—that can liberate us from prejudice and oppression.

Democratic Values

It may seem paradoxical, and yet it is not, that the values that have grown increasingly strong in modern times—equality and justice, individual freedom and integrity, the equal value of all people—have many of their roots in religious traditions and collections of texts that also contain such problematic and discriminatory passages, as we have discussed in this book. From one point of view, this is not surprising, since the culture (or cultures) in which we find ourselves today are continuations and developments of the cultures that harbor the texts we have studied. Representatives of religion may have opposed many of the social and scientific revolutions that have come to light in recent centuries, but the initiators of these upheavals are standing with their feet in the same soil as their opponents.

We have previously pointed out that human "nature," or at least the biological conditions for human survival as a social species, provide the raw material for hierarchical oppression and violence as well as for egalitarian and empathetic social construction. Similarly, cultures and religions carry the potential for both. Democratic values, like everything else, are the result of humanity's continuous negotiation with its biological conditions and social constructs in the light of its historical experiences. Those negotiations continue.

As far as same-sex relationships are concerned, all democratic values point unequivocally in the same direction. Moreover, the Christian tradition, which is an important part of the culture from which democratic values have emerged, should have good resources to contribute positively to further negotiations between the past and the future: two thousand years of experience in interpreting, reinterpreting, and applying ancient tradition in new contexts; an approach based on Judaism in which individuals and their needs and exigencies take precedence over tradition and cultural patterns; a habit of sorting out overarching principles and applying them pragmatically. Sometimes the church rises to that challenge. Sometimes it does not even come close.

The Death of Hierarchy and the Opportunity of Love

Throughout this book, we have repeatedly encountered hierarchical structures and mindsets. Virtually all the texts we have analyzed, with some exceptions, have a view of sexuality and sexual acts as some form of domination. Even in cases where sexuality does not seem to fit into clear hierarchical structures, as in the case of Sappho and her poems, we have seen how early interpreters quite soon pilot the exceptions into a hierarchical mainstream. Against this backdrop, it is not difficult to understand why homoerotic expressions throughout history have almost never had a chance to be understood on their own terms or to develop beyond hierarchical and culturally constructed frameworks.

What all the main themes that we have examined have in common is that they belong to a hierarchical worldview. Superiority and subordination in sexual relationships in general, and in same-sex relationships in particular, were associated with honor and shame. Notions of purity and impurity could be used rhetorically to reinforce negative values and vilify people who deviated from prevailing hierarchical norms.

Hierarchy can be seen as a form of organization. For sorting data files, a hierarchical folder system is practical. But the hierarchies of a society are not only practical. They are intimately linked to all the repression and suppression of people with dissenting ideas and practices of which history is so full. The history of hierarchy is a subject in itself that has occupied many scholars and writers. Like the expressions of sexuality, different forms of social hierarchies can be explained both in terms of human evolutionary conditions and as social and cultural constructs.

In the Christian tradition, there is an anti-hierarchical element that is particularly evident in the Jesus stories. This trait goes back to the Jewish prophetic tradition and its recurrent protests against powerful elites and their abuse of power, against injustice and exploitation of vulnerable groups, against violence and oppression of minorities. The Jesus narratives return time and again to various incidents where people and their situation are prioritized over the system and norms. Some of these stories turned out not to be entirely comfortable as the early Christians had to adapt to become respectable in the Roman Empire. Parts of the New Testament epistolary literature struggle quite hard to cope with and contain some of the unruly and radical tendencies that the Jesus stories seem to have engendered. But with the various tools of the hierarchy, the trend was controlled, and most people fell in line.

In our time, it has finally become impossible to maintain hierarchies while defending people over systems and traditions. Through the study of some ancient texts and contexts, we have seen the effects of hierarchical structures and relational patterns in the field of sexuality and their consequences in different types of same-sex relationships. Based on democratic values and a basic understanding of the human condition, all hierarchical systems and patterns become problematic. Many become even harmful.

Same-sex relationships meet human needs for closeness, attachment, and care in the same way as any other relationship. Another word for this is love. Love and respect for the integrity and basic needs of every human being is a necessary condition for the well-being of the individual, for the further development of human beings as a social species, and for the continued coexistence and survival of humankind on a common planet. In such a future, there is no place for the categorization of the other as unclean or disgusting. In such a future, superiority and subordination need to be replaced by coordination and equality. In such a future, our relationships cannot be governed by status or based on notions of honor and shame. The death of hierarchy is the opportunity of love.

NOTES ON SOURCES

Chapter 1

For the translation of *pornoi*, see note to chapter 2.

For the evolutionary connection between the development of human sexuality and characteristics that have promoted human survival as a social species, see Taylor 1996; Hill and Hurtado 2009; Neill 2009. For a discussion of biological functionality and the adaptive function of various emotions and behaviors, see Nussbaum 2004; Bártova and Valentová 2012. For relevant aspects of the perennial question of the relationship between nature and nurture, biology and culture, essentialism and constructivism, see Barber 1998; Butler 1999; Stein 1999; Kauth 2000; Bem 2001; Prestage 2003; Kyle 2009. Research on how the formatting of the brain's signaling system is affected throughout childhood is reported in, for example, Haidt 2001; Preston and de Waal 2002.

On the concept of sexuality as a modern construction and the history of the concept of homosexuality, see Foucault 1978, 1985, 1986; Halperin 1990, 2002; Mondimore 1996; Garton 2004; Lugones 2007. Interesting discussions of different understandings of gender identity and transgender identities in history can be found in Butler 2004.

Various theories of how homoeroticism may have arisen—hormonal, genetic and adaptive (evolutionary biological and prehistoric) explanatory models—are discussed in Greenberg 1988. Research on the behavior of various primates, in particular on the differences between chimpanzees and bonobos in terms of dominant males, the role of sexuality in conflict resolution and group dynamics, and possible conclusions regarding human evolution, are presented in Boehm 1999.

Chapter 2

For current research on the content, origin, and dating of the Pentateuch, in particular regarding the legal material, see, for example, Achenbach 2003; Römer 2005, 2014; Kratz 2005, 2015; Nihan 2007; Schmid 2012. Comprehensive summaries can be found in Kazen 2011, 2019.

The biblical texts in this chapter are discussed by a large number of scholars in biblical commentaries as well as in books and articles dealing especially with Leviticus and Paul's letters. I do not refer to the vast amount of available commentaries existing, nor do I include them in the bibliography. Nissinen 1998 has become a classic that discusses the most important ancient material, both biblical and ancient West Asian, Greek, and rabbinic sources. Something similar applies to Brooten 1996. See also Davies 1985; Stowers 1994; Martin 1995, 1996; Römer and Bonjour 2005.

Regarding Leviticus and the prohibitions of the Holiness Code, Olyan 1994 provides a very good review of the evidence, to which most biblical scholars continue to refer. Among other things, Olyan clarifies the meaning of the expression *miškabê 'iššâ* (which I translate as "woman-lays") as referring to, or assuming, anal penetration. Many other scholars have since commented and argued about the nuances of this discussion. Two recent articles argue for other interpretations. Wells 2020 suggests that the phrase *miškabê 'iššâ* should not be taken as an adverbial accusative of manner but of location: a man may not have sex with another man who belongs to the domains of a woman, that is, who is married. Töyräänvuori 2020 suggests that the prohibition does not concern same-sex activities as such but two men simultaneously having sex with a woman, which would confuse paternity issues. Tiemeyer 2023 seems to side with Töyräänvuori. I find neither of them convincing, as they both require too much speculation and depend on several weak links in the chains of evidence. The discussion of the relationship between the Holiness Code's view of same-sex acts and the purity laws, including the specific terminology used, continues in chapter 3.

The ancient West Asian legal texts referred to are readily available in Roth 2000. The Book of the Dead exists in many versions, editions, and translations. See for example Allen and Hauser 1974. The *Vendidād* in Darmesteter's translation (1895) is available online (https://ia800206.us.archive.org/5/items/zenda vestavolumoounkngoog/zendavestavolumoounkngoog.pdf). The history and age of the *Vendidād* is disputed as the language exhibits late features, but many scholars believe that the content dates back to the Achaemenid era when the Pentateuch was also compiled (fifth to fourth century BCE).

The question of cult prostitution in ancient Israel is controversial, but today many scholars are inclined to believe that many of the earlier assumptions are misconceptions and speculations based on the polemic of certain biblical texts against foreign cults as well as Greek slander against Eastern religion. See the articles in Faraone and McClure 2006, especially Bird 2006 and Roth 2006. For an older view, see for example van der Toorn 1989. For a systematic discussion that perhaps exaggerates the criticism somewhat, see Budin 2008. On the Ishtar/ Astarte cult and its cult servants, see Nissinen 1998; Peled 2014; Esztári and Vér 2015. The fourth-century BCE temple inscription from Cyprus (the Kition tariffs) is listed in *Canaanite and Aramaic Inscriptions* (CIS I 86/KAI 37, B.10).

Interpretations of the story of Ham and Noah are discussed for example in Aaron 1995; Bergsma and Hahn 2005; Goldenberg 2005. A thorough study of how the stories of Sodom and Giva have been interpreted and how the interpretation has developed over time is Carden 2004. See also Stone 1995, 1996; Jordan 2009.

It is not self-evident how to translate words formed on the Greek root *porn-*, like *porneia, pornos, pornē*, and *(ek)porneuō*. In the past they were often translated with "fornication," "fornicator," and "fornicate," but these words are rather archaic and imprecise. In classical Greek, *porneia* basically meant "prostitution," but during the time of Paul it was used to label illicit sex and indecent and shameful sexual behavior in general. The meaning is thus quite broad but is tied to the status of the woman and the shame involved. Cf. Harper 2012.

The section on same-sex sexual acts in Romans 1 has generated an enormous amount of text, and I am barely referring even to a fraction of it. Most scholars discuss the obvious parallel in the Wisdom of Solomon. Brooten 1996 is an important classic study. Other examples are Stowers 1994; Davies 1995; Martin 1995, 1996; Good 2000; Römer and Bonjour 2005. Cf. also Kazen 2006.

Chapter 3

For overviews of purity laws and purity practices in Israelite society and Second Temple Judaism, see Kazen 2010a, 2010b, 2011, 2021. A few examples of major (and often classic) works are Paschen 1970; Neusner 1973; Sanders 1990; Milgrom 1991; Wright 1992; Harrington 1993; Maccoby 1999; Frevel and Nihan 2013. The literature is vast. The first chapter of Kazen 2021 also contains a thorough discussion of scholarship on purity and impurity with an extensive bibliography.

For examples of the New Testament use of purity terminology in discourse on moral virtue, see for example Matt 5:8; Mark 7:1–23 and parallels; John 15:3; Rom 1:24; 6:19; 1 Cor 6:17; 7:1, 14; 2 Cor 12:21; Gal 5:19–20; Eph 4:19; 5:3, 5; Col 3:5; 1 Thess 2:3; 4:7; 1 Tim 1:5; 2 Tim 2:21–22; Titus 1:15; 2:14. For the concept of moral impurity in an Israelite context, see Klawans 2000 (cf. Kazen 2021 for a different view), and Hayes 2002 for "genealogical" impurity (intermarriage). For inner purity concepts in Greece, see Chaniotis 2012; Petrovic and Petrovic 2016.

For the development of stepped pools for ritual bathing, see now Adler 2022. For a discussion of various innovations, including an additional, initial bath to lessen impurity levels, see Baumgarten 1995; Milgrom 1995; Lawrence 2006; Kazen 2010, chap. 4.

Paul Rozin's nine elicitors of disgust are presented in Rozin, Haidt, and McCauley 2000. Kazen 2011 interprets various categories of impurity through the lens of emotional disgust. The discussion is subsequently taken further by applying cognitive metaphor theory and conceptual blending theory to conceptions, practices, and texts of purity and impurity; see several of the articles now collected in Kazen 2021 with references. A classic introducing conceptual metaphor theory is Lakoff and Johnson 1980. For blending theory, see Fauconnier and Turner 2002; cf. Coulson and Oakley 2000.

Other reasons than taboo for not raising pigs in Iron Age Israel are discussed by Hesse and Wapnish 1997.

A possible underlying understanding of the spilling of semen to no avail as sinful is discussed for example in Milgrom 1991. Satlow 1994 suggests it is a rather late idea that appears in redactional strata of the Babylonian Talmud. For illicit mixtures of defiling emissions, see Olyan 1994. For the mixing of seed in relation to holiness, although not within a discussion of same-sex activities, see Koltun-Fromm 2010.

The meaning of "set apart" in Deut 22:9 is disputed. The Hebrew says *tiqdaš*, which literally means "sanctified." It could mean that the produce would accrue to the sanctuary, or that it would be "set apart" in the sense of forfeited or even defiled. In any case it is no longer at the disposal of the owner.

Chapter 4

For different approaches to women and slaves and sexual behavior toward them, both in ancient West Asia in general and in ancient Israel, see for example Collins 1997; Rooke 2009; Démare-Lafont 2011; Sassoon 2011. A recent study that highlights the relationship between identity (personhood) and violence, including issues of sexuality and violence, is Lemos 2017.

The language of Lev 19:20 is conspicuous. The example of a man who has sexual intercourse with a woman literally says that he lies with her a *šikbat-zeraʿ*, that is, he impregnates her with his semen. The word for the "damages" (*biqqōret*) he must pay occurs only here in the Hebrew Bible and opinions differ as to its meaning: either "inquiry," "investigation," or the compensation resulting from an investigation.

In Exod 22:16–17(15–16), the "virgin" is literally a "young woman," but the context suggests a woman with no previous sexual experience. The male recipient of the bridewealth is not explicitly stated in the sentence, but can hardly be anyone except the woman's father, who appears in the subsequent sentence.

In Deut 22:28–29 it is not entirely clear who is "young," the man or the girl. The phrase "when a man comes across a young (*naʿărâ*) virgin girl" can also be read as "when a young man (*naʿar*) comes across a virgin." The Masoretic text has "what is written" (*ketiv*) and "what is read" (*qere*) traditions: the former reads the word as masculine (*naʿar*) and the latter as feminine (*naʿărâ*). The word can thus be related either to the masculine subject or to the feminine object. When the word recurs, identifying the young person's father as the recipient of the compensation money, we once again find the same difference between *ketiv* and *qere*. Since it is quite clear that it is the *girl's* father and not the young man's who is compensated, we should go for the *qere* (the feminine *naʿărâ*) in both cases.

Examples of research on same-sex behavior among other primates, with a bearing on the question of the evolution of homoerotic attraction in humans, can be found in Boehm 1999; de Waal 1999. See Bethe (1907) 1988; Greenberg 1988; Mondimore 1996; Barber 1998; Gowdy 1998; Crompton 2003; Hill and Hurtado 2009; Neill 2009, for examples of homoeroticism in hunter-gatherer societies. The discussion of ritualized homoeroticism and homoerotic initiation rites as the origin of ancient pederasty is somewhat of a minefield. The chains of evidence are weak or have missing links. All reasoning therefore remains highly speculative, and the validity of comparisons with contemporary "homosexual" initiation rites is difficult to assess. For an overview of such rites in Melanesia, see Herdt 1984. Cross-gender sexuality in shamanistic cultures is also discussed by several of the studies mentioned above.

Same-sex relationships in heroic sagas such as Gilgamesh and Enkidu, Achilles and Patroclus, and David and Jonathan are the focus of several studies, including Ackerman 2005; Jennings 2005; Heacock 2011; and most recently Tiemeyer 2023. The Gilgamesh epic is available in many editions and translations, such as Dalley 1989; George 1999; Foster 2001; Warring and Kantola 2001.

Drawing lines between headhunters, manhood rites, initiation rites, warrior societies and homoerotic practices from widely differing cultures and eras is very difficult and speculative. Neill 2009 manages to make the source material look more coherent than it really is.

Two very useful text collections of ancient relevant material are Hubbard 2003 and Larson 2012. In these collections, virtually all the ancient Greek and Roman texts referred to above are readily available in English translation. Rich visual materials (mainly vase paintings, but also other images) are provided by Lear and Cantarella 2008.

Xenophon several times mentions Greek mercenaries with young lovers (e.g., *Anab.* 2.6.28; 4.6.3; 7.4.7–11). Thebes's "Sacred Band" (*hieros lochos*) is described by Plutarch in *Pel.* 18–19, but there are scholars who are doubtful whether Plutarch's description corresponds to reality. Plutarch is also one of the sources of information about Sparta (e.g., *Lyc.* 17.1; 18.4), together with Xenophon (*Lac.* 2.12–14), Aelian (*Var. hist.* 3.12) and book 2 of Aristotle's *Politics.* Aristotle compares Sparta and Crete and argues that the Spartans adopted many customs from the Cretans. Both Plato and Xenophon make special mention of Elis and Boeotia/Thebes in their respective versions of Socrates's tabletalk when reflecting the views of Pausanias (Plato, *Symp.* 182; Xenophon, *Symp.* 8.34). For contemporary scholarly discussions and controversies surrounding the view of initiatory insemination as a ritual practice with Doric or wider Indo-European origins, see Bethe (1907) 1988; Dover 1978; Bremmer 1980; Patzer 1982; Sergent 1986; Percy 1996; and the problematizing discussions in Halperin 2002 (see Appendix: Questions of Evidence) and Skinner 2014. Strabo's account of an abduction of boys in Crete can be found in *Geogr.* 10.4.20–21; he borrowed the material from Ephorus (frag. 149). The Minoan drinking cup is described for example by Koehl 1986, and the mentioned bronze statuette from Kato

Syme on Crete is discussed in Lear 2014; Skinner 2014. Both are depicted in Hubbard 2003. For abductions and same-sex relationships in Greek mythology, see Sergent 1986. Treating the carvings on the far edge of ancient Thera as evidence for ritualized or initiatory same-sex sexual acts, see Bethe (1907) 1988; Brongersma 1990; Cantarella 2002; Lear 2014. This must be considered an overinterpretation given both their nature and their location; see Marrou 1956; Dover 1978; Skinner 2014; Martín González 2014.

The relationship between the worship of the body, sports, hero cult, aesthetics and same-sex sexual acts is thoroughly discussed in Scanlon 2002 (cf. Fisher 2014). Vase paintings with the epithet *kalos* are also discussed in Scanlon 2002, and for example in Lear and Cantarella 2008. Motifs with same-sex sexual scenes are collected in Dover 1978; Hubbard 2003; Lear and Cantarella 2008. Some examples from Aristophanes's comedies that suggest male behavior at wrestling schools and gymnasia are *Nub.* 949–1113; *Vesp.* 1023–1028; and *Pax* 762–763; cf. Plato, *Lysis*.

The status and definition of the *hetaira*—a woman outside the regular family structures who acted as a sexual and, at times, intellectual "companion"—is debated. See for example articles in Faraone and McClure 2006; Kapparis 2017.

There is a lively debate between those who argue that ancient homoerotic expressions were based on asymmetrical relationships as part of a power game between superiority and subordination with a focus on penetration (for example, Dover 1978; Halperin 1990, 2002; cf. Foucault 1985), and those who argue that there was also room for equal relationships or that the situation was at least more complicated and multifaceted (for example Hubbard 2000b, 2014), which, on the other hand, the former rarely deny. At times, the debate can take on an apologetic character that downplays the basic premises of pederastic practices (cf. Davidson 2007). For further discussion, see Skinner 2014.

The text from *Phaedrus* is full of ambiguities. For example, it talks of the lover "having been admitted and received both with regard to *logon* and *homilian*," which I have rendered above as "conversation" and "company." *Homilia* can, however, also mean sexual intercourse, although in this text it is clear that the relationship has not (yet) reached that point. Perhaps the best translation is "in word and deed" (cf. the use of the idiom in Hippocrates, *Artic.* 10).

Williams 2010 does for Rome what Dover did for Greece (see annotations in the bibliography), and the collections of texts by Hubbard 2003 and

Larson 2012 also contain Roman material. The concept of *stuprum* and the rather poorly documented Roman legislation *Lex Scatinia* (or *Scantinia*) are discussed in Cantarella 2002 and Williams 2010, who also consider differences between the views of same-sex sexual acts in Rome and Greece. For the idea that *Lex Scatinia* was only referred to in cases of hubris against a boy (*puer*) after *Lex Iulia* took care of other issues, see Williams 2010, 103–36.

For discussions of the Stoics Seneca and Musonius Rufus, see for example Valantasis 1999; Sellars 2006; and Thorsteinsson 2010. Brooten 1996; Engberg-Pedersen 2000; Rasimus, Engberg-Pedersen, and Dunderberg 2010 analyze Paul as a Stoic, including his views on nature.

Chapter 5

The interplay of honor and shame and the importance of status in ancient societies is addressed by many historians. See, for example, Fisher 1992, whose major study focuses on the concept of hubris, and Cairns 1993, whose equally major work on the Greek concept of *aidōs* in ancient literature is important. For application to the texts of the Hebrew Bible, Stone 1995, 1996 can be mentioned. For New Testament texts and historical settings, DeSilva 2000 is useful. Finney 2012 applies these insights to 1 Corinthians. The classic is otherwise Malina 1993; however, Malina has been criticized for simplifications and generalizations. On the relationship of shame to politics and law in the contemporary world, see Nussbaum 2004. For a discussion of the concept of honor and its relationship to violence with a view to the cultural and literary history of the West, see Miller 1993.

Plutarch's text on women's courage can be found in the tract *On the Bravery of Women* (*Mulierum virtutes*) in the collection *Moralia* (Babbitt 1931).

In Sir 41:17–20, the Greek reads "from truth, God, and covenant" (*apo alētheias theou kai diathēkēs*), as one of the items associated with feelings of shame. The phrase can alternatively be translated "before the truth of God and the covenant." The Hebrew versions, however, read "[o]ath and/or covenant" (אלה° וברית) (Genizah fragment B XI Recto), and "before breaking oath and covenant" (מהפר אלה וברית) (Masada fragment 3). The phrase about placing your elbow in the food can also be read as stretching your elbow over the bread. The curse over receiving and giving translated the Greek *skorakismou*, which is formed from the verb *skorakizō*, which is derived from *es korakas*, "to the crows," or, in more explicit English, "go to hell!" The meaning is to dismiss and curse people who either ask for a gift or to abusively deny the reciprocity that is manifested in mutual gift giving.

The archaic depiction of two women with wreaths can be seen in Hubbard 2003. The depiction of Sappho with a lyre from around 500 BCE can be found in Snyder 1997.

There is an extensive literature on Sappho and her poetry, of which only a fraction can be presented here. Many of her texts are only preserved as fragments in later works, and some have been "discovered" more recently. Textual editions of Sappho are Lobel and Page 1955; Campbell 1990; and Voigt 1971, whose Greek text and revised numbering are commonly used today. Examples of English translations are Burnett 1983 (which translates parts of Sappho); Campbell 1990; Snyder 1997 (which translates all known fragments); and Rayor and Lardinois 2014 (which translate all available fragments, including those published in 2004 and the most recent ones identified in 2014).

Ancient information about Sappho (*testimonia*) can be found in, among others, Strabo, Eusebius, Herodotus, Horace, Cicero, and Seneca. Claims about her family relationships originate from the *Suda*, a Byzantine encyclopedia from the tenth century. The veracity of much of this information is questionable, and later smearing tendencies are evident. These *testimonia* are collected in Campbell 1990. The inscription from Paros (The Parian Marble) can be studied at http://www.ashmolean.museum/ash/faqs/q004/. The particular information about Sappho can be found in Campbell 1990. Campbell also includes the contemporary Alcaeus's description of Sappho, which can also be found in other editions of Alcaeus's fragments. The fragment S/A 16 (Sappho or Alcaeus) that has been used for various speculations can be found in both Campbell 1990 and Rayor and Lardinois 2014.

Modern interpretations of Sappho's "school" have varied over time. Older interpretations of Sappho as the leader of a "school of girls" (the most elaborate is Wilamowitz-Moellendorff 1913) or of a ritual society (*thiasos*), and various ways of modifying these conceptions, are discussed and criticized in Parker 1993. See also the articles in Greene 1999. Alcman's *partheneia* are translated into English in Rayor 1991; the first song is also reproduced in Hubbard 2003. For an alternative translation, see Davenport 1969. Anacreon's poem (frag. 358) is also found in Hubbard 2003 in translation. For the Greek text, see for example Campbell 1988. See also the editions listed in the bibliography, under primary texts, for the various texts referred to. For a discussion of the interpretation of the Soranos fragment quoted by Caelius Aurelianus, see Brooten 1996.

The Babylonian Talmud exists in many translations. See for example Epstein 1960–1990. An English translation of the Palestinian (Jerusalem) Talmud is Neusner 1984–1995 and the Sifra is translated by Neusner 1988. See also sefaria .org. For a more detailed discussion of the rabbinic texts, see Brooten 1996.

Self-control and moderation as ancient virtues are discussed by many historians and classicists. Examples are found in the articles collected in Bobonich and Destrée 2007. Sellars 2006 provides good overviews of Stoicism, and the articles in Kamesar 2009 does the same for Philo's thought. See especially North 1977 on *sōphrosynē*, and Schofield 2013 on the cardinal virtues and their history in Greek philosophy. Paul's views on sexual relations and self-restraint have been addressed by many exegetes. For some examples, see Stowers 1994; Martin 2006; Finney 2012. For abstinence and self-restraint as virtues in the early Christian movement, see for example the articles in Wimbush and Valantasis 1995; Vaage and Wimbush 1999; Moore and Anderson 2004.

The traditional interpretation of 1 Cor 11:4–5 is that both men and women shame their "head" by violating gender roles—men by praying *with* something on their head and women by doing it *without* something on their head. Recent research, however, suggests that Roman tradition at prayer and mantic activities included covering one's head (*capite velato*), so that the shame here incurred by men may have more to do with pagan practice, and that it is mainly the instructions for women to cover their heads (anyway) that have to do with gender roles. See Nõmmik, forthcoming.

Chapter 6

For discussions of the relationship between biological factors and social or cultural constructs, see references in the note to chapter 1. For biological and psychological links between sex and violence, see Myers et al. 2006. Nongbri 2013 offers a problematizing discussion of religion as part of culture rather than a separate category. The anti-hierarchical tendency in the Christian tradition has always lived its own life alongside power structures and dogmas. Its roots can be found in the Jewish prophetic tradition and the Jesus stories. See for example Kazen 2013.

BIBLIOGRAPHY

Ancient Texts

Primary texts are sorted by editors and translators as opposed to ancient authors.

Ancient West Asian and Egyptian Texts

Allen, Thomas George, and Elizabeth Blaisdell Hauser. 1974. *The Book of the Dead, or, Going Forth by Day: Ideas of the Ancient Egyptians concerning the Hereafter as Expressed in Their Own Terms*. Chicago: University of Chicago Press.

Dalley, Stephanie. 1989. *Myths from Mesopotamia: A New Translation*. Oxford: Oxford University Press.

Darmesteter, James. 1895. *The Vendîdâd*. Part 1 of *The Zend-Avesta*. 2nd ed. Sacred Books of the East 4. Oxford: Clarendon.

Foster, Benjamin R. 2001. *The Epic of Gilgamesh: A New Translation, Analogues, Criticisms*. New York: Norton.

George, Andrew. 1999. *The Epic of Gilgamesh: The Babylonian Epic Poem and Other Texts in Akkadian and Sumerian*. London: Penguin.

Roth, Martha T. 1997. *Law Collections from Mesopotamia and Asia Minor*. 2nd ed. Writings from the Ancient World 6. Atlanta: Scholars Press.

Jewish and Christian Texts

Aland, Barbara, Kurt Aland, Johannes Karavidopoulos, Carlo M. Martini, and
Bruce M. Metzger, eds. 2012. *Novum Testamentum Graece*. 28th rev. ed. Stuttgart: Deutsche Bibelgesellschaft.

Elliger, Karl, and Wilhelm Rudolph, eds. 1983. *Biblia Hebraica Stuttgartensia*. Stuttgart: Deutsche Bibelgesellschaft.

Epstein, I. 1960–1990. *The Soncino Hebrew-English Edition of the Babylonian Talmud*. 30 vols. London: Soncino.

Neusner, Jacob. 1984–1995. *The Talmud of the Land of Israel: A Preliminary Translation and Explanation*. 35 vols. Brown Judaic Studies. Atlanta: Scholars Press.

———. 1988. *Sifra: An Analytical Translation*. 3 vols. Brown Judaic Studies 138–140. Atlanta: Scholars Press.

Roberts, Alexander, and James Donaldson. 1987. *Fathers of the Second Century: Hermas, Tatian, Athenagoras, Theophilus, and Clement of Alexandria*. Vol. 2 of *The Ante-Nicene Fathers: Translations of the Writings of the Fathers down to A.D. 325*. 1885. Repr., Grand Rapids: Eerdmans.

Schaff, Philip. 1975. *Saint Chrysostom: Homilies on the Acts of the Apostles and the Epistle to the Romans*. Vol. 11 of *A Select Library of the Nicene and Post-Nicene Fathers of the Christian Church*. 1889. Repr., Grand Rapids: Eerdmans.

Schneemelcher, Wilhelm, ed., and M. McL. Wilson, trans. 1992. *Writings Relating to the Apostles: Apocalypses and Related Subjects*. Vol. 2 of *New Testament Apocrypha*. Rev. ed. Cambridge: Clarke; Louisville: Westminster John Knox.

Stählin, Otto. 1972. *Protrepticus und Paedagogus*. Vol. 1 of *Clemens Alexandrinus*. 3rd ed. Berlin: Akademie-Verlag.

Turcan, Marie. 2007. *Tertullien: Le Manteau (De pallio): Introduction, texte critique, traduction, commentaire et index*. Sources Chrétiennes 513. Paris: Cerf.

Greek and Roman Texts

Adams, Charles Darwin. 1919. *The Speeches of Aeschines: Against Timarchus. On the Embassy. Against Ctesiphon*. Loeb Classical Library. London: Heinemann; New York: Putnam's Sons.

Babbitt, Frank Cole. 1931. *Plutarch. Moralia, Volume III: Sayings of Kings and Commanders. Sayings of Romans. Sayings of Spartans. The Ancient Customs of the Spartans. Sayings of Spartan Women. Bravery of Women*. Loeb Classical Library. Cambridge: Harvard University Press.

————. 1936. *Plutarch. Moralia, Volume IV: Roman Questions. Greek Questions. Greek and Roman Parallel Stories. On the Fortune of the Romans. On the Fortune or the Virtue of Alexander. Were the Athenians More Famous in War or in Wisdom?* Loeb Classical Library. Cambridge: Harvard University Press.

Bailey, D. R. Shackleton. 1993. *Martial: Epigrams.* 3 vols. Loeb Classical Library. Cambridge: Harvard University Press.

Brownson, Carleton L. 1921. *Xenophon: Hellenica, Books VI and VII. Anabasis, Books I–III.* Loeb Classical Library. London: Heinemann; New York: Putnam's Sons.

Brownson, Carleton L., and O. J. Todd. 1922. *Xenophon: Anabasis, Books IV–VII. Symposium and Apology.* Loeb Classical Library. London: Heinemann; New York: Putnam's Sons.

Bury, R. G. 1926. *Plato: Laws.* 2 vols. Loeb Classical Library. London: Heinemann; New York: Putnam's Sons.

Campbell, David. 1982. *Greek Lyric, Volume I: Sappho and Alcaeus.* Loeb Classical Library. Cambridge: Harvard University Press.

————. 1988. *Greek Lyric, Volume II: Anacreon. Anacreontea. Choral Lyric from Olympus to Alcman.* Loeb Classical Library. Cambridge: Harvard University Press.

Colson, F. H., and G. H. Whitaker. 1929–1943. *Philo.* 10 vols. Loeb Classical Library. Cambridge: Harvard University Press.

Corcoran, Thomas H. 1971. *Seneca, Natural Questions, Volume I: Books 1–3.* Loeb Classical Library. Cambridge: Harvard University Press.

Davenport, Guy. 1969. "Alkman: Partheneia and Fragments." *Arion: A Journal of Humanities and the Classics* 8:477–99.

Drabkin, I. E. 1950. *Caelius Aurelianus: On Acute Diseases and On Chronic Diseases.* Chicago: University of Chicago Press.

Edmonds, J. M. 1922–1927. *Lyra Graeca: Being the Remains of All the Greek Lyric Poets from Eumelus to Timotheus Excepting Pindar.* 3 vols. Loeb Classical Library. London: Heinemann; New York: Putnum's Sons.

Fowler, Harold North. 1914. *Plato: Euthyphro; Apology; Crito; Phaedo; Phaedrus.* Loeb Classical Library. London: Heinemann; New York: Putnam's Sons.

Gow, A. S. F., and Denys L. Page. 1965. *Introduction, Text, and Indexes of Sources and Epigrammatists.* Vol. 1 of *The Greek Anthology: Hellenistic Epigrams.* Cambridge: Cambridge University Press.

Gummere, Richard M. 1925. *Seneca: Ad Lucilium epistulae morales.* Vol. 3. Loeb Classical Library. London: Heinemann; New York: Putnam's Sons.

Henderson, Jeffrey. 1998. *Aristophanes: Acharnians. Knights.* Loeb Classical Library. Cambridge: Harvard University Press.

————. 1998. *Aristophanes: Clouds. Wasps. Peace.* Loeb Classical Library. Cambridge: Harvard University Press.

————. 2000. *Aristophanes: Birds. Lysistrata. Women at the Thesmophoria.* Loeb Classical Library. Cambridge: Harvard University Press.

————. 2002. *Aristophanes: Frogs. Assembly Women. Wealth.* Loeb Classical Library. Cambridge: Harvard University Press.

Hett, W. S. 1936. *Aristotle: Problems.* 2 vols. Loeb Classical Library. London: Heinemann; New York: Putnam's Sons.

Hiller von Gärtringen, F. 1898. *Inscriptiones Symes, Teutlussae, Teli, Nisyri, Astypalaeae, Anaphes, Therae et Therasiae, Pholegandri, Meli, Cimoli.* Vol. 3 of *Inscriptiones insularum maris Aegaei praeter Delum.* Inscriptiones Graecae 12. Berlin: Reimer.

————. 1904. *Supplementum.* Supplemental vol. of *Inscriptiones insularum maris Aegaei praeter Delum.* Inscriptiones Graecae 12. Berlin: Reimer.

Hubbard, Thomas K. 2003. *Homosexuality in Greece and Rome: A Sourcebook of Basic Documents.* Berkeley: University of California Press.

Hudson-Williams, T. 1910. *The Elegies of Theognis and Other Elegies Included in the Theognidean Sylloge.* London: Bell and Sons.

Jones, Horace Leonard. 1928. *The Geography of Strabo: Books 10–12.* Loeb Classical Library. London: Heinemann; New York: Putnam's Sons.

Lamb, W. R. M. 1925. *Plato: Lysis. Symposium. Gorgias.* Loeb Classical Library. London: Heinemann; New York: Putnam's Sons.

Larson, Jennifer. 2012. *Greek and Roman Sexualities: A Sourcebook.* London: Bloomsbury.

Lobel, Edgar, and Denys Page, eds. 1955. *Poetarum lesbiorum fragmenta.* Oxford: Clarendon.

Lutz, Cora. 1947. *Musonius Rufus: "The Roman Socrates."* Yale Classical Studies 10. New Haven: Yale University Press.

Macleod, M. D. 1961. *Lucian: Dialogues of the Dead. Dialogues of the Sea-Gods. Dialogues of the Gods. Dialogues of the Courtesans.* Loeb Classical Library. Cambridge: Harvard University Press.

Marchant, E. C., and O. J. Todd. 2013. *Xenophon: Memorabilia. Oeconomicus. Symposium. Apology.* Revised by Jeffrey Henderson. Loeb Classical Library. Cambridge: Harvard University Press.

Marchant, E. C., and G. W. Bowersock. 1925. *Xenophon: Scripta Minora.* Loeb Classical Library. London: Heinemann; New York: Putnam's Sons.

Minar, Edwin L., F. H. Sandbach, and W. C. Helmbold. 1961. *Plutarch. Moralia,*

Volume IX: Table-Talk, Books 7–9. Dialogue on Love. Loeb Classical Library. Cambridge: Harvard University Press.

Murray, A. T. 1995. *Homer: The Odyssey.* Revised by George E. Dimock. 2 vols. Loeb Classical Library. Cambridge: Harvard University Press.

———. 1999. *Homer: Iliad.* Revised by William F. Wyatt. 2 vols. Loeb Classical Library. Cambridge: Harvard University Press.

Oldfather, W. A. 1925. *Epictetus: The Discourses as Reported by Arrian, the Manual, and Fragments. Volume 1: Discourses, Books I and II.* Loeb Classical Library. London: Heinemann; New York: Putnam's Sons.

Page, Denys L. 1962. *Poetae Melici Graeci.* Oxford: Clarendon.

Paton, W. R. 1918. *The Greek Anthology. Volume 4: Books X–XII.* Loeb Classical Library. London: Heinemann; New York: Putnam's Sons.

Perrin, Bernadotte. 1914. *Plutarch's Lives: Theseus and Romulus. Lycurgus and Numa. Solon and Publicola.* Loeb Classical Library. London: Heinemann; New York: Putnam's Sons.

———. 1917. *Plutarch's Lives: Agesilaus and Pompey. Pelopidas and Marcellus.* Loeb Classical Library. London: Heinemann; New York: Putnam's Sons.

Rackham, H. 1926. *Aristotle: The Nicomachean Ethics.* Loeb Classical Library. London: Heinemann; New York: Putnam's Sons.

———. 1932. *Aristotle: Politics.* Loeb Classical Library. London: Heinemann; New York: Putnam's Sons.

Rayor, Diane J. 1991. *Sappho's Lyre: Archaic Lyric and Women Poets of Ancient Greek.* Berkeley: University of California Press.

Rayor, Diane J., and André Lardinois. 2014. *Sappho: A New Translation of the Complete Works.* Cambridge: Cambridge University Press.

Rusten, Jeffrey, I. C. Cunningham, and A. Knox. 1929. *Theophrastus: Characters. Herodas: Mimes. Cercidas and the Choliambic Poets.* Loeb Classical Library. Cambridge: Harvard University Press.

Voigt, Eva-Maria. 1971. *Sappho et Alcaeus: Fragmenta.* Amsterdam: Polak & van Gennep.

Way, Arthur S. 1912. *Euripides: Iphigeneia at Aulis. Rhesus. Hecuba. The Daughters of Troy. Helen.* Loeb Classical Library. London: Heinemann; New York: Putnam's Sons.

Winterbottom, M. 1974. *Seneca the Elder: Declamations, Volume I: Controversiae, Books 1–6.* Loeb Classical Library. Cambridge: Harvard University Press.

Wilson, N. G. 1997. *Aelian: Historical Miscellany.* Loeb Classical Library. Cambridge: Harvard University Press.

Whittaker, Molly. 1982. *Tatian: Oratio ad Graecos and Fragments*. Oxford Early Christian Texts. Oxford: Clarendon.

Zanker, Graham. 2009. *Herodas: Mimiambs*. Aris & Philips Classical Texts. Oxford: Oxbow.

Secondary Literature
Annotations partly by Ida Simonsson.

Aaron, David H. 1995. "Early Rabbinic Exegesis on Noah's Son Ham and the So-Called 'Hamitic Myth.'" *Journal of the American Academy of Religion* 63.4:721–59.

The author discusses, as the title suggests, early rabbinic interpretations of the story of the drunken Noah and his son Ham, who sees him lying naked in the tent.

Achenbach, Reinhard. 2003. *Die Vollendung der Tora: Studien zur Redaktionsgeschichte des Numeribuches im Kontext von Hexateuch und Pentateuch*. Wiesbaden: Harrassowitz.

A thorough study of the redaction history of the book of Numbers within the framework of how many scholars today understand the emergence of the Pentateuch after the Babylonian exile, during the Persian period.

Ackerman, Susan. 2005. *When Heroes Love: The Ambiguity of Eros in the Stories of Gilgamesh and David*. New York: Columbia University Press.

In this study of the controversial (homo)erotic undertones in the stories of David and Jonathan, and Gilgamesh and Enkidu, Ackerman suggests that, despite their similarities, the two stories should be understood from two different interpretive frameworks. Gilgamesh and Enkidu are best understood as liminal figures whose equal relationship is an exception in an otherwise hierarchical view of sexuality. The eroticizing language in the story of David and Jonathan, on the other hand, has political connotations and, according to Ackerman, aims to undermine Jonathan's masculinity—and thus his potential claim to the royal throne—by portraying him as David's lover.

Adler, Yonatan. 2022. *The Origins of Judaism: An Archaeological-Historical Reappraisal*. New Haven: Yale University Press.

Original and innovative study on the formation of Judaism during the Hasmonean period. Contains important sections on purity issues informed by the author's archaeological work.

Arnold, John H., and Sean Brady, eds. 2011. *What Is Masculinity? Historical Dynamics from Antiquity to the Contemporary World*. Gender and Sexualities in History. London: Palgrave Macmillan.

In this anthology, a number of researchers examine how masculinities have been portrayed from ancient Athenian pederasty to the soldiers of the First World War. Methodological and theoretical questions about the conditions of masculinity research are also addressed.

Asher-Greve, Julia M. 2002. "Decisive Sex, Essential Gender." Pages 11–26 in S. Parpola and R. M. Whiting, eds., *Sex and Gender in the Ancient Near East*.

Asher-Greve examines how biological sex and gender roles were understood in ancient West Asia. She argues that three genders can be discerned, men and women whose gender roles are inscribed at birth, and a diffuse third gender. The third gender could be "biological" (deviant genitalia) or "social" (deviant behavior).

Barber, Nigel. 1998. "Ecological and Psychological Correlates of Male Homosexuality: A Cross-Cultural Investigation." *Journal of Cross-Cultural Psychology* 29:387–401.

The results of this study indicate that homosexuality is less common in hunter-gatherer cultures and more common in settled farming communities and urban environments. According to the author, this could be interpreted as environmental factors triggering a genetic predisposition to homosexuality, and this could explain how homosexuality has survived evolution despite reducing the chances of reproduction.

Bártova, Klara, and Jaroslava Valentová. 2012. "Evolutionary Perspective of Same-Sex Sexuality: Homosexuality and Homosociality Revisited." *Anthropologie* 50.1:61–70.

The article addresses the question of how homosexuality can be understood from an evolutionary perspective, as same-sex sexuality reduces an individual's reproductive chances. According to the authors, it is reasonable to think that an individual may have different types of sexual relationships throughout life, and that the gender of the partner is less important than other beneficial aspects of the relationship that may be of a social nature.

Baumgarten, Joseph M. 1995. "The Laws about Fluxes in 4QTohoraa (4Q274)." Pages 1–8 in *Time to Prepare the Way in the Wilderness*. Edited by D. Dimant and L. H. Schiffman. Studies on the Texts of the Desert of Judah 16. Leiden: Brill.

One of the best-known editors of the Dead Sea Scrolls discusses a fragment about purification rituals within a broader context.

Bergsma, John Sietze, and Scott Walker Hahn. 2005. "Noah's Nakedness and the Curse of Canaan (Genesis 9:20–27)." *Journal of Biblical Literature* 124:25–40.

Two scholars analyze and interpret the text about Noah getting drunk and the behavior of his sons in the situation.

Bem, Daryl. 2001. "Is Half an Interactional Theory Still an Interactional Theory?" Review of *True Nature: A Theory of Sexual Attraction*, by Michael R. Kauth. *The Journal of Sex Research* 38:263–65.

In a critical review of Kauth's book *True Nature*, Bem argues that Kauth, who rejects both essentialist and constructivist understandings of gender and sexuality, fails to provide a credible alternative of his own.

Berg, Henrik. 2011. "Masculinities in Early Hellenistic Athens." Pages 97–113 in J. H. Arnold and S. Brady, eds., *What Is Masculinity?*

Berg's contribution to the anthology *What Is Masculinity?* consists of a study of masculinities in comedies written in Hellenistic Athens (323–275 BCE) but also addresses more general methodological issues. Masculinity is described differently depending on age, ethnicity, and status, which raises questions about whether intersectional perspectives should be included in an analysis of historical material.

Bethe, Erich. (1907) 1988. "Die dorische Knabenliebe: Ihre Ethik und ihre Idee." Pages 17–57 in A. K. Siems, ed., *Sexualität und Erotik in der Antike*.

A classic 1907 article on Greek pederasty, which avoids moralizing and takes a historical and anthropological perspective. Beliefs about the ritual background of pederasty, as well as the introduction of the practice by the Doric (Spartan) tribes in Greece, are highly controversial today.

Bird, Phyllis A. 2006. "Prostitution in the Social World and the Religious Rhetoric of Ancient Israel." Pages 40–58 in Christopher A. Faraone and Laura K. Mc-Clure, eds., *Prostitutes and Courtesans in the Ancient World.*

Bird shows that in biblical texts, prostitutes often appear as an image of an Israel that is "unfaithful" to God rather than in their own right. But when prostitutes are included in the stories as characters rather than symbols, it is often in a way that goes against cultural expectations. For example, the quarrelling presumed mothers who want Solomon to judge between them turn out to be prostitutes.

Bobonich, Christopher, and Pierre Destrée, eds. 2007. *Akrasia in Greek Philosophy: From Socrates to Plotinus.* Philosophia Antiqua 106. Leiden: Brill.

A collection of essays in which various scholars discuss the view of *akrasia* and *enkrateia* (lack of self-control and self-restraint) in classical and Stoic philosophers.

Boehm, Christopher. 1999. *Hierarchy in the Forest: The Evolution of Egalitarian Behavior.* Cambridge: Harvard University Press.

Anthropologist Boehm seeks to find the roots of the democratic lifestyle with its fundamental egalitarian values in human prehistory. He examines political and moral aspects of the behavior of chimpanzees, gorillas, and bonobos, and studies social structures in hunter-gatherer societies and in contemporary societies. The conclusion is that humans are politically flexible creatures.

Boyarin, Daniel. 1997. *Unheroic Conduct: The Rise of Heterosexuality and Jewish Masculinity.* Berkeley: University of California Press.

In this personal text, Boyarin examines how Jewish masculinity is portrayed both in the Talmud and in the American culture in which he was raised. He argues that heterosexuality emerged as an aspect of Jewish masculinity only in modern times.

Boyarin, Daniel. 2006. "What Do We Talk about When We Talk about Platonic Love?" Pages 3–22 in V. Burrus and C. Keller, eds., *Towards a Theology of Eros.*

"Platonic love" is an expression that has taken on a life of its own in Western culture and is sometimes used with little or no connection to Plato's own texts. In this article, Boyarin shows that in the *Symposium*, Plato contrasts his own understanding of *erōs* with the Athenian understanding of physical eroticism as a means to a higher love of the good. According to Boyarin, Plato sees physical sexuality as animal, separate from the pursuit of the true and good.

Boyarin, Daniel. 2007. "Against Rabbinic Sexuality: Textual Reasoning and the Jewish Theology of Sex." Pages 131–46 in G. Loughlin, ed., *Queer Theology*.

Boyarin argues through discussions of biblical texts and rabbinic interpretations that there is no reason to assume that there were any systems for understanding sexuality in terms of objects of desire in biblical or talmudic Judaism. On the contrary, the texts show a very different way of looking at sexuality than the modern concepts of hetero- and homosexuality.

Brawley, Robert L., ed. 1996. *Biblical Ethics and Homosexuality: Listening to Scripture*. Louisville: Westminster John Knox.

Here a number of different voices meet in an anthology consisting of two parts focused on two themes: the first part reflects on how the Bible can be used normatively for Christians today; the second part provides different perspectives on the theme of the Bible and sexuality.

Bremmer, Jan. 1980. "An Enigmatic Indo-European Rite: Paederasty." *Arethusa* 13:279–98.

Based on cross-cultural and anthropological material, Bremmer argues that Greek pederasty has its roots in initiation rites. The inscriptions in Thera are indeed graffiti but point to a connection with initiation rites.

Brongersma, Edward. 1990. "The Thera Inscriptions: Ritual or Slander?" *Journal of Homosexuality* 20.4:31–40.

Inscriptions on a rock on ancient Thera (the Greek island of Santorini) have given rise to different interpretations. Is their homoerotic content evidence of ritual acts, or are they pornographic graffiti? Brongersma argues in favor of the first option, which is highly contested today.

Brooten, Bernadette J. 1996. *Love between Women: Early Christian Responses to Female Homoeroticism.* Chicago: University of Chicago Press.

Brooten argues in this classic study that erotic love between women was part of the cultural sphere in which the early Christian church emerged. However, this sexuality was perceived by the normative forces of society as unnatural because the "natural" sexual role of the woman was to be passive. Brooten argues that the early church's condemnation of sex between women as unnatural is consistent with the views of the surrounding society and is based on the same hierarchical understanding of gender.

Budin, Stephanie Lynn. 2008. *The Myth of Sacred Prostitution in Antiquity.* Cambridge: Cambridge University Press.

Budin's work is an important mythbuster, tracing notions of cult prostitution from ancient West Asia to early Christian rhetoric and deconstructing what she believes is a myth. This is done based on a relatively narrow definition of prostitution as sex for payment, and Budin has been criticized for exaggerating her case somewhat.

Burnett, Anne Pippin. 1983. *Three Archaic Poets: Archilochus, Alcaeus, Sappho.* Cambridge: Harvard University Press.

This book analyzes poems and fragments from the three relatively contemporary poets mentioned in the title. The section on Sappho contains detailed analysis of some selected poems, including discussion of the Greek text and translation.

Burrus, Viriginia, and Catherine Keller, eds. 2006. *Towards a Theology of Eros: Transfiguring Passion at the Limits of Discipline.* New York: Fordham University Press.

A range of theologians and philosophers reflect on the transformative power of eroticism and its place in religious life and theological thought.

Butler, Judith. 1999. *Gender Trouble: Feminism and the Subversion of Identity.* 2nd ed. New York: Routledge.

Literary scholar and philosopher Judith Butler, whose thinking has pioneered the theoretical field known as queer theory, argues in this theoreti-

cally dense and linguistically distinctive book that gender is performative. By
performativity, she means that our gender roles are, so to speak, copies without originals, that through our behavior we actually create masculinity and
femininity. She also argues that the biological body is never unmediatedly
available for neutral or objective study, but that all our scientific knowledge
is always already human culture.

Butler, Judith. 2004. *Undoing Gender.* New York: Routledge.

This collection of essays centers on and refines the question from *Gender
Trouble* about how gender is "made," constructed and deconstructed. Butler
explores how people conform to norms in order to be recognized, but also how
the conditions of recognition can become unbearable for some people—including a case study of an intersex person whose life tragically ends in suicide.

Cairns, Douglas L. 1993. *Aidōs: The Psychology and Ethics of Honour and Shame in
Ancient Greek Literature.* Oxford: Clarendon.

In a major study of ancient Greek literature from Homer to Aristotle, the
author discusses various aspects of honor and shame, with a particular focus
on the difficult-to-translate key concept of *aidōs.*

Cantarella, Eva. 2002. *Bisexuality in the Ancient World.* 2nd ed. New Haven: Yale
Nota Bene.

Classicist Cantarella draws on a wide range of source material, from legal
texts to poetry and philosophy, to examine and compare how bisexuality
was lived and portrayed in ancient Rome and Athens.

Capomacchia, Anna Maria G. 2002. "Eros in Heroic Times." Pages 79–84 in S. Parpola and R. M. Whiting, eds., *Sex and Gender in the Ancient Near East.*

Capomacchia examines the role of *erōs* as a fundamental aspect of human
life in the mythological worlds of the ancient Near East.

Carden, Michael. 2004. *Sodomy: A History of a Christian Biblical Myth.* London:
Equinox.

Carden analyses how the two parallel stories of Sodom and Gomorrah
(Genesis 19) and the gang rape in Giva (Judges 19) have been interpreted in

Christian and Jewish tradition. The author shows that early interpretations focus on lack of hospitality and xenophobia. Only with Philo does the sexual motif gain importance, which is the basis for later Christian interpretations of "sodomy."

Cartledge, Paul. (1981) 1988. "The Politics of Spartan Pederasty." Pages 385–415 in A. K. Siems, ed., *Sexualität und Erotik in der Antike*.

The author of the article argues that pederasty played an important role in the coming of age of boys or young men during the heyday of Sparta.

Chaniotis, Angelos. 2012. "Greek Ritual Purity: From Automatisms to Moral Distinctions." Pages 123–39 in *How Purity Is Made*. Edited by P. Rösch and U. Simon. Wiesbaden: Harrassowitz.

An outline of the development of the idea of purity of mind or soul and its relationship to impurities of the body in ancient Greek thought.

Clines, David J. A. 1995. *Interested Parties: The Ideology of Writers and Readers of the Hebrew Bible*. Journal for the Study of the Old Testament Supplement Series 205. Sheffield: Sheffield Academic.

A collection about the impact of ideology on the texts of the Hebrew Bible. One chapter discusses the masculinity of the figure of David.

Cobb, L. Stephanie. 2008. *Dying to Be Men: Gender and Language in Early Christian Martyr Texts*. New York: Columbia University Press.

By using social identity theory, a theory of identity formation based on social belonging, Cobb reads the stories of early Christian martyrs as a way of creating a Christian identity. In this identity, certain virtues become important that coincide with the Roman Empire's ideal of masculinity, such that even women who die as martyrs are described in the stories as male. In this way, according to Cobb, the Roman death penalty was reformulated as a positive means of identification for early Christians.

Cohen, Edward E. 2000. *The Athenian Nation*. Princeton: Princeton University Press.

In this book, Cohen challenges what he perceives as the modern scholarly myth of ancient Athens as a primarily political society. According to him, this myth includes the understanding of sexuality in political terms, where one party is dominant and active, especially the free man with citizenship, and one is subordinate and passive, a role assigned to women, slaves, and prostitutes who are imagined to be without citizenship. This understanding, which otherwise completely dominates all research on ancient Greece, is simply a prejudice, says Cohen, who prefers to interpret Athens in terms of a market with basic legal protection against abuse for all. However, this interesting approach is somewhat undermined by the fact that the market as a theoretical concept is a modern phenomenon, and Cohen does not present any arguments for why the economy of ancient Athens would have functioned in accordance with the theories of modern neoclassical economics.

Collins, John J. 1997. "Marriage, Divorce, and Family in Second Temple Judaism." Pages 104–62 in *Families in Ancient Israel*. Edited by L. G. Perdue. Louisville: Westminster John Knox.

An overview article on marriage and family in Israelite society.

Connell, R. W. 2005. *Masculinities*. 2nd ed. Berkeley: University of California Press.

Classic and seminal study on masculinity that, among other things, introduces the four concepts of hegemony, subordination, complicity, and marginalization.

Coulson, Seanna, and Todd Oakley. 2000. "Blending Basics." *Cognitive Linguistics* 11:175–96.

Short introduction to conceptual blending theory.

Creanga, Oividiu, ed. 2010. *Men and Masculinity in the Hebrew Bible and Beyond*. Sheffield: Sheffield Phoenix.

This anthology discusses the representation of the masculinity of a range of biblical and postbiblical figures, including Moses, Job, Samson, and Jeremiah. Attention is also paid to the understanding of masculinity by both authors and readers.

Crompton, Louis. 2003. *Homosexuality and Civilization*. Cambridge: Belknap.

This work covers a huge area, both geographically and temporally, in a kind of history of homosexuality. There are chapters on same-sex sexuality in ancient Greece; Israel from 900 BCE to 600 CE; China from 500 BCE to 1849; and Spain during the Inquisition among others. The focus is on large empires, the "civilizations" of the book's title, and individual people in an almost cinematic narrative style. The question of what is "civilization" and why the selection of civilizations looks the way it does may be asked in the light of the postcolonial criticism of recent decades.

Davidson, James. 2007. *The Greeks and Greek Love: A Radical Reappraisal of Homosexuality in Ancient Greece*. London: Weidenfeld & Nicolson.

This brick of over six hundred pages is quite arrogant in tone and full of criticism of other scholars, not least Kenneth Dover's classic study. But the author in turn has been heavily criticized for everything from mistranslations to distorted historiography. Davidson paints a picture of ancient Greece where sexual relations with boys under eighteen were not physical, male prostitution was condemned, and gay men lived in monogamous marriages. Thomas Hubbard (see below) writes: "there are actually many valuable observations within the book, but one must wade through an insufferable cesspool of dross to find them."

Davies, Margaret. 1995. "New Testament Ethics and Ours: Homosexuality and Sexuality in Romans 1:26–27." *Biblical Interpretation* 3:315–31.

Davies presents two arguments against using Romans 1:26–27 today to argue normatively against same-sex sexuality. First, Paul's overall argument undermines the theoretical basis for his condemnation of same-sex sexuality in Romans 1:26–27, a condemnation that can thus be seen as a result of prejudice rather than theology. Second, she argues that we now have knowledge of human biology that indicates that gender and sexuality should be understood as continuums rather than binaries.

Démare-Lafont, Sophie. 2011. "The Status of Women in the Legal Texts of the Ancient Near East." Pages 109–32 in *Torah*. Edited by Irmtraud Fischer, Mercedes Navarro Puerto, and Andrea Taschl-Erber. Vol. 1.1 of *The Bible and*

Women: An Encyclopaedia of Exegesis and Cultural History. Atlanta: Society of Biblical Literature.

> The author discusses the ambivalent legal status of women in ancient West Asia.

DeSilva, David A. 2000. *Honor, Patronage, Kinship and Purity: Unlocking New Testament Culture*. Downers Grove, IL: InterVarsity.

> A historical-exegetical study that discusses the role of the ancient concepts of honor and shame in New Testament texts.

Dodd, David B. 2000. "Athenian Ideas about Cretan Pederasty." Pages 33–41 in T. K. Hubbard, ed., *Greek Love Reconsidered*.

> A short article on how the Athenian historian Ephorus (fourth century BCE) describes and interprets pederasty as part of an abduction ritual from Crete.

Dover, Kenneth J. 1978. *Greek Homosexuality*. London: Duckworth.

> This is the first major scholarly study of homoerotic relationships in ancient Greece and has become a classic in the field. Using vase paintings, legal speeches, drama, and philosophical and literary texts, Dover examines how same-sex sexuality was perceived. The currently dominant view among scholars in the field, that sexual behavior in ancient Greece was linked to social hierarchies, was established here.

Esztári, Réka, and Ádám Vér. 2015. "The Voices of Ištar: Prophetesses and Female Ecstatics in the Neo-Assyrian Empire." Pages 3–39 in *Religion and Female Body in Ancient Judaism and Its Environment*. Edited by Géza Xeravits. Deuterocanonical and Cognate Literature Studies 28. Berlin: de Gruyter.

> The authors analyze the role of female prophets in the Ishtar cult, including the cross-gender roles of *assinu* and *kurgarrû*.

Faraone, Christopher A., and Laura K. McClure, eds. 2006. *Prostitutes and Courtesans in the Ancient World*. Madison: University of Wisconsin Press.

> This anthology deals with a range of topics related to prostitution in antiquity, a field in which lively research is being carried out, entailing that some

of the articles may have lost some of their relevance. Topics include various aspects of the links between prostitution and religious rhetoric and practice, as well as legal, economic, and moral aspects of ancient prostitution, including the distinction between sex slaves and free prostitutes. Several articles also discuss the prostitute as a literary figure.

Fauconnier, Gilles, and Mark Turner. 2002. *The Way We Think: Conceptual Blending and the Mind's Hidden Complexities.* New York: Basic Books.

An elaborate introduction to conceptual blending theory.

Feinstein, Eve Levavi. 2014. *Sexual Pollution in the Hebrew Bible.* Oxford: Oxford University Press.

Feinstein examines how ritual purity terminology is used in the Hebrew Bible to describe sexual acts. Moral aspects are insufficient to explain notions of sexual "pollution." Instead, the author draws on research on disgust and argues in favor of rhetorical uses of impurity language. The study analyzes key texts such as Genesis 18 and 34 as well as Ezekiel 18, 22, and 36.

Finney, Mark T. 2012. *Honour and Conflict in the Ancient World: 1 Corinthians in Its Greco-Roman Social Setting.* Library of New Testament Studies 460. London: Bloomsbury.

The author makes an exegetical analysis of 1 Corinthians based on the ancient concept of honor. The book provides a useful overview of ancient understandings of honor, not least in relation to sexuality, from Homer to Roman culture.

Fisher, N. R. E. 1992. *Hybris: A Study in the Values of Honour and Shame in Ancient Greece.* Warminster: Aris & Phillips.

Fisher's major study on hubris discusses the concepts of honor and shame in ancient Greek literature from Homer to Aristotle.

Fisher, N. R. E. 2014. "Athletics and Sexuality." Pages 244–64 in T. K. Hubbard, ed., *A Companion to Greek and Roman Sexualities.*

The author analyzes the role of nudity in sport competitions and the erotic aspects of sport. Both boys' and girls' sports are discussed.

Foucault, Michel. 1978. *The History of Sexuality.* Vol. 1: *An Introduction.* Translated by Robert Hurley. New York: Pantheon.

In the first volume of *The History of Sexuality,* Foucault starts with the question of why we believe that in recent centuries power has "oppressed" sexuality with a moralism from which we must liberate ourselves. Becoming "sexually liberated" turns into a demand that paradoxically weighs many contemporary people down with guilt rather than, as the phrase promises, leads to liberation. Foucault argues that in recent centuries, the discourse on sexuality has grown with an increasingly refined terminology, and that this has to do with political motives and the fact that those in power have had to deal with large human populations. Human reproduction, and thus human sexuality, then becomes politically interesting. Foucault examines the dynamics of power, ideology, and knowledge in relation to the field of sexuality.

Foucault, Michel. 1985. *The History of Sexuality.* Vol. 2: *The Use of Pleasure.* Translated by Robert Hurley. New York: Pantheon.

In the second volume of the series, Foucault looks at sexuality in Greek antiquity, particularly Xenophon, Plato, and Aristotle. He argues that sexuality as a concept is a contemporary invention, while the ancient Greeks rather spoke of *aphrodisia,* a term that had to do with moral care as well as pleasure in love.

Foucault, Michel. 1986. *The History of Sexuality.* Vol. 3: *The Care of the Self.* Translated by Robert Hurley. New York: Pantheon.

Here Foucault examines the sexual ethics of the Stoics and Epicureans. He argues that here the individual emerges more clearly as a moral subject, and the art of living as an object of ethical reflection gives way to ethical commandments and requirements and an ascetic attitude to life. Foucault's intention was to move from here to the sexual ethics of early Christianity, but he never finished this work before his death.

Frevel, Christian, and Christophe Nihan, eds. 2013. *Purity and the Forming of Religious Traditions in the Ancient Mediterranean World and Ancient Judaism.* Dynamics in the History of Religion 3. Leiden: Brill.

This multiauthored collection of articles covers purity concepts all over the ancient Near East and the Greco-Roman world: ancient Mesopotamia,

Egypt, Anatolia, Phoenicia, Iran, Greece, Rome. It also has separate chapters on Leviticus, Numbers, Deuteronomy, Ezekiel, Ezra-Nehemiah, Hellenistic Judaism, Qumran, and archaeology of the late Second Temple period.

Garton, Stephen. 2004. *Histories of Sexuality: Antiquity to Sexual Revolution*. London: Equinox.

A book about the history of sexuality but with a focus on the modern era.

George, Mark K. 2010. "Masculinity and Its Regimentation in Deuteronomy." Pages 64–82 in O. Creanga, ed., *Men and Masculinity in the Hebrew Bible and Beyond*.

George examines how the ideal Israelite man is portrayed in Deuteronomy—his relationship to God, family structures, diet, time cycles, and so on.

Goldenberg, David M. 2005. "What Did Ham Do to Noah?" Pages 257–66 in *"The Words of a Wise Man's Mouth Are Gracious" (Qoh 10,12): Festschrift for Günther Stemberger on the Occasion of His 65th Birthday*. Edited by Mauro Perani. Berlin: de Gruyter.

The article discusses mainly rabbinic interpretations of the story of Noah getting drunk: Did Ham castrate or rape him, and what does the curse on Canaan mean?

Good, Deirdre. 2000. "The New Testament and Homosexuality: Are We Getting Anywhere?" *Religious Studies Review* 26:307–12.

Good discusses a number of volumes that address the issue of the New Testament and homosexuality, but she also discusses the discussion itself, or rather the debates that are taking place about same-sex marriage and the ordination of openly gay people as priests and ministers. She wonders whether these debates have become too central and caused too much conflict and suggests a moratorium on them for a period of reflection.

Gowdy, John, ed. 1998. *Limited Wants, Unlimited Means: A Reader on Hunter-Gatherer Economics and the Environment*. Washington, DC: Island.

Collection of articles on various aspects of hunter-gatherer societies, including issues of gender roles and hierarchies.

Greene, Ellen, ed. 1996. *Reading Sappho: Contemporary Approaches*. Berkeley: University of California Press.

A rich anthology with fifteen Sappho scholars discussing everything from Sappho's language and literary context to her historical and social environment—and of course her expression of eroticism between women.

Greenberg, David F. 1988. *The Construction of Homosexuality*. Chicago: University of Chicago Press.

The author takes a broad approach in his attempt to understand homosexuality and the modern Western ban on homosexuality. He examines same-sex relationships in clan-based societies, antiquity, and feudal societies as well as the construction of modern homosexuality.

Greenberg, Steven. 2004. *Wrestling with God and Men: Homosexuality in the Jewish Tradition*. Madison: University of Wisconsin Press.

This book is the result of the author's own wrestling as a homosexual and Orthodox rabbi. The focus is more on using traditional Jewish interpretive methods, discussing many alternative interpretive models, than on finding clear-cut answers to the question of how the Bible deals with homosexuality. In addition to readings of biblical texts, he also examines the Talmud and medieval Jewish texts.

Gruber, Thibaud, and Zanna Clay. 2016. "A Comparison between Bonobos and Chimpanzees: A Review and Update." *Evolutionary Anthropology* 25:239–52.

The article reviews research that compares western and eastern chimpanzees with bonobos and discusses what updated data means for the reconstruction of our last common ancestor. Among other things, attention is given to the lower aggression and female-centric character of bonobo societies.

Haidt, Jonathan. 2001. "The Emotional Dog and Its Rational Tail: A Social Intuitionist Approach to Moral Judgement." *Psychological Review* 108:814–34.

Based on a number of psychological studies, the author argues that people usually make moral decisions based on emotions and intuition and then rationalize them.

Halperin, David M. 1990. *One Hundred Years of Homosexuality: And Other Essays on Greek Love.* New York: Routledge.

Classicist Halperin approaches ancient Greek texts on male love, but without classifying them according to our modern object-oriented understanding of sexuality, that is, as expressions of homosexual or heterosexual eroticism. Instead, Foucault's historical understanding of sexuality becomes Halperin's theoretical framework.

Halperin, David M. 2002. *How to Do the History of Homosexuality.* Chicago: University of Chicago Press.

Here, Halperin builds on and updates the arguments from his earlier book *One Hundred Years of Homosexuality.* Inspired by Foucault, he argues in favor of a historical or constructivist rather than a biological understanding of sexuality and, like Foucault, suggests that sexuality has to do with human subjectivity rather than classifications.

Halperin, David M., John J. Winkler, and Froma I. Zeitlin, eds. 1990. *Before Sexuality: The Construction of Erotic Experience in the Ancient Greek World.* Princeton: Princeton University Press.

In fifteen essays, classicists and cultural historians discuss sexual norms and practices, but also how the understanding of what counts as a sexual activity has changed over time.

Harper, Kyle. 2012. "Porneia: The Making of a Christian Sexual Norm." *Journal of Biblical Literature* 131:363–83.

A thorough discussion of the development of the meaning of *porneia* in antiquity. Harper outlines a trajectory for a shift of meaning from classical Greek texts, through the LXX and Jewish Greek literature, to early Christian usage. A key point is the association of *porneia* with concerns for society, reproduction, and shame.

Harrington, Hannah K. 1993. *The Impurity Systems of Qumran and the Rabbis: Biblical Foundations.* Society of Biblical Literature Dissertation Series 143. Atlanta: Scholars Press.

Thorough comparative study of ritual purity and impurity in Qumran and rabbinic literature.

Hayes, Christine E. 2002. *Gentile Impurities and Jewish Identities: Intermarriage and Conversion from the Bible to the Talmud.* Oxford: Oxford University Press.

Hayes distinguishes between ritual, moral, and genealogical impurity. While all sources understand gentiles as capable of generating moral impurity, Hayes argues that the concept of genealogical impurity, which makes assimilation or conversion impossible, was introduced by Ezra and became prominent for some Second Temple groups.

Heacock, Anthony. 2011. *Jonathan Loved David: Manly Love in the Bible, and the Hermeneutics of Sex.* Sheffield: Sheffield Phoenix.

Heacock reviews and discusses various historical and contemporary interpretations of the story of David and Jonathan and proposes his own interpretation using the exegetical method of reader-response criticism.

Herdt, Gilbert H., ed. 1984. *Ritualized Homosexuality in Melanesia.* Berkeley: University of California Press.

Eight anthropologists present research on same-sex sexual rites from New Guinea and Melanesia.

Hesse, Brian, and Paula Wapnish. 1997. "Pots and People Revisited: Ethnic Boundaries in the Iron Age I." Pages 216–37 in *The Archaeology of Israel: Constructing the Past, Interpreting the Present.* Edited by N. A. Silberman and D. Small. Journal for the Study of the Old Testament Supplement Series 237. Sheffield: Sheffield Academic.

The authors claim that pig avoidance was not unique for any one group in the ancient Near East and argue that only in the Hellenistic period, with consumption of pigs in urban settings, could pig avoidance become a boundary marker.

Hill, Kim, and A. Magdalena Hurtado. 2009. "Cooperative Breeding in South American Hunter-Gatherers." *Proceedings of the Royal Society of Biological Sciences* 76:3863–70.

This study addresses the evolutionary biological hypothesis that hunter-gatherer societies throughout history have practiced what is known as co-operative breeding, that is, that people jointly took care of their children in a group, and that not all adults had children themselves. The hypothesis is tested here on two South American hunter-gatherer societies, where it was found that each reproductive couple was helped to care for the children by an average of 1.3 nonreproductive adults.

Holmes, Brooke. 2012. *Gender: Antiquity and Its Legacy*. London: I. B. Tauris.

A book about gender in antiquity and how Greek and Roman thoughts and beliefs have shaped the development of gender as a modern concept.

Howson, Richard, and Jeff Hearn. 2020. "Hegemony, Hegemonic Masculinity, and Beyond." Pages 41–51 in *Routledge International Handbook of Masculinity Studies*. Edited by L. Gottzén, U. Mellström, and T. Shefer. London: Routledge.

The authors discuss the concepts of hegemony and hegemonic masculinity, arguing against a static view and power as mere domination and pointing to the importance of legitimacy for authority being acknowledged.

Hubbard, Thomas K., ed. 2000a. *Greek Love Reconsidered*. New York: Hamilton.

Four scholars discuss whether Greek pederasty was about mentoring and a boy's transition to adulthood, or about the exploitation of the powerless by the powerful. The book contains important contributions but was published by the North American Man/Boy Love Association (NAMBLA), which discredited it.

Hubbard, Thomas K. 2000b. "Pederasty and Democracy: The Marginalization of a Social Practice." Pages 1–11 in T. K. Hubbard, ed., *Greek Love Reconsidered*.

The author discusses historical approaches to Greek pederasty. However, the article has an unclear apologetic conclusion.

Hubbard, Thomas K. 2011. "Athenian Pederasty and the Construction of Masculinity." Pages 189–22 in J. H. Arnold, and S. Brady, eds., *What Is Masculinity?*

A very common interpretation of the ancient ideal of masculinity is that it is part of a strictly hierarchical culture of honor, where sexual relations are determined by superiority and subordination. Hubbard argues that this image is grossly generalized and also compromisingly coincides with the traditional North American and Northern European racist image of the "other." He argues that ancient Athenian pederasty does not fit this stereotype of a superior and subordinate party, but is instead about the older man nurturing the boy into an active masculinity.

Hubbard, Thomas K., ed. 2014. *A Companion to Greek and Roman Sexualities.* Chichester: Wiley-Blackwell.

A series of essays discussing various sexual practices and discourses represented in a variety of genres in Roman and Greek antiquity, taking into account both continuity and discontinuity across time and space.

Jackson, Samuel A. 2008. *A Comparison of Ancient Near Eastern Law Collections Prior to the First Millennium BC.* Gorgias Dissertations 35. Piscataway, NJ: Gorgias.

Similarities in the ancient West Asia's various laws on sex have often led scholars to assume that there is some sort of basic recipe that would have disseminated along with the spread of cuneiform writing. Jackson argues that the similarities are less than many have assumed, and that there is no reason to assume a common basis for the laws of the different peoples.

Jennings, Theodore W., Jr. 2005. *Jacob's Wound: Homoerotic Narrative in the Literature of Ancient Israel.* London: Continuum.

Jennings claims to hear homoerotic overtones in many of the stories in the Hebrew Bible, not only David and Jonathan, but also David and Saul, Samuel and Saul, Elijah and Elisha, and so on.

Jordan, Mark D. 2009. "The Discovery of Sodom." Pages 292–305 in B. Krondorfer, ed., *Men and Masculinities in Christianity and Judaism.*

The chapter is taken from Jordan's previous book, *The Invention of Sodomy in Christian Theology* (1997) and deals with the concept of "sodomy" in the Middle Ages but also discusses the emergence of the concept from the time of the Bible onward.

Jost, Renate. 2006. *Gender, Sexualität und Macht in der Anthropologie des Richterbuches*. Stuttgart: Kohlhammer.

The author analyzes key parts of the book of Judges based on issues of power, gender, and sexuality. The book includes a discussion of the emergence of patriarchal society colored by social anthropology.

Kapparis, Konstantinos. 2018. *Prostitution in the Ancient Greek World*. Berlin: de Gruyter.

Recent and comprehensive study on prostitution in ancient Greece with special attention to the figure of the *hetaira*.

Katz, Jonathan Ned. 1995. *The Invention of Heterosexuality*. New York: Dutton.

The author clarifies the historical background of the terms "heterosexuality" and "homosexuality" and argues that heterosexuality is also a social convention.

Kauth, Michael R. 2000. *True Nature: A Theory of Sexual Attraction*. New York: Kluwer Academic.

The author discusses the three main models used to understand human sexuality—psychology, social constructivism, and biology—and rejects all three as too one-sided, instead presenting his own proposal that synthesizes all three models.

Kazen, Thomas. 2006. "Tolkning och respekt: Om bibeltolkning och homosexualitet." Pages 182–94 in *Spår av Gud*. Edited by Lars Ingelstam, Johnny Jonsson, and Berit Åqvist. Studia theologica Holmiensia 14. Stockholm: Teologiska högskolan.

This short article is, in some ways, a precursor to this book.

Kazen, Thomas. 2008. "Dirt and Disgust: Body and Morality in Biblical Purity Laws." Pages 43–64 in *Perspectives on Purity and Purification in the Bible*. Edited by B. J. Schwartz and D. P. Wright. Library of the Hebrew Bible/Old Testament Studies 474. London: T&T Clark.

In this article, the author argues that all three main types of impurity in the Pentateuchal legal material are linked to emotional disgust.

Kazen, Thomas. 2010a. *Issues of Impurity in Early Judaism*. Coniectanea Biblica: New Testament Series 45. Winona Lake, IN: Eisenbrauns.

A collection of articles on purity and impurity in the Second Temple period. The second chapter summarizes the author's "psycho-biological" model for interpreting purity and impurity within a framework of emotional disgust.

Kazen, Thomas. (2002) 2010b. *Jesus and Purity Halakhah: Was Jesus Indifferent to Impurity?* Corrected reprint edition. Coniectanea Biblica: New Testament Series 38. Winona Lake, IN: Eisenbrauns.

The author's doctoral thesis on the historical Jesus's approach to the concepts of purity and impurity. The book includes overviews of purity rules and practices during the Second Temple period. Now available in a second reprint edition (Stockholm: Enskilda Högskolan Stockholm, 2021).

Kazen, Thomas. 2011. *Emotions in Biblical Law: A Cognitive Science Approach*. Hebrew Bible Monographs 36. Sheffield: Sheffield Phoenix.

A biblical study with interdisciplinary features. The author uses cognitive science insights (evolutionary biology, neuroscience and developmental psychology) in analyzing the role of different emotions in selected texts from the Hebrew Bible's legal material. This includes discussions on the role of disgust in various ideas of impurity.

Kazen, Thomas. 2013. *Scripture, Interpretation, or Authority? Motives and Arguments in Jesus' Halakic Conflicts*. Wissenschaftliche Untersuchungen zum Neuen Testament 1.320. Tübingen: Mohr Siebeck.

A study of the halakic development (interpretation and application of Jewish law) in the centuries around the beginning of our era from the situation reflected in the Qumran texts to later rabbinic reasoning. Three disputed areas are focused on: Sabbath, purity, and divorce.

Kazen, Thomas. 2019. "The Role of Law in the Formation of the Pentateuch and the Canon." Pages 257–74 in *The Oxford Handbook of Biblical Law*. Edited by Pamela Barmash. Oxford: Oxford University Press.

An overview article on the role of legal materials in the evolution of the Pentateuch.

Kazen, Thomas. 2021. *Impurity and Purification in Early Judaism and the Jesus Tradition.* Resources for Biblical Studies 98. Atlanta: SBL Press.

> The author's collection of a decade of articles on purity and impurity. In chapter 2 ("Purity and Impurity"), the author defines and discusses the concepts of purity and impurity with a particular focus on Israelite religion and Second Temple Judaism. In chapter 4 ("Purity and Persia") he argues that some of the purity laws and practices in Leviticus and Numbers emerge under the influence of Persian culture and religion during the early Second Temple period. In chapters 5 and 6 ("The Role of Disgust in Priestly Purity Law"; "Disgust in Body, Mind, and Language"), he builds on his previous interpretation of the relationship between purity concepts and disgust with insights from cognitive metaphor theory, particularly conceptual blending, to understand and explain how the concept of impurity is sometimes used rhetorically and evocatively. In chapter 7 ("Purification"), the author discusses purification rituals in ancient West Asia, Greece, and Rome with a particular focus on early Judaism and in the context of emerging Christian rituals. Various ritual theory and cognitive science perspectives are included.

Klawans, Jonathan. 2000. *Impurity and Sin in Ancient Judaism.* Oxford: Oxford University Press.

> Klawans's influential study on ritual and moral impurity argues that the Qumran sectarians conflated the two types.

Koehl, Robert B. 1986. "The Chieftain Cup and a Minoan Rite of Passage." *The Journal of Hellenic Studies* 106:99–110.

> The author of the article analyzes the imagery on a Minoan cup. He argues that the image represents a so-called rite of passage—perhaps linked to the custom described by the ancient writer Ephorus, where a young boy was taken away to be taught by an older lover for two months before becoming an adult.

Kohn, Eli. 2006. "Drunkenness, Prostitution and Immodest Appearances in Hebrew Bible Narrative, Second Temple Writings and Early Rabbinic Literature: A Literary and Rhetorical Study." PhD diss., University of the Free State.

> The exhaustive title of the work clearly indicates the subject of the thesis. The question driving the investigation is how the early rabbis understood

the embarrassing or even deeply provocative behavior of important biblical figures, such as Lot getting drunk with his daughters and sleeping with them.

Koltun-Fromm, Naomi. 2010. *Hermeneutics of Holiness: Ancient Jewish and Christian Notions of Sexuality and Religious Community*. Oxford: Oxford University Press.

Study of the relationship between purity, sexuality, and holiness in early Jewish, Christian, and rabbinic literature. The author discusses aspects such as procreation and the mixing of holy and unholy seed.

Kratz, Reinhard G. 2005. *The Composition of the Narrative Books of the Old Testament*. London: T&T Clark. (Originally in German: *Die Komposition der erzählenden Bücher des Alten Testaments*. Göttingen: Vandenhoeck & Ruprecht, 2000.)

A redaction-critical study in the German tradition of the development of the narrative books of the Hebrew Bible.

Kratz, Reinhard G. 2015. *Historical and Biblical Israel: The History, Tradition, and Archives of Israel and Judah*. Oxford: Oxford University Press. (Originally in German: *Historisches und biblisches Israel: Drei Überblicke zum Alten Testament*. Tübingen: Mohr Siebeck, 2013.)

In this book, Kratz places the emergence of the Hebrew Bible in a historical and sociological context.

Krondorfer, Björn, ed. 2009. *Men and Masculinities in Christianity and Judaism: A Critical Reader*. London: SCM.

In this comprehensive anthology, Krondorfer has collected thirty-five key texts in research on masculinity and the Judeo-Christian tradition. Each text is introduced by Krondorfer and provided with further reading tips, making the volume an accessible entry point into masculinity research in relation to religious studies and theology.

Kyle, Rebecca. 2009. "What Accounts for Cross-Cultural Variation in the Expression of Homosexuality?" *Chrestomathy* 8:99–114.

Kyle argues that population pressure is one of several factors that influences whether or not homosexuality is practiced in a culture. High population pressure tends to be associated with a range of cultural practices that reduce human reproduction, of which homosexual behavior could be one.

Lakoff, George, and Mark Johnson. 1980. *Metaphors We Live By.* Chicago: University of Chicago Press.

The now-classic introduction to conceptual metaphor theory.

Lawrence, Jonathan D. 2006. *Washing in Water: Trajectories of Ritual Bathing in the Hebrew Bible and Second Temple Literature.* Atlanta: Society of Biblical Literature.

This book is a study of ritual washing (in a broad sense) in the Hebrew Bible and Second Temple literature, including the Dead Sea Scrolls. This includes washing for cultic purposes, for initiation, and in metaphorical contexts. The author also discusses the historical development of ritual bathing practices.

Lear, Andrew. 2014. "Ancient Pederasty: An Introduction." Pages 102–27 in T. K. Hubbard, ed., *A Companion to Greek and Roman Sexualities.*

The author discusses historical, archaeological, and literary evidence for pederasty in ancient Greece and Rome.

Lear, Andrew, and Eva Cantarella. 2008. *Images of Ancient Greek Pederasty: Boys Were Their Gods.* London: Routledge.

The authors discuss how male pederastic relationships were portrayed on pottery in ancient Greece from courtship to intercourse. The book is richly illustrated with images of the paintings.

Lemos, Tracy M. 2017. *Violence and Personhood in Ancient Israel and Comparative Contexts.* Oxford: Oxford University Press.

Lemos analyses the relationship between "personhood" and (ritualized) violence, focusing on social recognition, legal rights and action. The author discusses the dominance of men in relation to strangers, women, slaves, and children.

Levine, Baruch A. 2002. "'Seed' Versus 'Womb': Expressions of Male Dominance in Biblical Israel." Pages 337–43 in S. Parpola and R. M. Whiting, ed., *Sex and Gender in the Ancient Near East.*

Levine analyzes the male-dominated language of the Hebrew Bible regarding fertility and reproduction, seeing it as an expression of the patriarchal order— the womb is understood as a kind of container for the life that males give rise to.

Loader, William. 2013. *Making Sense of Sex: Attitudes towards Sexuality in Early Jewish and Christian Literature*. Grand Rapids: Eerdmans.

In this book, Loader summarizes his research on early Jewish and Christian understandings of sexuality in the centuries around the beginning of the common era. Loader has previously written a series of books in which he carefully examines text group after text group and maps their views on sexuality.

Loughlin, Gerard, ed. 2007. *Queer Theology: Rethinking the Western Body*. Oxford: Blackwell.

This anthology of contributions of varying quality includes strict textual interpretations as well as thoughtful biblical meditations and less thoughtful analyses of queer theory. A good entry point for those who are curious about queer theology.

Lugones, María. 2007. "Heterosexualism and the Colonial/Modern Gender System." *Hypatia* 22.1:186–209.

In this theoretically dense article, Lugones examines what she calls the colonial/modern gender system, a system that she argues has been used to classify people in terms of race/gender that naturalizes relations of superiority and subordination. She argues that the binary gender system developed under colonialism and is intertwined with a racialization process that has given rise to a multiplicity of hierarchically ordered genders and races, where "a woman" was assumed to be white, upper class, and heterosexual, whereas "a black" person was assumed to be male, heterosexual, and so on. According to Lugones, this interpretive grid has rendered invisible both large groups of people and the sexual practices of other cultures, which she examines in some historical detail.

Maccoby, Hyam. 1999. *Ritual and Morality: The Ritual Purity System and Its Place in Judaism*. Cambridge: Cambridge University Press.

Maccoby provides an overview of the ritual purity system in the Hebrew Bible in conversation with Jacob Milgrom, Jacob Neusner, and Mary Douglas.

Among other things he claims that impurity ascribed to idols and evil deeds is metaphorical only.

Malina, Bruce J. 1993. *The New Testament World: Insights from Cultural Anthropology.* Louisville: Westminster John Knox.

A classic book by a New Testament scholar who is known as a pioneer in introducing social anthropological perspectives into New Testament research. The book includes a section on honor and shame in the "Mediterranean world," but Malina has also been criticized for overgeneralizing and oversimplifying.

Marrou, Henri Irénée. 1960. *Histoire de l'education dans l'antique.* 5th ed. Paris: Seuil.

A major work on education in antiquity. Among other things, the author takes a stand against the interpretation that the inscriptions at Thera reflect an initiation rite.

Martin, Dale B. 1995. "Heterosexism and the Interpretation of Romans 1:18–32." *Biblical Interpretation* 3:332–55.

In this article, Martin discusses the subject with other researchers, in particular biblical scholar Richard B. Hays. The aim is to expose "heterosexist" interpretations of the first chapter of Romans. Also in Martin 2006, 51–64.

Martin, Dale B. 1996. "*Arsenokoitēs* and *Malakos*: Meanings and Consequences." Pages 117–36 in R. L. Brawley, ed., *Biblical Ethics and Homosexuality.*

Arsenokoitēs and *malakos* are two words on which the supposed New Testament condemnation of homosexuality largely rests (1 Cor 6:9). Here Martin examines the uses and meanings of both words. *Arsenokoitēs* may be used for sexual exploitation, while *malakos* is an insult suggesting that someone is feminine. Martin's point is that interpreting this as a condemnation of male homosexuality requires interpretation. Moreover, whatever the words "really" mean, there are profound ethical problems with using Bible verses as moral rules today. For example, if "feminine" is an insult, what does it say about the view of women? Also in Martin 2006, 37–50.

Martin, Dale B. 2006. *Sex and the Single Savior.* Louisville: Westminster John Knox.

A collection of articles dealing in different ways with issues of sexuality in New Testament texts, including the two articles above and another classic on different ways of interpreting Jesus as "single."

Martín González, Elena. 2014. "The Drawings on the Rock Inscriptions of Archaic Thera (IG XII 3, 536–601; IG XII 3 Suppl. 1410–1493)." Unpublished paper presented at the 145th Annual Meeting of the Society for Classical Studies. Washington, DC, January 3–5, 2014.

Unlike most others who discuss the inscriptions on the rock wall behind the Temple of Apollo and the gymnasium in Thera (Santorini), the author examines the images associated with the inscriptions. The conclusion is that it is unequivocally graffiti.

McCaffrey, Kathleen. 2002. "Reconsidering Gender Ambiguity in Mesopotamia: Is a Beard Just a Beard?" Pages 379–91 in S. Parpola and R. M. Whiting, eds., *Sex and Gender in the Ancient Near East.*

Gender and gender roles in Mesopotamia are seen as confusing by contemporary scholars. In mythology, gods may have one gender at one time, and another at another time. In art and in archaeological excavations, people who appear anatomically one gender may have cultural markers belonging to the other gender. Here, McCaffrey hypothesizes that the confusion arises when researchers interpret the material in accordance with our contemporary understanding of gender as biologically determined and binary and try to interpret the material with the understanding that gender in Mesopotamia functioned differently from us.

Milgrom, Jacob. 1991. *Leviticus 1–16: A New Translation with Introduction and Commentary.* Anchor Bible 3. New York: Doubleday.

Major commentary on Leviticus with elaborate discussions of Israelite ritual purity laws.

Milgrom, Jacob. 1995. "4QTohoraa: An Unpublished Qumran Text on Purities." Pages 59–68 in *Time to Prepare the Way in the Wilderness.* Edited by D. Dimant and L. H. Schiffman. Studies on the Texts of the Desert of Judah 16. Leiden: Brill.

Leviticus scholar Milgrom discusses a Dead Sea Scrolls fragment about purification rituals within a broader context.

Miller, William Ian. 1993. *Humiliation: And Other Essays on Honor, Social Discomfort, and Violence*. Ithaca: Cornell University Press.

William Miller, a law professor and scholar of Icelandic literature, discusses the concept of honor and its relationship to violence.

Mondimore, Francis Mark. 1996. *A Natural History of Homosexuality*. Baltimore: Johns Hopkins University Press.

A social, biological, and political history of sexuality with a particular focus on homosexuality.

Moore, Stephen D., and Janice Capel Anderson, eds. 2003. *New Testament Masculinities*. SBL Semeia Studies 45. Atlanta: Society of Biblical Literature.

On male images and ideals in New Testament texts and the world. Many of the articles discuss views on self-restraint and moderation.

Myers, Wade C., et al. 2006. "The Motivation behind Serial Sexual Homicide: Is It Sex, Power, and Control, or Anger?" *Journal of Forensic Sciences* 51.4:900–907.

Four researchers examine hypotheses of sexual violence and present both theoretical and empirical evidence (evolutionary as well as physiological) that sadistic pleasure is a primary motivation for sexual serial killers. Secondarily, power and control have a reinforcing effect, while anger is not found to be a key component.

Neill, James. 2009. *The Origins and Role of Same-Sex Relations in Human Societies*. Jefferson, NC: McFarland.

An exposé of the history of homosexuality. The author examines sexual expression in different animal species, in different human cultures in history and today. He concludes that humans as a species are "ambisexual," and that prohibitions against homosexuality are the exception rather than the rule in human history. The book is very comprehensive but relatively dependent on other secondary literature and sometimes overinterpretive.

Neusner, Jacob. 1973. *The Idea of Purity in Ancient Judaism*. Leiden: Brill.

Neusner's classic study on ritual purity and impurity, which also—although more as an aside—suggests an underlying role of disgust for conceptions of impurity.

Nihan, Christophe. 2007. *From Priestly Torah to Pentateuch: A Study in the Composition of the Book of Leviticus*. Forschungen zum Alten Testament 2.25. Tübingen, Germany: Mohr Siebeck.

One of the best and most thorough studies of how Leviticus evolved and was shaped during the Persian period.

Nissinen, Martti. 1998. *Homoeroticism in the Biblical World: A Historical Perspective*. Minneapolis: Fortress.

This book has become something of a classic on the subject. Nissinen presents an excellent overview of attitudes toward homoerotic behavior in ancient Mesopotamia, Israel, Greece, Rome, rabbinic Judaism, and early Christianity. He argues that same-sex eroticism was also understood within a framework of superiority and subordination, just like sexual relations in general. The biblical texts on homoeroticism are placed in this broad cultural context.

Nõmmik, Aldar. Forthcoming 2025. *Praying and Prophesying with a Garment Hanging Down from the Head: Robes, Romans, and Rituals in 1 Corinthians 11:2–16*. Stockholm: Enskilda Högskolan Stockholm.

The author interprets 1 Cor 11 within the context of the Roman ritual practice of covering one's head (*capite velato*) at prayer and mantic activities. This means that the shame incurred by men had more to do with pagan practice and that it was mainly the instructions for women to cover their heads (anyway) that had to do with gender roles.

Nongbri, Brent. 2013. *Before Religion: A History of a Modern Concept*. New Haven: Yale University Press.

The author argues that the understanding of religion as a separate sphere, distinct from politics, economics, science and society in general, is a modern construct.

North, Helen F. 1977. "The Mare, the Vixen, and the Bee: *Sophrosyne* as the Virtue of Women in Antiquity." *Illinois Classical Studies* 2:35–48.

A classic article on *sōphrosynē* (moderation) and its importance as a female virtue in Greek literature. The author published a major study on *sōphrosynē* already in 1966.

Nussbaum, Martha. 2004. *Hiding from Humanity: Disgust, Shame and the Law.* Princeton: Princeton University Press.

Nussbaum examines how political ideologies and written and unwritten laws relate to our emotions. Emotions such as shame and disgust and their functions in relation to norms and legal systems are examined.

Nussbaum, Martha. 2010. *From Disgust to Humanity: Sexual Orientation and Constitutional Law.* Oxford: Oxford University Press.

The author shows how, in reality, disgust underlies many of our values and argues that it should not be allowed to govern legislation, as it leads to people being deprived of their human rights. Instead of a "politics of disgust" we need a "politics of humanity" that not only respects others but also tries to see the world from their perspective because they are fellow human beings.

Nussbaum, Martha, and Juha Sihvola, eds. 2001. *The Sleep of Reason: Erotic Experience and Sexual Ethics in Ancient Greece and Rome.* Chicago: University of Chicago Press.

In this anthology, the authors want to understand two questions together: what sexual experiences are reflected in classical texts, and what sexual ethical judgements are present in the same texts? The idea is that sexual experiences go beyond reason while being subject to reasoning. Taking these aspects together, the authors of the anthology find that for the ancient Romans and Greeks, sex was not only about control and power but also about love and reciprocity.

Olyan, Saul. 1994. "'And with a Male You Shall Not Lie the Lying down of a Woman': On the Meaning and Significance of Leviticus 18:22 and 20:13." *Journal of the History of Sexuality* 5:179–206.

Olyan analyzes the literal meaning of the two verses of the so-called Holiness

Code mentioned in the title of the article and what they may have meant in their cultural context. As the commandment does not appear outside the Holiness Code, Olyan concludes that the prohibition related to purity concerned penetration by one man of another and is analogous to the prohibition of a man to have penetrative sex with a menstruating woman. At an earlier stage, only the penetrator was condemned.

Ormand, Kirk. 2009. *Controlling Desires: Sexuality in Ancient Greece and Rome*. Westport, CT: Praeger.

Ormand provides an accessible and relatively comprehensive account of how sexuality is treated in some texts from ancient Greece and Rome. Like many other researchers in the field, he argues that our contemporary view of sexuality cannot be applied to the ancient material.

Page, Denys L. 1955. *Sappho and Alcaeus: An Introduction to the Study of Ancient Lesbian Poetry*. Oxford: Clarendon.

Cambridge scholar Page analyzes texts by Sappho and her contemporary, Alcaeus, who was also from Lesbos. The book includes the original text, translation, and detailed commentary on twelve of Sappho's poems.

Parker, Holt N. 1993. "Sappho Schoolmistress." *Transactions of the American Philological Association* 123:309–51.

In an article of over forty pages, the author refutes a large number of myths about Sappho and concludes that most of what we think we know about her is wrong or at least unsubstantiated speculation. This applies both to ideas about Sappho as head of a girls' school and to those about ritual associations (*thiasoi*).

Parpola, S., and R. M. Whiting, eds. 2002. *Sex and Gender in the Ancient Near East: Proceedings of the 47th Rencontre Assyriologique Internationale, Helsinki, July 2–6, 2001*. Helsinki: Neo-Assyrian Text Corpus Project.

This very comprehensive collection of scholarly articles deals with a variety of issues related to sexuality and gender in ancient West Asia. Some of the articles with particular relevance to the present volume are mentioned separately in the bibliography.

Patzer, H. 1982. *Die griechische Knabenliebe*. Wiesbaden: Steiner.

The author modifies Bethe's theory that anal insemination was a Doric custom and argues that the practice was universal throughout Greece.

Paschen, Wilfried. 1970. *Rein und Unrein: Untersuchung zur biblischen Wortgeschichte*. Studien zum Alten und Neuen Testaments 24. Munich: Kösel-Verlag.

This is an early study of the concepts of ritual purity and impurity.

Peled, Ilan. 2014. "*Assinu* and *Kurgarrû* Revisited." *Journal of Near Eastern Studies* 73.2:283–97.

Peled partly reevaluates previous research on the cross-gender cult servants of the goddess Ishtar and argues that together they represented the sexual aspects of the goddess: Ishtar had both male and female attributes.

Percy, William A. 1996. *Pederasty and Pedagogy in Archaic Greece*. Urbana: University of Illinois Press.

Percy outlines the historical controversies surrounding the theory that Greek pederasty originated in an Indo-European initiation rite involving anal insemination. He argues instead that the background is to be found in Crete in aristocratic contexts, where teenage boys became lovers of young warriors. The development of the custom was linked to overpopulation.

Petrovic, Andrej, and Ivana Petrovic. 2016. *Inner Purity and Pollution in Greek Religion*. Vol. 1: *Early Greek Religion*. Oxford: Oxford University Press.

A collection of material on the conceptualization of inner pollution and purity in ancient Greek religion.

Pitt-Rivers, Julian. 1977. *The Fate of Schechem or the Politics of Sex: Essays in the Anthropology of the Mediterranean*. Cambridge: Cambridge University Press.

A collection of anthropological studies focusing on the concept of honor.

Pomeroy, Sarah B. 1975. *Goddesses, Whores, Wives, and Slaves: Women in Classical Antiquity*. London: Hale.

A now classic study of women's roles and lives in ancient Greece and Rome by historian and classicist Sarah Pomeroy.

Pomeroy, Sarah B. 1997. *Families in Classical and Hellenistic Greece: Representations and Realities*.

The author analyzes family structures and values in ancient Greece.

Prestage, Garreth. 2003. Review of *True Nature: A Theory of Sexual Attraction*, by Michael R. Kauth. *Culture, Health & Sexuality* 5:95–98.

In this review, Kauth's book is presented as somewhat sloppy in its argumentation and theoretically underdeveloped as well as disproportionately interested in same-sex sexuality and to a lesser extent in heterosexuality—but still worth reading for those who are curious about a discussion of sexuality from biological, psychological, and social aspects.

Preston, Stephanie D., and Frans B. M. de Waal. 2002. "Empathy: Its Ultimate and Proximate Bases." *Behavioural and Brain Sciences* 25:1–72.

Using different experiments, two researchers show how human empathy is multilayered and how what we often call nature and nurture interact even in the development (i.e., "wiring") of our brains.

Reynolds, Margaret. 2003. *The Sappho History*. Houndmills: Palgrave Macmillan.

This book is on the reception of Sappho in modern literature.

Römer, Thomas. 2005. *The So-Called Deuteronomistic History: A Sociological, Historical and Literary Introduction*. London: T&T Clark.

Römer examines the so-called Deuteronomistic history, a widely accepted thesis among biblical scholars that Deuteronomy, Joshua, Judges, 1–2 Samuel, and 1–2 Kings were compiled during and after the Babylonian exile by a school of scribes with a particular perspective. Römer asks how this school emerged, what ideological forces were at play, and how the perspective came to influence Jewish identity in the Second Temple period.

Römer, Thomas. 2014. "Der Pentateuch." Pages 53–116 in *Die Entstehung des Alten Testaments*. Edited by Walter Dietrich et al. Theologische Wissenschaft: Sammelwerk für Studium und Beruf 1. Rev. ed.Stuttgart: Kohlhammer.

An overview of the origins and development of the Pentateuch by one of the foremost representatives of the newer approaches dominant among European biblical scholars.

Römer, Thomas, and Loyse Bonjour. 2005. *L'homosexualité dans le Proche-Orient ancien et la Bible*. Essais Biblique 37. Geneva: Labor et Fides.

This popular science book discusses several well-known biblical texts as well as other ancient material related to same-sex sexuality. The intention is not to provide new biblical scholarship but rather to present the current state of research to a French-speaking audience.

Rooke, Deborah W., ed. 2009. *A Question of Sex? Gender and Difference in the Hebrew Bible and Beyond*. Sheffield: Sheffield Phoenix.

A collection that discusses various aspects of the socially and culturally determined roles of men and women in the Hebrew Bible.

Roth, Martha T. 2006. "Marriage, Divorce, and the Prostitute in Ancient Mesopotamia." Pages 21–39 in Christopher A. Faraone and Laura K. McClure, eds., *Prostitutes and Courtesans in the Ancient World*.

Roth addresses and refutes the persistent myth of ritualized or sacred prostitution in Mesopotamia before going on to discuss the relationship between sex within and outside of marriage. The latter seems not to have been understood as morally wrong but as a threat to the economic function of marriage.

Rozin, Paul, Jonathan Haidt, and Clark McCauley. 2000. "Disgust." Pages 637–53 in *Handbook of Emotions*. Edited by M. Lewis and J. M. Haviland-Jones. 2nd ed. New York: Guildford.

This article presents empirical psychological research on the role of disgust conducted by Rozin and colleagues. The text includes a model of different types of distaste and nine very common elicitors.

Sanders, E. P. 1990. *Jewish Law from Jesus to the Mishnah: Five Studies*. London: SCM.

These studies, in which Sanders continually argues with Neusner, focus on Jesus, the Pharisees, and Jewish law, with a separate study on whether the Pharisees ate ordinary food in purity, and another on purity and food in the diaspora.

Sanders, Ed, Chiara Tymiger, Chris Carey, and Nick J. Lowe, eds. 2013. *Erôs in Ancient Greece*. Oxford: Oxford University Press.

A collection of articles by various researchers. The background is a conference in London on *erōs* as an emotion in ancient Greek culture and how *erōs* overlaps with other emotions.

Sassoon, Isaac. 2011. *The Status of Women in Jewish Tradition*. Cambridge: Cambridge University Press.

Sassoon discusses the status of women in relation to marriage, law, and gender equality in early Jewish tradition.

Satlow, Michael L. 1994. "'Wasted Seed,' the History of a Rabbinic Idea." *Hebrew Union College Annual* 65:137–75.

Satlow suggests that the notion that nonprocreative emission of semen would have been considered sinful is a rather late idea appearing in the redactional stratum of the Babylonian Talmud.

Scanlon, Thomas F. 2003. *Eros and Greek Athletics*. Oxford: Oxford University Press.

This study of ancient Greek sport and body culture, and how it was intertwined with religiosity, ethics, gender roles, and sexuality, is the first to explore these fascinating connections.

Schmid, Konrad. 2012. *The Old Testament: A Literary History*. Minneapolis: Fortress. (Originally in German: *Literaturgeschichte des Altes Testaments*. Darmstadt: WBG, 2008).

Schmid provides a clear overview of the emergence and development of the Hebrew Bible from a continental perspective. The focus is on the exilic and Persian periods.

Schofield, Malcolm. 2013. "Cardinal Virtues: A Contested Socratic Inheritance." Pages 106–27 in *Plato and the Stoics*. Edited by A. G. Long. Cambridge: Cambridge University Press.

The article discusses the Stoic version of the four cardinal virtues and how these were developed and discussed by Stoic thinkers over time.

Sellars, John. 2006. *Stoicism*. Chesham: Acumen.

This book is an overview of ancient Stoicism.

Sergent, B. 1984. *L'homosexualité dans la mythologie grecque*. Paris: Payot.

The author discusses Strabo's (and Ephorus's) record of the abduction of young boys in Crete, seeing traces of Indo-European origins, and examines same-sex relationships and sexuality in Greek mythology.

Siems, Andreas Karsten, ed. 1988. *Sexualität und Erotik in der Antike*. Wege der Forschung 605. Darmstadt: Wissenschaftliche Buchgesellschaft.

An anthology of both older and later contributions, most of which are in German but some in English. These include Erich Bethe's classic article on Doric boy love (see separate entry) and a review article by Kenneth Dover.

Skinner, Marilyn B. 2014. *Sexuality in Greek and Roman Culture*. 2nd ed. Chichester: Wiley-Blackwell.

A thorough and pedagogical overview of different approaches to sexuality in ancient Greece and Rome. The author discusses developments and relates them to the present. The dialogue with other scholars on controversial issues is well balanced. The book also includes discussion questions.

Snyder, Jane McIntosh. 1989. *The Woman and the Lyre: Women Writers in Classical Greece and Rome*. Bristol: Bristol Classical Press.

This is a classic study of women writers in antiquity from Sappho onward. The book discusses mainly female poets in the classical and Hellenistic periods but also female philosophers and writers in the Roman period.

Snyder, Jane McIntosh. 1997. *Lesbian Desire in the Lyrics of Sappho*. New York: Columbia University Press.

A thematic and very detailed analysis of Sappho's poems focusing on the role of erotic desire. The analysis is based on the author's own translation of all (then known) Sappho fragments. The book includes the Greek text and the author's translation.

Stein, Edward. 1999. *The Mismeasure of Desire: The Science, Theory, and Ethics of Sexual Orientation*. Oxford: Oxford University Press.

When this book was published, there had been extensive discussions for decades about gender and sexuality—what is innate and what is cultural? Stein examines metaphysical beliefs, scientific research, and ethical issues related to the question. He argues that neither essentialism, which holds that gender and sexuality are innate, nor constructivism, which holds that they are cultural and social constructs, are credible ways of approaching the question of what shapes our sexuality. Rather, he argues that there are multiple factors at play, about which we actually know very little.

Stone, Ken. 1995. "Gender and Homosexuality in Judges 19: Subject-Honor, Object-Shame?" *Journal for the Study of the Old Testament* 67:87–107.

The story of the particularly brutal gang rape in Judges 19 has been examined with different methods and from different perspectives. Stone here tries to bring together several different perspectives in what he calls an anthropological reading. Using honor-shame culture as a framework for interpretation, he argues that the rape of the unnamed woman is part of a power play between the men in the story.

Stone, Ken. 1996. *Sex, Honor, and Power in the Deuteronomistic History*. Journal for the Study of the Old Testament Supplement Series 234. Sheffield: Sheffield Academic.

Stone examines several biblical (Deuteronomistic) texts that deal with sexual, often violent acts, including his article on Judges 19 referenced above. The framework for his interpretive tool is anthropological studies that show that sex and male status and power are linked.

Stowers, Stanley K. 1994. *A Rereading of Romans: Justice, Jews, and Gentiles.* New Haven: Yale University Press.

Stowers argues here that Romans is not, as commonly assumed, about sin and salvation, but instead about the lack and perfection of self-control—an important feature of Greco-Roman culture.

Taylor, Timothy. 1996. *The Prehistory of Sex: Four Million Years of Human Sexual Culture.* London: Fourth Estate.

Taylor uses archaeological material to sketch the prehistory of sexuality. Contraception and reproduction, homoeroticism and transsexuality, patriarchal structures and destruction of the environment are some of the many topics covered in the book.

Thorsteinsson, Runar M. 2010. *Roman Christianity and Roman Stoicism.* Oxford: Oxford University Press.

The author compares the morality of first-century Christians in Rome with that of their Stoic neighbors, finding both similarities and differences.

Tiemeyer, Lena-Sofia. 2023. *In Search of Jonathan: Jonathan between the Bible and Modern Fiction.* Oxford: Oxford University Press.

An exegetical and reception-critical study of the character of Jonathan, which also includes a chapter on "Jonathan, Homoeroticism, and Masculinity."

Toorn, Karel van der. 1989. "Female Prostitution in Payment of Vows in Ancient Israel." *Journal of Biblical Literature* 108:193–205.

The author argues that women, lacking the resources to fulfill their vows to God, were driven to prostitution, which he believes can shed light on the phenomenon of cultic prostitution. This type of interpretation of cultic prostitution is today highly questioned.

Töyräänvuori, Joanna. 2020. "Homosexuality, the Holiness Code, and Ritual Pollution: A Case of Mistaken Identity." *Journal for the Study of the Old Testament* 45:1–32.

The author suggests that Lev 18:22 and 20:13 do not refer to sexual acts between two males but prohibit a "threesome"—two males simultaneously
having sex with the same woman.

Vaage, Leif E., and Vincent L. Wimbush, eds. 1999. *Asceticism and the New Testament.*
New York: Routledge.

Over twenty scholars discuss different approaches to asceticism and abstinence in New Testament texts.

Valantasis, Richard. 1999. "Musonius Rufus and Roman Ascetical Theory." *Greek,
Roman, and Byzantine Studies* 40:207–31.

Musonius Rufus lived and worked in first-century Rome and has been called
the Socrates of Rome. Valantasis focuses here on the role of asceticism in the
philosopher's teachings and sees him as part of the broader asceticism of his
time, which also includes early Christian ascetics—a type of asceticism that,
Valantasis argues, cannot be interpreted on either the basis of the ascetic
ideals of late antiquity or our divisions of ancient philosophers into different
schools, but must be read in its own right.

Verstraete, Beerte C., and Vernon L. Provencal, eds. 2005. *Same-Sex Desire and Love
in Greco-Roman Antiquity and in the Classical Tradition of the West.* Bingham-
ton, NY: Haworth.

This anthology deals with what the title promises—same-sex eroticism and
love in text and image in Greco-Roman antiquity and the classical tradition. It also examines how Western culture has been inspired by these texts
and images.

Waal, Frans B. M. de. 1999. "Apes from Venus: Bonobos and Human Social Evolution." Pages 39–68 in *Tree of Origin: What Primate Behavior Can Tell Us
about Human Social Evolution.* Edited by Frans B. M. de Waal. Cambridge:
Harvard University Press.

One of the world's leading primate researchers analyzes the role of same-sex
sexuality in bonobo social interactions.

Waetjen, Herman C. 1996. "Same-Sex Relations in Antiquity and Sexuality and Sexual Identity in Contemporary American Society." Pages 103–16 in R. L. Brawley, ed., *Biblical Ethics and Homosexuality*.

The author tries to understand same-sex relationships in antiquity from the perspective of how the ancient binary taxonomies of humans are based on biological differences. The biblical texts are based on the same kind of taxonomies as other ancient texts. Plato's androgynous myth is discussed and questions about sexual identity and sexual orientation are raised. The conclusion is that the biblical texts cannot be used to discuss what we mean by homosexuality. In addition, the author argues that the kingdom of God has canceled the validity of any notion of purity for ethical issues.

Wells, Bruce. 2020. "On the Beds of a Woman: The Leviticus Texts on Same-Sex Relations Reconsidered." Pages 123–58 in *Sexuality and Law in the Torah*. Edited by H. Lipka and B. Wells. Library of Hebrew Bible/Old Testament Studies 675. London: T&T Clark.

The author criticizes Olyan's influential interpretation and argues, based on grammar and language, that the prohibitions of Lev 18:22 and 20:13 only concern intercourse with a man who belongs to the sexual domain of another woman.

Williams, Craig A. 2010. *Roman Homosexuality*. 2nd ed. Oxford: Oxford University Press.

In this book, Williams does for Rome what Dover did for Greece. He examines in particular the ideals of manhood and masculinity in ancient Rome, within which certain same-sex sexual behaviors could be accommodated. He argues that hierarchical structures determine who is thought to be active (male) and passive (female/slave), and breaking this hierarchical structure in one's sexual behavior was not looked upon favorably.

Wimbush, Vincent L., and Richard Valantasis, eds. 1995. *Asceticism*. Oxford: Oxford University Press.

This book contains some forty essays on asceticism in antiquity.

Winter, Bruce W. 2003. *Roman Wives, Roman Widows: The Appearance of New Women and the Pauline Communities*. Grand Rapids: Eerdmans.

The book analyzes women's roles in the first century, especially in the light of new Roman female ideals and Roman legislation.

Wilamowitz-Moellendorff, Ulrich von. 1913. *Sappho und Simonides: Untersuchungen über griechische Lyriker*. Berlin: Weidmannsche Buchhandlung.

A classic analysis of some Sappho poems. The author is usually credited with the persistent idea of Sappho as headmistress of a girls' school.

Wilson, Lyn Hatherly. 1996. *Sappho's Sweetbitter Songs: Configurations of Female and Male in Ancient Greek Lyric*. London: Routledge.

Wilson compares Sappho's poetry with examples from male poets to examine how gender differences were constructed in antiquity and compare with theories of how the feminine has been conceptualized in the late twentieth century.

Wright, David P. 1992. "Unclean and Clean (Old Testament)." Pages 729–41 in vol. 6 of *Anchor Bible Dictionary*. Edited by David Noel Freedman. 6 vols. New York: Doubleday.

This seminal dictionary article is on purity and impurity in the Hebrew Bible.

INDEX OF ANCIENT NAMES AND PLACES

INDEX OF SUBJECTS

INDEX OF SCRIPTURE
AND OTHER ANCIENT SOURCES